THE REAL TEST OF INTELLIGENCE

For years, intelligence tests have served as "divine" indicators of intellect. But do they accurately evaluate intelligence or, more important, our ability to achieve success?

In *Successful Intelligence*, Yale University professor Robert Sternberg challenges the notion of these intelligence tests. He explains why IQ tests are poor predictors of how individuals will succeed in life because they focus on "inert" knowledge, thereby excluding a whole range of intellectual abilities. And he argues that what's needed are new tools with which to evaluate intelligence and broaden its definition. Complete with personal anecdotes and practical new ways to promote goal-oriented action, this enlightening and inspiring book is essential reading for anyone interested in maximizing their strengths and fulfilling their life's ambitions.

"Questions just how smart those IQ tests really are."
—*Detroit News/Free Press*

"Offers characteristics of the kind of intelligence that solves
real-world problems."
—*Kansas City Star*

"A fine addition to the growing literature that refutes the long-held
idea that there is such a thing as 'general' intelligence and
that it can be quantified."
—*Kirkus Reviews*

ROBERT J. STERNBERG is an award-winning professor who holds the IBM chair in psychology and education at Yale University. One of the world's leading researchers and authorities on intelligence, he is also a fellow of the American Academy of Arts and Sciences, and has written more than forty books.

ROBERT J. STERNBERG

SUCCESSFUL INTELLIGENCE

HOW PRACTICAL

AND CREATIVE

INTELLIGENCE

DETERMINE

SUCCESS IN LIFE

℗ A PLUME BOOK

PLUME
Published by the Penguin Group
Penguin Putnam Inc., 375 Hudson Street, New York, New York 10014, U.S.A.
Penguin Books Ltd, 27 Wrights Lane, London W8 5TZ, England
Penguin Books Australia Ltd, Ringwood, Victoria, Australia
Penguin Books Canada Ltd, 10 Alcorn Avenue, Toronto, Ontario, Canada M4V 3B2
Penguin Books (N.Z.) Ltd, 182–190 Wairau Road, Auckland 10, New Zealand

Penguin Books Ltd, Registered Offices: Harmondsworth, Middlesex, England

Published by Plume, an imprint of Dutton Signet,
a member of Penguin Putnam Inc.
This is an authorized reprint of a hardcover edition published by Simon & Schuster.
For information address Simon & Schuster,
1230 Avenue of the Americas, New York, NY 10020.

First Plume Printing, October, 1997
10 9 8 7 6 5 4 3 2 1

 REGISTERED TRADEMARK—MARCA REGISTRADA

LIBRARY OF CONGRESS CATALOGING-IN-PUBLICATION DATA
Sternberg, Robert J.
Successful intelligence : how practical and creative intelligence
determine success in life / Robert J. Sternberg.
p.   cm.
Originally published: Simon & Schuster, 1996.
Includes bibliographical references (p.   ) and index.
ISBN 0-452-27906-2
1. Intellect.   2. Intelligence tests.   3. Creative thinking.
4. Common sense.   5. Success—Psychological aspects.   I. Title.
[BF431.S73826   1997]
153.9—dc21   97–17800
                                                           CIP

Original hardcover design by Jeanette Olender.

Printed in the United States of America

BOOKS ARE AVAILABLE AT QUANTITY DISCOUNTS WHEN USED TO PROMOTE PRODUCTS OR SERVICES.
FOR INFORMATION PLEASE WRITE TO PREMIUM MARKETING DIVISION, PENGUIN PUTNAM INC.,
375 HUDSON STREET, NEW YORK, NY 10014.

To Mrs. Alexa, my fourth-grade teacher

at Tuscan Elementary School in Maplewood, New Jersey.

Thank you for turning my life around.

CONTENTS

Preface

This book has a very simple point. Almost everything you know about intelligence—the kind of intelligence psychologists have most often written about—deals with only a tiny and not very important part of a much broader and more complex intellectual spectrum. It deals with *inert intelligence*. What's that? According to *The American Heritage Dictionary of the English Language* (Third Edition, 1992), *inert* means: "1. Unable to move or act . . . not readily reactive with other elements." Inert intelligence is what you show when you take an IQ test, or the Scholastic Assessment Test, or the American College Test, or any of a large number of similar tests used for college and graduate-school admissions. Many people do well on these tests, thereby showing impressive potential academic prowess, at least according to those who believe in the tests. But the intelligence measured is inert—it doesn't lead to goal-directed movement or action. As a result, these people's most impressive accomplishments may well be their test scores, or their grades in school. Those who can recall facts, who may even be able to reason with those facts, don't necessarily know how to use them to make a difference, either to themselves or to anyone else.

In this book, I will be concerned with inert intelligence only as it is related to what really matters in life: what I call *successful intelligence.* Successful intelligence is the kind of intelligence used to achieve important goals. People who succeed, whether by their own standards or by other people's, are those who have managed to acquire, develop, and apply a full range of intellectual skills, rather than merely relying on the inert intelligence that schools so value. These individuals may or may not succeed on conventional tests, but they have something in common that is much more important than high test scores. **They know their strengths; they know their weaknesses. They capitalize on their strengths; they compensate for or correct their weaknesses.** That's it.

Successfully intelligent people realize that no one is good at everything. Einstein wasn't. Lincoln wasn't. Da Vinci wasn't. Galileo wasn't. The idea that there is a general factor of intelligence that can be measured by IQ and similar tests is a myth that is supported only because the range of abilities they measure is narrow. As I will show, once you expand the range of abilities that are measured, the general IQ factor disappears.

There is nothing wrong with good test scores. I want to emphasize this: Good test scores don't preclude successful intelligence. But neither do they assure it. Indeed, some people with good scores become so enamored of those scores that they never develop the other skills they will need to be successfully intelligent.

I consider myself lucky. I'm a full professor with an endowed chair at Yale. I've won many awards, published over six hundred articles and books, and been awarded about $10 million in research grants and contracts. I am a fellow of the American Academy of Arts and Sciences and am listed in *Who's Who in America.* I have a terrific wife and two wonderful kids. Odd, then, that my greatest luck in life may well have been a failure. I bombed IQ tests when I was a kid. Why was that so lucky? Because I learned in elementary school that if I was going to succeed, it wasn't going to be because of my IQ. And I also learned soon thereafter that just as low scores on tests of inert intelligence don't preclude success, neither do high scores guarantee it. And from these lessons and the questions they raised, I would eventually begin my quest to explore and try to define the kind of intelligence that is an accurate predictor of success.

Some psychologists have finally started to recognize that there is more to intelligence than IQ. For example, Daniel Goleman's book *Emotional Intelligence* is an examination of the emotional component of intelligence: how feelings affect thoughts and how to deal with them. Howard Gardner writes of musical, bodily kinesthetic, and a number of other kinds of intelligence. I can't possibly review in this book the many forms of intelligence that psychologists have proposed. Some of them are very specific, such as musical intelligence, which may be important in the lives of some people but matters quite a bit less to others. Here, I will focus on the kind of intelligence that matters to everyone in reaching important life goals, and that's successful intelligence.

PART I

What Counts? IQ, Intelligence, or Successful Intelligence?

CHAPTER ONE

Beyond IQ
to Successful Intelligence

If IQ rules, it is only because we let it. And when we let it rule, we choose a bad master. We got ourselves into the test mess; we can get ourselves out of it. It's a mess from which I personally had to extricate myself.

My Life as a Dum-dum

As an elementary-school student, I failed miserably on the IQ tests I had to take. I was incredibly test-anxious. Just the sight of the school psychologist coming into the classroom to give a group IQ test sent me into a wild panic attack. And by the time the psychologist said, "Go!" to get us started, I was in such a funk that I could hardly answer any of the test items. I still remember being on the first couple of problems when I heard other students already turning the page as they sailed through the test. For me, the game of taking the test was all but over before it even started. And the outcome was always the same: I lost.

Of course, countless test publishers, teachers, administrators, and school psychologists will swear that there is no such thing as "failing" an IQ test; that there is no such thing, really, as "winning" or "losing" on an IQ test. Maybe not—and maybe the Pope isn't Catholic. But for all practical purposes, you fail the test and lose the game when as a result of the exercise you are labeled *dumb*.

You don't need to be a genius to figure out what happens next. No one expects much from a dum-dum. My teachers in the early elementary-school grades certainly didn't expect much from me. And I, like many students, wanted to please my teachers. So I gave them what they expected. I wasn't a very good student in my first three years of elementary school. Were the teachers disappointed? Not on your life. They were happy that I was giving them what they expected, and I was happy they were happy. So everyone was happy, and I was just one more loser in the game of life.

Was it that I just didn't have the gray matter to be a high achiever, or was it in fact a self-fulfilling prophecy that resulted from the teachers' knowledge of my IQ test score? Most of the time, we never really find out, because once the student starts down the road to low achievement, he or she quickly discovers that it is a one-way street to the academic twilight zone. And as in the show by that name, few people who enter the twilight zone ever leave it.

I was lucky, damn lucky, in a way few students are. In fourth grade, when I was nine years old, I ended up in Mrs. Alexa's class. Whereas my teachers in the early primary grades had all been older and deeply dug into the trenches of the testing field, Mrs. Alexa was fresh out of college and either didn't know or didn't care much about IQ test scores. She believed I could do much better than I was doing, and she expected more of me. No, she demanded more of me. And she got it. Why? Because I wanted to please her, even more than I had wanted to please my teachers in the first three grades. (In fact, I would have proposed marriage to her on the spot if she hadn't been just a little too old and, inconveniently, already married.)

Mrs. Alexa didn't seem particularly surprised, but I was astonished when I actually exceeded her expectations. I became a straight-A student very quickly. For the first time, I saw myself as someone who could be an A student, and I was one thereafter. But at the time, it never occurred to me that I had become an A student because I was truly smart, despite the rotten scores on my IQ tests. On the contrary, I felt certain that I had become an A student despite my low intelligence. After careful reflection, I came to the conclusion that it was because I went to bed early. (I still go to bed early.)

Obstacles to the Development of Successful Intelligence

As I learned from my own experience, one of the biggest obstacles to the development of what I call successful intelligence is negative expectations on the part of authority figures. When these authority figures, whether they are teachers, administrators, parents, or employers, have low expectations, it often leads to their getting from an individual what they expect. The process may start in school, but it usually doesn't end there. Low grades become a ticket to life's slow lane. Thus, it's not a low IQ per se that can so easily lead us down the road to ruin, it's the negative expectations that are generated.

As a college senior, I sought advice from my dean at Yale regarding future plans. I told him I was interested in psychology graduate school. He suggested that such a plan seemed overly ambitious to him, because, he said, I was basically a technician and should find a career path appropriate for someone with a technician's mentality. I was hurt. But my reaction to his advice was: Thanks but no thanks. I went to graduate school in psychology. As important to successful intelligence as knowing when to accept advice is knowing when to reject it.

Successfully intelligent people defy negative expectations, even when these expectations arise from low scores on IQ or similar tests. They do not let other people's assessments stop them from achieving their goals. They find their path and then pursue it, realizing that there will be obstacles along the way and that surmounting these obstacles is part of their challenge.

A second big obstacle to successful intelligence is one's own flagging sense of self-efficacy. It's not just other people's negative expectations that get in the way. These expectations can be contagious and ultimately rob a person of working up to his or her own potential for success.

For years, I was convinced that I had no sense of direction when it came to finding my way through the streets of New Haven, even a few blocks from where I worked. One night, I was scheduled to give a talk at a school in a particularly bad area of the city. As I drove to the school, it was still light, and I carefully noted the streets onto which I was turning. The route was complicated. When I left that school, well after ten at night, I found my way out of the maze of dangerous streets without a single wrong turn. I couldn't believe it. I realized that the main reason I had become lost in the past was that I was so convinced I would get lost that I had never paid the careful attention needed to let me find my way around. When I told myself I could do it, I did it.

Successfully intelligent people are self-efficacious. They have a can-do attitude. They realize that the limits to what they can accomplish are often in what they tell themselves they cannot do, rather than in what they really cannot do.

A third obstacle to the realization of successful intelligence is lack of role models. Successfully intelligent people can often point to one or several powerful people in their lives who have helped them fulfill their potential or, in many cases, turn off the path toward failure and onto the path toward success. It's not enough just to have such people in their lives. What makes the difference is that they make the most of what is offered.

Mrs. Alexa was such a turnaround figure for me. Had I had some other fourth-grade teacher, I might today be cleaning my office at Yale rather than working in it. That's no exaggeration. Once you start down the wrong path, it becomes harder every year to get off it. Fourth grade was still early enough for me to find a better path.

Successfully intelligent people actively seek out role models. Throughout their lives, they may have several such models, and their own success represents a unification of the best attributes of

the various models. In other words, they do not slavishly follow any one model but rather form their own distinctive identity. They also observe people who fail, and note why they fail, and then make sure they do things differently.

Like Father, Like Son

My own not-so-happy experiences with IQ tests transpired in the 1950s, during the ancient days of Nikita Khrushchev and the International Communist Conspiracy; Elvis Presley and the International Rock-and-Roll Conspiracy; and Dick, Jane, Sally, and the International Conspiracy to Bore Schoolchildren to Death. How times have changed! Khrushchev is dead; Presley is dead; and Dick, Jane, and Sally are still trying posthumously to figure out why they were fired from their lead roles in reading texts. But maybe they are laughing at us from their graves, because in the domain of testing, nothing has changed a whole lot.

My son, Seth, was an elementary-school student in the not-so-distant eighties, thirty years after my own soporific adventures with Dick and Jane. Seth was in a good school and then, because of a move, had to transfer to another good school. The schools were very similar in every respect, right down to their physical appearances. But for Seth, there was one stunning difference. In the first school, he was in the top reading group, whereas in the second school, he was in the bottom reading group. It was hard for me to believe that a kid could have got so dumb over the summer.

What had happened was that when Seth arrived at his new school, the teachers needed to place him in a reading group. They weren't just going to take the word of the first school that he should be in the top reading group. They took what they viewed as a more scientific approach. The first day of school, they gave Seth a test of reading ability (which, by the way, correlates pretty highly with tests of intellectual ability). Seth bombed the test. It was his first day in a new school with a new building, a new teacher, new children, plus a new house and all the new problems that come with any move. He was scarcely in a position to concentrate on any serious kind of test at all. So it really was no surprise that he didn't do well.

The effect of the low score was immediate, and it was profound. Seth was dumped with the other waste products in the garbage pail of the reading groups. But after a while, his teacher noticed that Seth was reading better than other children in the group, an observation that was scarcely surprising, since he had already learned the skills he was being taught at his other school. So you might think the school would bump him up to the middle reading group. Instead, Seth was given the reading test again.

This time, his performance was better. He scored at a higher level on the reading test, so he was placed in the second reading group. Soon, though, the teacher noticed that Seth was reading better than the children in the second reading group, and so, by the same logic, he was given the reading test again. And this time, he scored at the level of the children in the first reading group. Perhaps you can guess what the school did.

You probably guessed wrong. Seth was left in the middle reading group. Seth's mother and I certainly guessed wrong. We couldn't understand why, the first two times, his teachers took the scores on the reading test to be divine revelations and, the third time, they crassly ignored the score. We had a conference with the heavyweights —the principal, the school psychologist, the reading teacher. They explained to us that although Seth had indeed done well on the reading test, he was now a full book behind the kids in the top group. If he were advanced to the top group, he would miss all the skills in that book.

Talk about self-fulfilling prophecies! Because Seth had been understandably distracted on his first day in the new school, he had been placed in a low-level reading group with low-level expectations, and as far as the school was concerned, he was now stuck. Multiply what happened to Seth by a few hundred million or so, and you will have a good picture of what is happening to children in schools all over this country in a given year. Start with low expectations, act in a way to generate those expectations, get what you expected, and "confirm" what you believed in the first place.

The underlying message in Seth's predicament was that the test—the predictor of reading performance—was more important than the performance it was supposed to predict: namely, reading. It would be rather like saying that a forecast tells us more about the weather than the weather itself—if the weather forecaster says it's going to rain, that's what matters, not whether it actually rains. This kind of backward logic is not limited to reading. We sometimes refer to people whose achievement is higher than we would expect from their IQ as *overachievers*. Again, the predictor becomes more important than the achievement itself, and instead of acknowledging that there is something wrong with the test, we conclude that there must be something wrong with the person.

Much of the research that is done in psychology curiously mirrors the kind of self-fulfilling prophecy that plagued Seth. Research is done that shows IQ only weakly to predict later outcomes. But instead of concluding that IQ isn't very important, certain researchers then strangely conclude that the abilities measured by IQ cause the later successes or failures. The research does not show this. It shows a statistical relation, not a causal one.[1]

What we have seen is that low test scores set in motion a chain of events that can lead to poor later outcomes, independent of the abilities the tests measure. Once a child is labeled as stupid, his opportunities start to dry up, and forces in the environment conspire to lead to the outcomes that would be expected and appropriate for a stupid person. Teachers expect less. Placements in lower tracks, reading groups, or, later, colleges reflect the reduced expectations. Good work is viewed with suspicion: Maybe the individual cheated, or at least got outside help. Labels are not just descriptions of reality; they contribute toward shaping reality.

IQ is about the label that is supposed to predict whether a person will be able to do certain work, whether that work is reading, writing, or creating a business plan. Intelligence is about the skills that truly enable a person to read, write, or create a technically flawless business plan, whatever the test may say. Successful intelligence is about writing the story or report that not only is technically good but makes a difference to people because it changes the way they think; it's about designing the business plan that not only is flawless but launches a successful business in a competitive world. The whole concept of relating IQ to life achievement is misguided, because IQ is a pretty miserable predictor of life achievement. We make IQ more important by determining kids' paths, even from elementary school, based upon their scores on these and similar tests. The child who might someday have been a great writer never gets the chance to develop the verbal skills that would enable him to fulfill that potential. Why? Because one day in first grade he bombed a reading test.

There is a story of a man who dies and goes straight to heaven. Saint Peter gives him a brief tour of the premises and points to an individual, mentioning that he was the greatest poet of his time. The man looks at Saint Peter, incredulous. "Excuse me," he says, "but I knew that man. He was nothing more than a humble shoemaker. He never even went to school or learned how to write." "Precisely so," responds Saint Peter. Never given the chance to develop his writing skills, the man's prodigious talent went to waste. The story would be more humorous if it weren't so true of so many people.

Successfully intelligent people realize that the environment in which they find themselves may or may not enable them to make the most of their talents. They actively seek an environment where they can not only do competent work but make a difference. They create their own opportunities rather than let their opportunities be limited by the circumstances in which they happen to find themselves.

Getting In

What happened to Seth, to me, and to many other people at the elementary-secondary level happens as well at the level of college, graduate, and professional schools. If you want to go to college these days, chances are pretty good that you will have to take either the SAT (Scholastic Assessment Test) or the ACT (American College Test). These tests differ primarily in the parts of the country where they are most widely used—the SAT primarily in the East and the West, the ACT more often in the Midwest and parts of the South—and in the exact types of problems they contain. Neither test has the word *intelligence* in its title, a deliberate decision on the part of each of the test publishers, but both tests are used as tests of intelligence, or at least of the intellectual abilities believed to lead to success in college. If you don't do well on these tests, you can pretty much kiss good-bye your chances of admission to a selective college.

Of course, if you want to go to business school, you need to take the Graduate Management Admission Test (GMAT); if you want to go to law school, it's the Law School Admission Test (LSAT); for medical school, it's the Medical College Admission Test (MCAT); and if you don't test well, chances are pretty good you won't get to where you want to go, regardless of the level of your intelligence or education.

One of the sadder things I experience as a faculty member is watching the hopes and dreams of aspiring graduate students being shattered on the crags of tests whose validity is questionable anyway. Recently, I received a two-page, single-spaced letter from a woman who had hoped to come to Yale to do graduate study in psychology. The hopes of a lifetime were dashed in a three-hour test. As she put it:

I took the GRE [Graduate Record Examination] last week: Not only did I go down in defeat, I crashed and burned in a blaze of glory. Two hundred hours of intensive preparation could not banish . . . years of test anxiety. . . . Since the beginning of summer, I have invested my time and resources exclusively to doing well on the GRE. . . . I gave up family, friends and flying. . . . I invested in a PowerBook to practice the computer exam, taking six computer versions of the GRE to become familiar with the computerized format. . . . Everything was fine until the first question appeared on the screen, a relatively simple verbal analogy. I started shaking and my mind went blank. . . . The clock was ticking, and I could not breathe. . . . I felt sick. I was devastated. My heart was pounding. . . . And then, with no warning, the screen went white. Time's up. Too bad. . . .

And so that was it. Bye-bye GRE, bye-bye graduate school.

Why are Americans so preoccupied with intelligence tests? There are few countries in the world that count on them so much. Other countries may count tests of achievement as much as or more than we do. But tests of achievement measure what you know. One can understand why people would value what you know. What is less clear is why people would value a test that measures what you may, or may not, come to know.

IQ is about scores on various tests used in schools and business. Intelligence is about what you really can achieve. And successful intelligence is about what you really can achieve that will make a difference to you and others. It's what separates those who just achieve from those who excel. Successfully intelligent people who don't test well, recognizing the overreliance our society places on tests, study to do better and thus increase the opportunities they will be given to achieve their goals. If they cannot raise their scores to the desired levels, they find alternative paths to their goals.

Successfully intelligent people seek to perform in ways that not only are competent but distinguish them from ordinary performers. They realize that the gap between competence and excellence may be small but the greatest rewards, both internal and external, are for excellence.

Three Traditions in American Education

If tests so often stand in the way of people performing at their peak levels, and low test scores prevent them from being allowed to seek their goals, what kind of thinking in American education has led us to place such heavy reliance on them? Historically, there are three sociopolitical traditions in America that have filtered down into education, but the third and most positive force has been lost in a battle between the traditional right and left wings in American politics. Each of these traditions stems from a somewhat different point of view on, and has had different implications for, American education and the phenomenon of testing.

The Hamiltonian Tradition

The right wing, both in education and in politics, I will refer to as the *Hamiltonian tradition*. I don't equate its beliefs precisely with those of Alexander Hamilton, but they stem from the spirit if not the letter of his views. What, then, is the Hamiltonian tradition? "Hamilton wished to concentrate power. . . . Hamilton feared anarchy and thought in terms of order. . . . Hamilton believed republican government could only succeed if directed by a governing elite." [2] The critical aspect of the Hamiltonian tradition, from an educational standpoint, is that people cannot be trusted to govern themselves and need the rule of a governing elite. In their book *The Bell Curve*, Herrnstein and Murray share that belief when they write about the emergence of a cognitive (high-IQ) elite, which eventually will have to take responsibility for the irresponsible masses of nonelite (low-IQ) people, who cannot take care of themselves. The less-endowed intellectually, in this view, need a paternalistic government that will take good care of them as they live out their lives in their largely separate but well-regulated enclaves. Left to themselves, they would create, as indeed they have always created, chaos.

Books such as *The Bell Curve* only put into print once more what has been said many times since the beginning of the twentieth century by Carl Brigham, Henry Goddard, and others. And many of the same ideas go even farther back, to Hamilton and even to Plato, with his idea of a class of intellectual philosopher-kings who would rule in a wise and just fashion over their less intellectually endowed brethren.

But who are the intellectual elite? How could they be found, and how should they be educated? The simplest answer to these questions is by some form of testing that would measure intelligence. And those who scored well on these tests would gain admission to the institutions of higher education. Thus, over time, the use of intelligence testing in the Hamiltonian tradition got a strong foothold in education, in general, and in admissions to higher education, in particular. Ironically, in college admissions, test scores became really important only in the 1960s as a means of protecting society against ruling elites. In the 1950s, SAT scores at Harvard were about 100 points lower than they were ten years later. The ticket to a good college in the fifties was good family connections—wealth, social status, contacts. When Inslee Clark at Yale started counting SATs heavily, it was so that those without such connections would have a shot at getting in. Curiously, then, it was, if anything, an anti-Hamiltonian gesture. What happened?

As our society moved away from any overt admission that family background could count for much, it needed some other code to stamp on the ticket that would enable society's wealthy and privileged to follow the paths to success they always had. Tests became the next best thing. Why? Because it didn't take people long to realize that test scores are very highly correlated with socioeconomic class.[3] Not perfectly, but highly enough. So, more or less, you could continue to do what you had long been doing, but now under the banner of ability-based admissions.

Test scores didn't quite make it as a substitute, however. For example, in the college-admissions business, too many kids from New York City did well. Jews and Asians also scored disproportionately well, not only relative to their population numbers but relative to their numbers in the upper social classes, where they have never been terribly well represented.

Enter diversity considerations. Recognizing they could admit almost the whole class from the Bronx High School of Science, Stuyvesant High School, and Hunter High School—three first-rate public schools in New York—colleges started seeking "diversity" and required much better credentials from these applicants than from applicants going to other schools. Now mix in the exorbitant price of attending an elite college (over $30,000 per year in the late 1990s), and colleges have managed to leave room for the relatively wealthy but have squeezed out the middle class, while still leaving room for a few minorities and some relatively poor applicants.

And it doesn't stop there. Colleges could still give preference to "legacies" (applicants whose forebears went to that college) and to "development cases" (applicants whose parents are filthy rich), and the system of college admissions left the kids of the socioeconomic elite still pretty well protected. Not all of them, but enough. Society's moguls didn't really have too much to worry about, unless they had the misfortune to have had a real dummy for a child.

So what started out as an attempt to render college admissions democratic didn't stay that way, even though the intentions of the admissions officers of the schools and colleges that use tests are, for the most part, honorable. They are attempting to do their best. But they themselves are for the most part members of the Hamiltonian elite, and so they will look at things from their own, usually Hamiltonian, point of view.

The Hamiltonian tradition, in short, has become practically synonymous with testing. It preserves privilege, ironically through a means originally designed to overthrow it. The privileged tend to support testing because they have done well by it, and because their children tend to do well by it. So today the Hamiltonian tradition is also doing quite well, as is testing.

The Jacksonian Tradition

The left wing, in both education and politics, I will refer to as the *Jacksonian tradition,* again with the stipulation that its views do not necessarily exactly follow those of Andrew Jackson. What did Jackson believe? "Jacksonian democracy shared that contempt for intellect which is one of the unlovely traits of democracy everywhere. There was no contact between the political democracy of Jackson and the philosophical democracy of men such as Emerson. . . . The people become educated, knowledge extends, a middling ability becomes common. Outstanding talents and great characters are more rare. Society is less brilliant and more prosperous. . . . The common man gained active participation in government at all but the highest levels."[4]

Jackson believed that all people are equal, not only as human beings but in terms of their competencies—that one person would serve as well as another in government or on a jury or in almost any position of responsibility. In this view of democracy, people are essentially intersubstitutable. Translated into modern terms, it is represented by a well-known political scientist with whom I was once on a panel. He said to an audience of over a thousand that any test that leads to higher scores by members of one group than by members of another group is biased, by definition. Perhaps he also would have liked to see older and younger children performing at the same levels, in order to be fair to the younger children.

In this view, we do not need tracking or sectioning in schools, which do nothing more than grant artificial privileges to one group over another. Nor do we need intelligence and other ability tests, which do more of the same. If one group is not doing as well as another in gaining access to resources, and if efforts to bring this group to parity fail, then the group should be given benefits until it attains parity, regardless of performance—not regardless of ability, because in the Jacksonian view, everyone is equal, not only humanly but ultimately, in respect to ability. What matters is equality of outcome, rather than of the productive work that leads to these outcomes. Indeed, in this view, if outcomes are equalized, equality of productive work will somehow follow.

The Jacksonian view has wreaked havoc with our educational system. In the name of "full inclusion," children with severe emotional and physical handicaps who require the lion's share of a teacher's and a full-time aide's attention are mainstreamed into the regular classroom, leaving the rest of the children with only a fraction of the teacher's attention. Students who could excel are held back so that they will conform to the lower group norm, and children who can barely understand what is going on in the classroom are placed in it to serve some elusive and illusory egalitarian goal. Indeed, parents now even clamor to have their children labeled as "disabled" or "hyperactive" so that they will receive extra resources from the school. What system of allocating resources could be more perverse? We create a pretense that equality of opportunity means identical instruction for all, and we reap what we sow—an educational system that fully benefits almost no one.

The Jeffersonian Tradition

There is a third force in American political and educational thinking, which has somehow gotten lost, or at least has attracted less attention than it deserves. This is the force represented by the Jeffersonian tradition in American political thinking. Again, my goal here is not precisely to reproduce Thomas Jefferson's beliefs but to gather a part of their essence. "Jefferson feared tyranny and thought in terms of liberty. . . . Jefferson [believed] that a republic must be based on an agrarian democracy. The people, according to Jefferson, were the safest and most virtuous, though not always the most wise, depository of power, and education would perfect their wisdom. . . . Jefferson inherited the idealistic conception of the new world to which the French philosophers paid homage—a republic of mild laws and equal opportunity, . . . renouncing wealth and power to preserve simplicity and equality." [5]

In the Jeffersonian tradition, people are indeed all equal in terms of political and social rights and should have equal opportunities, but they do not necessarily avail themselves equally of these opportunities and are not rewarded equally for their accomplishments. People are rewarded for what they accomplish, given equal opportunity, rather than for what they might have, or should have, or could have accomplished. Those who fail are not rewarded equally, because they gave it a shot, with those who succeed.

In this view, the goal of education is not to favor or foster an elite but to allow children the opportunities to make full use of the skills they have. Testing no longer becomes synonymous with elitism, because what is tested becomes much broader than what we are testing now. Different children bring different talents into the classroom, just as different adults bring different talents into the workplace. We thus need to test children, but much more broadly than we have ever done in the past, to make sure we are not wasting talent, as, I believe, we almost certainly are today. We provide to any child the education that best suits that child, and to those children who excel in a given area we want to give the extra challenge that will propel them to the highest level of accomplishment of which they are capable.

My views on education and testing are from a Jeffersonian perspective. But it is the Hamiltonian perspective that now drives our use of testing, and the Jacksonian perspective that dominates in classroom instruction. In testing, we hang on to Hamiltonian elitism to protect ourselves from what we view as the chaos of the Jacksonian concept of democracy. In teaching, we hang on to Jacksonian populism in the false hope that someday all students will truly achieve equally. It is my argument that the Jeffersonian concept of democracy is what should motivate us, and what we should strive to implement in our schools and in the workplace.

The Jeffersonian tradition is the one that most allows successful intelligence to thrive. It is the only one consistent with my concept of successful intelligence. Hamilton was wrong: People can have successful intelligence, but it is not necessarily related to their years of formal education, their intellectualism, their birth or social class, or, for that matter, their IQ. Jackson was also wrong: Not everyone is equally successfully intelligent, if only because people do not equally make best use of their intellectual potential. Jefferson was right: Everyone has intellectual strengths that can be developed, but not everyone develops them equally.

Successfully intelligent people capitalize on their intellectual strengths and compensate for and correct their weaknesses. Parents, schools, and the workplace need to support the development of successful intelligence in whatever ways they can, and to view

intellectual abilities as dynamic and flexible rather than as static and fixed.

Test Dependency:
How We Became Addicted

People who build up a dependency on drugs begin to reach a point where they can't imagine life without them. They continue to use them not because of the high the drugs give them but to ward off the lows of withdrawal symptoms. That's what has happened in our society—we have developed an addiction to tests that measure inert intelligence, not achievement or the potential to achieve. We're afraid the sky will fall in if we stop using such tests. But when Bowdoin College stopped requiring the SAT, the sky didn't fall in. Why has our society become so addicted to tests that measure qualities that, in the long run, just aren't that important? One factor is a national addiction to precise measurements.

If you ask Mr. Spock, of *Star Trek* fame, what the temperature is outside and tell him that you prefer the measurement in Fahrenheit rather than Celsius or Kelvin, he will immediately reply, say, "72.849273 degrees." There is nothing like precision when it comes to knowing the temperature. In fact, in our society, there is nothing like precision when it comes to knowing practically anything, including measurement of intelligence. With standardized test scores, one is left with an overwhelming feeling of precision; indeed, of exactitude. We can speak of an IQ of 116—precise to three digits—or an SAT score of 580, or whatever. But there's a problem. Our abilities to measure temperature and to measure intelligence just aren't the same.

With temperature, we know exactly what we are measuring. With intelligence, we don't. Moreover, with temperature, the only thing that would prevent us from giving measurements with Spock-like accuracy is the mechanical precision of our instrument: With a precise enough thermometer, our measurement of temperature can be very close to exact. With IQ tests, because we don't know exactly what we are measuring, increasingly greater precision of measurement is largely an illusion. Put another way, an increasingly sharp image on a movie screen does not make the objects depicted any more real.

The value our society puts on precision is not limited to intelligence. When we note the Dow Jones industrial average for the day, we may think we have the "beat" of the stock market, because we know so precisely what happened. In fact, the Dow Jones average represents only a very small fraction of the stocks on the New York Stock Exchange, and none of the stocks on the American Stock Exchange or any of the many non-U.S. exchanges. Moreover, the average does not even represent an unbiased indicator of how the stock market has done.

During much of 1994, for example, large increases in the Dow Jones, which comprises stocks of large industrial concerns, hid the fact that the market as a whole was not doing particularly well. Any number of people were surprised to find that at the same time they were hearing great news about stock performance on the radio or television, their own stocks were going nowhere. The Standard & Poor's 500 index, more (although not totally) representative of the market as a whole, was hardly moving.

What's frightening is that people make important decisions on the basis of pseudoquantitative precision—information that is numerically precise but conceptually inaccurate. Certainly, stock pickers, with all their quantitative indexes, do not always do particularly well, and random-walk portfolios (essentially tied to the market average) generally do better than portfolios that are picked on the basis of very precise-sounding indicators. Indeed, professionally managed mutual funds only occasionally do better than the market as a whole.

Numbers hold sway in other domains as well. Consider one other wholly different domain, oil exploration. In speaking about the problem of pseudoquantitative precision to managers for a company that specializes in locating underground oil reserves, I was amazed to hear that oil-exploration firms face the same problems as testers in psychological measurement. They cannot say for sure whether oil will be found in a given location. What they can do is provide estimates of the likelihood of finding oil there. Because drilling dry wells is so expensive, oil companies have a strong incentive to drill only where there is actually oil. What the managers told me, however, is that they usually prefer precise, quantitative information to less quantifiable information, even if the less-precise-sounding information has proved in the past to be more accurate. Oil drillers, in other words, make the same mistakes in picking winners as do psychologists and educators. They prefer "hard data," even when the numbers are suspect.

Let there be no doubt that such mistakes are made. At Yale, we not infrequently encounter students whose performance in classes comes nowhere near to matching their stellar test scores. Indeed, one occasionally meets people who, within five minutes, have managed to slip into a conversation their IQ, their SAT scores, or their Miller Analogies Test score, or whatever suits them. But after a few minutes, it begins to appear that their high test scores were their last major accomplishment. When people are admitted to competitive programs because of their test scores, it often turns out that the only thing the tests predict for them are similar scores on more of the same kinds of tests.

IQ and like tasks may predict people's grades in college with pseudoquantitative precision, but they are not a measure of their intelligence—the mental qualities that actually produce these grades as well as other forms of performance. Nor do they measure successful intelligence—those mental qualities that lead to outstanding accomplishment.

Birds of a Feather

If people are suckers for precise-sounding numbers, thus overrelying on tests, that isn't the only factor that leads to mismeasurements of intelligence. They are also suckers for others like themselves.

Do birds of a feather really flock together? Absolutely. Few findings in the psychological literature are more thoroughly verified than the fact that we are attracted to people who are more rather than less like ourselves. Our friends tend to be similar to us, and our mates even more so. Indeed, psychometrically measured intelligence is one of the most prominent attributes of so-called assortative mating—our tendency to marry people who resemble ourselves.

That same factor is certainly at work in college admissions offices. If we want to predict whom admissions officers are likely to be attracted to, we would do well to ask what they themselves are like. The probability is that, like anyone else, they will be attracted to people who are similar to them.

A first-rate college isn't going to hire graduates of Podunk U. to fill openings in the admissions office. Most likely, it will hire its own graduates, who know the college and can also serve as good advertisements by talking to applicants about how great the college is. Alternatively, admissions officers may be from a similar and, quite likely, competitive college, in which case they can tell applicants that they have come to realize how the college for which they are recruiting is far superior to the overrated competitor from which they were graduated.

These admissions officers will have something else in common besides their respective alma maters, however: high or at least quite decent standardized test scores. Why? Because the colleges from which they were graduated required the tests for admission, and they are unlikely to have been admitted unless their test scores were, if not top-of-the-scale, certainly competitive.

Admissions officers are in a powerful position. They can make or break an applicant or, at the very least, have a major say in who gets admitted to a college or graduate program and who does not. In the nation's top schools, they are an elite group, likely to think that they are on the fast track, which they are. And they will want to admit candidates who, like themselves, are on the fast track, or at least show signs of gearing up for it. One of the things that put them on the fast track was their test scores, and because people tend to be attracted to others like themselves, they look for candidates ... with high test scores.

There is probably no one group that we need to educate more about successful intelligence than the admissions officers who control the pipelines into the university system of our country. But they are a particularly hard group to reach. First, they are spread out in myriad colleges and universities across the country. Second, most people don't stay in the job very long. It tends to be transitional, so that by the time they may start forming their own ideas rather than just listening to the ideas of others, chances are they are about to leave the system. Third, they are responsible not to society in general but rather to the university in particular. And the perhaps sad fact is that most college admissions officers find high-SAT types to be just the kind of students the professors want: good at memorizing material, competent in academic skills, and savvy in taking tests. As a result, admissions officers, under some pressure to give the professorate what it wants, give it what it wants—students high in inert intelligence.

That is not to say admissions officers will always look for people at or near the top of the IQ, SAT, or ACT scales. In fact, they themselves probably weren't straight-A students, or students with near 800s on their SATs or 34 on their ACTs. If they had been, they probably would be in medical school or law school or graduate school rather than in admissions offices. In my own experience working in the Yale admissions office, admissions officers are not, in fact, particularly turned on by the super-genius types, but for the same reasons, they are not turned on by the low scorers. They don't personally identify with either group. Thus, the super-scorers will often find themselves in the awkward position of having actually to compensate for their very high scores—to show they are not eggheads, or squares, or, quite simply, dorks.

If these super-scorers were well advised in high school, they will have developed a record of diverse extracurricular activities, which can then be translated, at college-admissions time, into a story of how well rounded they are. In some colleges—more likely state schools—high scorers don't have to worry, because admissions are done by formula: higher scores always serve to the students' benefit. But Ivy League colleges, among others, look for a well-rounded student body, so that scores have to be high but don't necessarily have to be right near the top.

For those who don't test well, the rest of their story is probably irrelevant. They don't need such a story, because at the competitive college, unless they are members of some special-status group (alumni children, children of very wealthy parents who are potential donors, superstar athletes, or members of groups targeted for affirmative action), they are likely to be in trouble. And even members of a special-status group are unlikely to be admitted if their scores are below some probably unspoken threshold.

Thresholds for admissions may be explicit or implicit. More often than not, there is no explicit minimal cutoff score for admission on a given test. But there may be implicit cutoffs. And in many schools, it is an open secret that the implicit cutoffs are different, depending on your ethnic group, state of origin (e.g., you would typically need substantially higher standardized test scores coming from New York City, New York, than from Mobile, Alabama), particular high school, and so on. If you are too far from the implicit cutoff, you don't make the grade.

The whole university-admissions system is a good example of the distinction between inert and successful intelligence. I read many applications for admission to our graduate program. The essay is very important, because it is supposed to distinguish those who are serious students from those who are fluffy wanderers, without aim or direction. Some of the most academically brilliant students totally blow it with essays that wouldn't get them into Fleabag University, whereas academically less brilliant students open doors into the graduate schools of their choice with essays designed to appeal to the people reading them. Successfully intelligent students tailor their essays and their other self-presentations to the goals they are trying to accomplish. Students who are high in inert intelligence may write perfect sentences that sell no one on their candidacies.

Successful intelligence is, in part, what is sometimes called business sense. It refers to knowing your customers. IQ doesn't measure this business sense at all. Indeed, many people with high IQs seem not to be aware either that they have customers or that these customers are important. Some don't even produce enough to have anything worth selling. Rather, they are consumers who take in knowledge in school but give little back in return.

The fact is that when there are products, there are always customers, from teachers in elementary school to bosses at work. A person can be high in inert intelligence but have virtually no realization of the importance of the customer. People high in successful intelligence, on the other hand, recognize that to achieve their goals, they have to tailor their presentations and their products to a particular set of customers (from teachers to admissions officers to bosses).

Yet many businesses—deceived into believing that inert intelligence makes a difference in job performance—use tests in much the same manner as do colleges. The goal is to find people who will perform well in particular jobs. The military uses tests as well. The testing game itself is big business, and tests are used to sort out those who are given better jobs and access routes to better jobs from those who are not. But it sorts them on IQ-type measures rather than on successful intelligence, which is what will truly determine who succeeds.

Three Strikes and You're Out

Getting a job has always been hard. Keeping a job has, in recent years, become a lot harder. The ups and downs of the economy, and a new mentality that says it's OK to let employees go to improve company bottom lines, have led people to spend more and more time watching their backs and less and less time actually getting the job done. Now consider the implications of this kind of back watching for those who make university-admission or job-hiring decisions. Their job—often their only job—is to select the best people for the available positions. If they guess wrong too often, they are out, or at least they should be. After all, picking winners is what they are paid for.

How do you know who the winners are going to be? If you are picking horses, you are likely to pick those that have winning records. What else do you have to go on? If you are a stock picker, you are likely to pick stocks that have been winners in the past. And if you are making college or job decisions, you are likely to pick people who have a winning record, and such a record, in our society at least, means high test scores. That is because test scores, for all their inadequacies, do predict school and job performance, although to a modest degree.

Unfortunately, the modest level of prediction of the tests is not reflected in admissions and hiring decisions. Why? Look at things from the point of view of the personnel officer (whether university or corporate). Let's consider two candidates—Tweedledum and Tweedledee. Tweedledum has great test scores, although his softer indicators—letters of recommendation, perhaps, or outside activities —are not particularly distinguished. Tweedledee has ho-hum test scores but looks really intriguing with regard to the softer indicators —great letters of recommendation and great outside activities, such as his successful climbing of Mount Everest in inclement weather. But you have a limited number of slots and can't take both Tweedledum and Tweedledee. You have to decide between the two.

Whom do you go with? When people are scared about keeping their jobs, they often resort to a decision-making process called the "minimax strategy." They minimize their maximum loss. Tweedledum's test scores suggest that, at the very least, he will be a decent student or worker. Tweedledee looks more exciting but is more of a risk. And in tough times, it's hard to take risks.

Fast-forward to the future, when the data are in. How do you cover your back if Tweedledum doesn't work out? In his case, it's pretty easy. You point to the high test scores and swear by all that's holy that you can't be held responsible for the failure of Tweedledum. After all, he had high test scores. The objective indicators were all way up there. No one can blame you; if anyone is to be blamed, it should be the testing company, for selling a test that doesn't make accurate predictions.

But how about Tweedledee? Suppose you chose him and he doesn't work out. Now you're in a bit more trouble. Your boss points out to you that Tweedledee, for all his mountain climbing, had pretty weak test scores. How could you ever have selected him in the first place? Indeed, if you did, there must be something wrong with you. You should have known better. So now you're in the uncomfortable position of looking bad yourself. From the boss's point of view, it wasn't Tweedledee who screwed up, it was you. You should never have taken him in the first place. Three strikes and you're out; or these days, maybe just two, or even one.

The conservative strategy will generally be to go with the hard data, because you can always cover your back with them. When people are insecure, they tend to lean more strongly on what appear to be the "hard indicators," with the result that those who don't measure up on those indicators will be sidetracked, probably not just by one university or one company but by a whole bunch of them.

If we want things to change, we have to reward rather than punish personnel officers—whether in colleges or in businesses—who take risks, who look for candidates and applicants who will be successfully intelligent rather than merely high in IQ. It may sound like an injustice to turn down someone who tests well in favor of someone with a broader and more intriguing set of credentials. But truly excellent universities and businesses do it all the time. Moreover, the person with the high test scores will be well placed somewhere else. The person with the more exciting record, ironically, may not get that chance if everyone focuses exclusively on a set of scores.

One year, I argued strongly for a candidate for our graduate program who didn't have the very highest test scores or quite the typical profile for admission. On the other hand, he had written major works of fiction. That's the kind of risk we should encourage personnel officers to take. Some risk. He was admitted and he did great. But he didn't look best on paper, and paper counts in our society.

The Paper Chase

Have you ever had anyone clean your house, tend your baby, or fix your toilet, and then, as you write out the check, announce that he or she accepts only cold cash? Of course, there are those who are afraid that the check will bounce, but there are a whole lot more who want to hide the income and know that the best way to do it is to avoid a paper trail. You can't hide the paper trail in every business. For example, if you work in a bank, everything's documented. Or is it?

Recently, an employee of a major Japanese bank managed to hide over a billion dollars in losses that he had incurred while trying to gain back a few hundred thousand dollars he had lost in bad trades. An employee of a British bank actually sank it with his bad trades, conducted from Singapore. These employees managed to work things out so that they could hide their losses for long periods of time. Curiously, it is much harder today to hide bad test scores than to hide bank losses.

Test scores are under constant scrutiny. Many private schools and colleges publish their average test scores, and those that don't are asked to 'fess up by companies that publish these averages, such as Barron's and Peterson's, both of which sell college guides. Because college test scores, as well as those of various kinds of graduate schools, are published, admissions offices are under great pressure to admit students with high scores, so that their universities will be able to compete in the public eye with other universities. If Yale starts admitting lots of people with low scores, then people will take one look at the averages and say they thought Yale was on the way down, but now they know it.

Public elementary and secondary schools are under equally great pressure. For example, in my own state, Connecticut, statewide mastery test score averages are public information and are published in various newspapers, district by district. In other states, similar kinds of information are to be found, which provide comparative data on different school districts, compelling them to keep scores up. Teachers whose students have low scores are blamed for their students' inadequacies; schools are blamed for their students' and teachers' inadequacies; districts further have to cope with the blame for their administrators' inadequacies. And test scores have become the cold, hard cash in the performance world of educational institutions.

Test scores do, in fact, convert to cold, hard cash—in the real estate market. I was recently in rural northern Illinois, looking at houses that in suburban northern Illinois, or in southern Connecticut, for that matter, would fetch between three and four times their price in rural northern Illinois. Many factors determine housing prices, but test scores are quickly becoming among the most important. Test scores measure what a school district is believed to be producing, and there is a premium on real estate in markets that can claim excellent test scores. You'll pay a lot more for a house in the New Trier School district in suburban Chicago than you will for a house in even some of the surrounding neighborhoods.

Business, with its push toward productivity, is no different. Although test scores may be confidential information, productivity generally isn't, at least in publicly held companies. And companies want to maximize their productivity, because today they need to do so or go under. For human resources departments, the productivity of workers is often closely linked to high test scores. The result is pressure to keep the scores high on the tests used to select candidates for jobs, and some of the best applicants won't make it because they don't have the test scores to get them over the top in the very competitive job market. But should high test scores really matter for their selection, or is the reliance on scores akin to a superstition, such as a rain dance?

Rain Dances, Elevator Buttons,
and Lucky Charms

Every once in a while, I'm invited to a fascinating place like the American Southwest or the Middle East, and I want to see all the tourist sights. I don't have time, though, so I have to hope I'll be invited again. The trouble is, I've already given my talks on intelligence or creativity or whatever, and they probably won't invite me back. As a result, I have to think up another angle.

I've got one ready to go. To get the invitation, I have to be responsive to needs—and what do they need more in the Middle East than water? It hardly ever rains there. Suppose I offer to make it rain. In fact, I guarantee it—double their money back if I can't make it rain. Desperate, they invite me, and the first morning after I get there, I do a rain dance. Does it rain? Of course not. They ask for double their money back. I say, "You must be kidding! This is the Middle East. Nothing ever gets done quickly here. You can't expect rain in a day."

So every morning at nine I do a rain dance, and then I spend the rest of the day sightseeing. Eventually, of course, it rains, I thank my hosts for their patronage, and I leave.

What's the point? The point is that people believed in rain dances for thousands of years, because if they kept doing them, eventually it rained. You may not believe in rain dances, but you probably have some comparable superstition or habit. Say, for example, you are in a hurry for an elevator to come. Someone is already standing there, and the button is lit up. But you push it anyway. Why? Because people are always rewarded for pushing the button—push it and, sooner or later, the elevator will in fact come.

I, of course, would never do such a thing. But I do have a lucky charm I almost always wear around my neck. Does it bring me good luck? I have no idea. But why risk taking it off? The only time I do take it off is for chest X-rays. Now, everyone knows that X-rays in high doses cause cancer. So I keep associating removal of my lucky charm with cancer. Why risk cancer? I never really give myself the chance to disprove my prior beliefs.

In like fashion, once an organization—an elementary school, a college, a business organization—believes in the power of a test to predict the future, try to get the organization to discontinue the test. It's hard, because if the organization only accepts students or hires employees who score over a certain point on their tests, then all of the successes they see—that's right, all—will have scores over the cutoff for selection. In other words, the organization is in the same position as the believer in the rain dance, elevator magic, or a lucky charm: With the system in place, they only allow for their beliefs to be confirmed. Nothing is ever permitted to happen that will disprove these beliefs.

The situation can be worse. Suppose just once, or maybe twice, you let someone in with a subthreshold score—a test case. Usually, everyone knows who the test cases are. They may have the "wrong" skin color, or clothes, or background, or accent. Will they do as well as everyone else, all things being equal? Who knows, because all things are virtually never equal. They are certainly not treated as equals. They are treated as special cases, as an experiment. They are different and are treated differently. The expectations for them aren't quite the same, and hence it's no surprise when they confirm those expectations. Often as not, they are set up for failure, and failure is what they achieve. Indeed, that is the term for what such persons accomplish: achieved failure. Again, why take that risk? Yet people have enormous capacity to develop and manifest successful intelligence; how strange that so often we don't let them.

Money Makes the World Go Round

One final factor makes test scores so important in our society: money. There are now any number of studies assessing the validity of tests to predict performance in a variety of jobs, and this work is couched in terms of how much money corporate America could save if it always used ability tests. These studies have concluded that corporate America could save millions.

I have nothing against corporate America saving millions, especially if it is translated into both higher productivity and a higher standard of living for all. But there are three important things to observe about tests that have an economic purpose. First, the value of tests is seen as monetary. The test users talk not about human values but rather about how test scores translate into dollars. In fact, other tests might save even more money, with less waste of human talent.

Second, all kinds of assumptions are made in translating test scores into economic terms, but these assumptions are never made clear. For example, suppose all organizations use tests uniformly for employment selection procedures. The result is that the same people keep losing out on jobs, because they do poorly on the tests used by all the organizations. Eventually, they may find themselves unemployed or, in many cases, underemployed. What are the costs to society of their unemployment or underemployment? Considerable.

Third, the value of the tests is expressed solely in terms of the profits to be made by the corporations or other institutions. Corporate profits are fine. But the point of view of the individual taking the tests is not considered at all. Thus, if the same person is repeatedly disqualified by the tests, that's tough. On average, the organizations will do better, even if certain people continually get the short end of the stick. How much people who work for organizations may gain or lose as a result of tests also is not considered. The issue underlying such tests is economic, but not for the individual worker. Rather, it is economic solely from the point of view of the organization. Certainly, both points of view are important.

The irony here is that what is better for the individual is also truly better for the organization. If we focused on a broader array of abilities, not only talented individuals would profit, so would organizations. They would end up hiring not necessarily those with the highest IQs but perhaps those with the highest successful intelligence, which ultimately would save them even more than would the high-IQ people. Failing to focus on an organization and the people that constitute it as a system leads to less than optimal outcomes for all.

We need to consider the hidden costs as well as the apparent benefits of testing, and that consideration has been glaringly absent among those who most vocally advocate tests. But just what, exactly, are they advocating? It is a view of individual differences in intelligence as a more or less fixed quantity. My view of successful intelligence is quite different from the conventional IQ-based view. Here are just a dozen of the main differences:

1. Conventional tests of intelligence are viewed as measures of only a small part of intelligence, not as measures of most or all of it. They focus on inert academic intelligence and not active successful intelligence.

2. Successful intelligence, as I view it, involves analytical, creative, and practical aspects. The analytical aspect is used to solve problems, the creative aspect to decide what problems to solve, and the practical aspect to make solutions effective. These three aspects are relatively independent of one another. Conventional intelligence tests measure only the analytical aspect of intelligence, and they don't even measure all of that.

3. Intelligence is viewed as modifiable. You are not stuck with a certain amount of intelligence. Rather, you can increase your intelligence; you can also decrease it. Successful intelligence is particularly susceptible to change.

4. Intelligence cannot possibly be measured in any large degree solely by the use of multiple-choice tests. Successful intelligence cannot be measured by such tests at all. Multiple-choice tests thus need to be supplemented by tests that require various kinds of responses. Different kinds of tests tend to benefit different people, so it is important to use a variety of test instruments.

5. Intelligence is primarily an issue not of amount but of balance, of knowing when and how to use analytic, creative, and practical

abilities. Intelligence is involved in seeking to reach any goal. Successful intelligence is involved in seeking the optimum balance for achieving one's own goals.

6. People who overuse their IQ-like analytic abilities often find themselves less effective in their lives than do people who moderate their use of these abilities because they apply only in limited situations.

7. Because intelligence tests don't measure creative or practical abilities, and because these abilities show weak or negligible correlations with conventional tests, we need to measure these other aspects of intelligence as well. They predict success in school and on the job at least as well as and sometimes better than conventional intelligence tests. We even need to measure analytical abilities more broadly than we do.

8. Schools tend to reward abilities that later in life are not very important. As a result, schools often discourage people from pursuing those things that they ultimately could do best. At the same time, they may encourage people to pursue options in which they will later find themselves to have limited competence. We need to make the demands of schools more closely match the demands of everyday life.

9. Intelligence is partially heritable and partially environmental, but it is extremely difficult to separate the two sources of variation, because they interact in many different ways. Trying to assign an average number to the heritability of intelligence is like talking about the average temperature in Minnesota. It can be as hot as the equator during the summer and cold as the North Pole during the winter. The heritability of intelligence varies depending on a number of factors. The heritability of successful intelligence has not even been studied, so we simply cannot say what role, if any, heredity plays.

10. Racial and ethnic differences in IQ reflect only a small part of intelligence as a totality, and the best evidence suggests that the differences are largely or entirely environmental in origin.

11. An important element of intelligence is flexibility. Thus, we need to teach children to see issues from a variety of viewpoints and,

especially, to see how other people and other cultures view issues and problems facing the world.

12. Successfully intelligent people figure out their strengths and their weaknesses, and then find ways to capitalize on their strengths —make the most of what they do well—and to correct for or remedy their weaknesses—find ways around what they don't do well, or make themselves good enough to get by.

These are some elements of a new view of intelligence that is sorely needed in our schools, universities, and places of business. It is a view of intelligence that will not generate the self-fulfilling prophecies of low IQ-test scores and will break the supposedly risk-free reliance on tests that measure intelligence, as it is traditionally viewed, with at best only pseudoscientific precision. It is a view of intelligence that is less exclusive, far more democratic, and with far wider application in the real world. And finally, it is a view of intelligence in all its aspects —analytical, creative, and practical—the use of which will bring rich rewards.

PART II

People Count IQ,
but IQ Doesn't Count

CHAPTER TWO

What IQ Tells Us

What, exactly, are IQ tests, and where do they come from? In order to speak intelligently about intelligence tests, you need to know the answer to these questions. To begin with, there are two traditions in the study of intelligence.

Francis Galton: The Great Hand Squeeze Is Squeezed Out

Certainly one of the most influential books of all time has been Charles Darwin's *Origin of Species* (1859). In it, Darwin proposed that the evolution of species and the development of humans could be traced to an evolutionary process of natural selection. The book profoundly affected many different kinds of scientific endeavors, one of which was the investigation of human intelligence and how it develops. After all, the book suggested that the capabilities of humans were in some sense continuous with those of lower animals. What, then, was the relationship between the capabilities of the lower animals and humans?

Darwin's cousin Sir Francis Galton was probably the first to explore the implications of Darwin's book for the study of human intelligence. Galton suggested that two general qualities distinguish people who are more intelligent from those who are less so. The first is energy, or the capacity for labor. Galton suggested that intellectually able people in a variety of fields are characterized by remarkable levels of energy. The second quality is sensitivity. According to Galton, the smarter we are, the more we are sensitive to the stimuli around us. All this may sound quite scientific, but Galton's early forays into the study of intelligence suffered from the same kind of conflating of science with prejudice that has dogged the field right until the present. For example:

The discriminative facility of idiots is curiously low; they hardly distinguish between heat and cold, and their sense of pain is so obtuse that some of the more idiotic seem hardly to know what it is. In their dull lives, such pain as can be excited in them may literally be accepted with a welcome surprise.[1]

For seven years—between 1884 and 1890—Galton ran a service at the South Kensington Museum in London where, for a small fee, people could have their intelligence checked out. The only problem was that the tests used were, to put it mildly, a curious hodgepodge that measured lots of things but certainly not intelligence in any meaningful sense. For example, Galton contrived a whistle that would tell him the highest pitch a person could perceive. A nice test of hearing sensitivity, but scarcely a test of intelligence. Or if it is, you can be sure that your cat, or anyone else's, is a heck of a lot smarter than you are.

Another test used several cases of gun cartridges filled with layers of either shot, wool, or wadding. The cases were identical in appearance and differed only in their weight. The game was to discriminate the lighter from the heavier. A test of weight sensitivity? Maybe. A test of intelligence? Hardly. Nor was Galton's test of sensitivity to the smell of rose plants. Obviously, this was one intelligence test to be avoided by someone with a cold or an allergy to roses.

You might think that Galton would have been laughed out of town for such ideas. Quite the contrary. He didn't become Sir Francis because he was a public laughingstock. People took him very seriously, and so far as we can tell, he turned a handsome profit in his testing operation. And it wasn't only the museum visitor looking for a scientific self-assessment who took Galton seriously. A famous psychologist named James McKean Cattell was so impressed that he brought Galton's ideas to the United States.

Cattell (1890) devised his own test, which basically consisted of more of the same. For example, in a dynamometer pressure test, people had to squeeze an instrument as hard as they could, and the hardness of their squeeze became one of several measures of their intelligence. Another test looked at how much pressure it took for a person to experience pain. This was one time in a person's life when being easily hurt could actually be a payoff—reaping a higher assessment of intelligence.

As you might expect, there was one problem with all these measures. They didn't work. Eventually, a student of Cattell's blew the whistle. Appropriately enough, his name was Wissler. He found that scores on Cattell's tests were related neither to each other nor to college grades at Cattell's and Wissler's university, Columbia. Wissler's study was not a paragon of scientific research, but it was enough to convince people that Cattell's approach was a bomb.

Unfortunately, the bomb proved to be a time bomb. As Santayana so appropriately pointed out, those who don't learn from history are doomed to repeat it. Today a crop of neo-Galtonians have resurrected the work of Galton and Cattell, and have created a kind of night of the living dead. They are using measures such as simple reaction time (how quickly you can press a button after seeing a light go on) and line identification time (how quickly you can recognize which of two lines is longer) to measure intelligence. In the intelligence business, never think that burying an idea means that it is gone for good. It may come back to haunt you.

Galton's ideas, inspired by Darwin's theory of evolution, made a certain kind of evolutionary sense. Forest animals with sensory deficits tend not to live long; forest animals with unusual sensory acuity fare better. Perhaps, many years ago, our human ancestors were at a great selective advantage if they had superior sensory abilities. But often what leads to selective advantages at one time is not particularly useful at another time. For example, dark- and light-colored moths in cities have been differentially advantaged and disadvantaged as a result of overall levels of air pollution: The dark-colored moths are less visible during times of high pollution because of their smoky coloring, whereas light-colored moths are more visible during these times. During times of low pollution, the relative advantages and disadvantages reverse. In our time, acute sensory abilities are no longer a major factor leading either to reproductive advantage or to survival in general. Some theories are prescient: They come before their time. In contrast, Galton's theory was many thousands of years too late.

Alfred Binet: The Adulation of Academic Abilities

In 1904, the minister of public instruction in Paris created a commission to find a way to distinguish truly mentally "defective" children from those who were not succeeding in school for other reasons. The charge of the commission? To ensure that children would be placed in classes for the mentally retarded only if they were "unable to profit, in an average measure, from the instruction given in the ordinary schools."[2] Alfred Binet and his colleague Theodore Simon devised tests to meet this placement need.

Notice that the work of Binet grew out of a desire to help and protect children, not to penalize them. Teachers who found certain students to be pains in the neck had an option that for them must have been a great relief: They could recommend that such children be placed in classes for the retarded. It was not that the teachers were rotten scoundrels who wanted to make their own lives easier, although no doubt the thought must have crossed their minds. Rather, there was no clear distinction in people's minds between children who were behavior problems and children who were mentally re-tarded. As a result, kids with behavior problems were treated as though they were retarded.

Binet and Simon's conception of intelligence and of how to mea-sure it differed quite a bit from Galton's and Cattell's. Referring to the others' tests as "wasted time," Binet and Simon spoke of the core of intelligence as "judgment, otherwise called good sense, practical sense, initiative, the faculty of adapting one's self to circumstances. To judge well, to comprehend well, to reason well, these are the essential activities of intelligence." [3]

Let's face it: Binet's notions made a lot more sense than Galton's. Binet cited the example of Helen Keller as someone whose scores on tests of visual and hearing sensitivity would have been abysmal and yet whose level of intelligence—known to be extraordinary—could scarcely be faulted. Binet designed tests on which a physically handi-capped individual could do well. For him, intelligence depended on mental judgment, not on sensory acuity.

Most people know of Binet only through his test; but he had a theory of intelligence too, and it was a good one. He suggested that intelligent thought has three distinct elements, which he called *direc-tion, adaptation,* and *criticism. Direction* involves knowing what has to be done and how to do it. *Adaptation* refers to customizing a strategy for performing a task, then keeping track of that strategy and adapting while implementing it. *Criticism* is the ability to critique your own thoughts and actions. So suppose you want to buy a new car. You would use direction to figure out what you need to know about cars and how to apply this information in going out and actually choosing a car. Adaptation would be involved in your then going out, making decisions, and possibly revising your strategy as you are looking—for example, deciding that maybe, after all, you don't need a television set for backseat riders to entertain themselves while you are driving. Criticism would be used in evaluating your own decision-making process and asking yourself whether you are using good strategies for deciding on a car and where to buy it.

Binet's ideas, like Galton's, were imported to the United States but, in this case, originally to California rather than New York. Lewis Terman, a professor of psychology at Stanford University, created an Americanized test based on Binet's theory and tests. The rest, as they say, is history. The Stanford-Binet is still a leading competitor in the intelligence-testing business.

Binet's ideas made sense in the context in which they were proposed: for predicting academic success. Unfortunately, like so many ideas that catch on, they came to be used far beyond the domain in which they worked best. Tests of academic abilities came to be used in nonacademic domains as well. Moreover, the tests had and still have limitations that render their results questionable even in many academic contexts.

Tests Based on Binet's Theory

What are the kinds of questions that actually appear on IQ tests? Many of us have heard about IQ tests, and many have taken one or more at some time in our life, but it may be difficult to remember exactly what appeared on them. In fact, too many people talk about IQ tests without knowing what's actually on them and what's actually wrong with them. Much of this huge amount of verbiage is based on political or social convictions rather than on facts. There is nothing wrong with drawing political or social implications from these tests —I do it myself. But first you have to understand the tests, and both what's right and what's wrong with them. So let me describe in some detail one of the two most widely used tests, the Stanford-Binet, as derived from the original tests of Alfred Binet.

The Stanford-Binet Intelligence Scale, Fourth Edition (SB IV), is the most recent in a series of scales that dates back to 1905.[4] The first revision (i.e., the second edition) of the Stanford-Binet appeared in 1937, and the third edition in 1960. The test can be given to children as young as two, and up to any age, although the actual tryouts of the test (called *standardization*) extended only up to people twenty-three years of age.

What's on the test? What does a Stanford-Binet look like? There are fifteen subtests in all, only six of which are given throughout the entire age range of the test. The subtests break down into four categories: verbal reasoning, quantitative reasoning, figural/abstract reasoning, and short-term memory. Consider some examples of the fifteen subtests:

1. Vocabulary.　Individuals are asked to name the meanings of words. At the lower levels, the words are presented via pictures. Later, they are presented in writing. For example, one might be asked what a word such as *pretentious* means. Vocabulary is given to individuals at all age levels. Vocabulary questions appear on many tests of intelligence and related constructs, such as "scholastic aptitude tests." The inclusion of such test items should help you understand the concerns some psychologists, as well as educators, have about labeling them as tests of *intelligence.*

First of all, you need to realize that the time-honored distinction between *intelligence tests,* on the one hand, and *achievement tests,* on the other, is largely mythical. Intelligence tests typically measure the achievements a person is supposed to have attained several years earlier. Intelligence tests clearly measure achievement—what else is vocabulary? No one, not even the most nativist, hereditarian of theorists, would argue that we are born with vocabulary words conveniently stored in our brains. Achievement tests also require intelligence to complete: You need, at minimum, the intelligence to have learned the material that is being tested.

Second, when you test vocabulary, you can chuck any fantasies you may have had about culture fairness. A test of English vocabulary is scarcely going to measure the same thing for a child brought up speaking Spanish or Vietnamese or Japanese as for a child brought up speaking English. In fact, the total number of words known by the bilingual child may be greater than the total number known by the English-speaking child. The problem is that the test gives credit only for the words known in English, bestowing an obvious advantage on the child whose native language is English.

Amazingly, those who want to use intelligence tests in countries other than those in which they are created (which usually means the United States, the world's biggest producer and consumer of such tests) will often translate them into the languages of those countries. In doing so, they are assuming that the words translate exactly; that the words, however they translate, are essentially equal in difficulty and importance in the other language; and that giving definitions of abstract words in other cultures is as familiar as it is in American culture. None of these assumptions is likely to be true, but this fact doesn't stop people from doing what are essentially mindless translations of American or other tests.

Third, the way vocabulary is tested is an example of a theme that will appear throughout this book—that intelligence tests measure an academic, decontextualized kind of intelligence. Just recently, I sat in on a class where a teacher was testing high-school students on their knowledge of vocabulary. Each student had to both define the word in the abstract and use it in a sentence. Consider two different responses for the word *allay:*

> to reduce in intensity . . . The doctor gave the child aspirin to allay the child's temperature.
>
> to decrease . . . The politician allayed the people's fears regarding a possible tax increase.

Notice that the first student's abstract definition is better than that of the second, which is too broad. But the second student, although he did not produce as precise an abstract definition, knows how to use the word in actual context. He is the one who will appear more intelligent in his day-to-day interactions and even in the classroom, whereas the first student will receive the credit on the IQ test.

Last but by no means least, consider what vocabulary tests have done to our educational system. Why were kids in a high-school class memorizing vocabulary words? This is no way to learn how to read or write, to speak or listen. The natural way to learn words is in context—in reading and in listening, for example. Ultimately, what's important in life is to know how to read, write, listen, and speak well, not to be able to spit back definitions. Memorizing vocabulary words not only is unnatural but rarely results in serious long-term retention of the words. Because they are learned out of meaningful context, they are quickly forgotten, much as is the content of most of the courses for which we cram in school. But because scholastic aptitude tests given in high school assess vocabulary through various kinds of fundamentally unnatural test items, teachers force millions of students to waste their time memorizing words they are likely not to know how to use and are equally likely quickly to forget. Teachers teach to the tests, and these tests aren't measuring what kids or adults need to know.

2. Comprehension.   Here, the individual has to show understanding of social and cultural norms—by explaining, say, why people sometimes borrow money, or why people vote. At first glance, a test such as this might seem to measure intelligence in real-world contexts, an ability we are certainly interested in. But does it measure real-world understanding, or a caricature of real-world understanding—a story we like to tell ourselves about the society we wish we lived in?

For example, why do people borrow money? Ostensibly because they need funds to buy something they cannot afford to pay for in full at the time. But why do people *really* borrow money? Sometimes, as in the case of buying a house, it may be to get a tax break. Sometimes it's because they want luxuries—cars, boats, mansions— that they not only can't but shouldn't buy. Sometimes it's to get extra cash that they have no intention of paying back. Sometimes it's to buy controlled substances, which ultimately will kill them. And sometimes, of course, it's for the reasons given in the answer key of the test.

Or why do people vote? In a country where 99.6 percent of the people vote for the incumbent dictator (the recent not so amazing victory margin of Saddam Hussein), it's because they have to vote for the government-approved candidate, or else. Sometimes it's because they want to show their dissatisfaction with all the offered candidates, as when a U.S. citizen writes in a preferred candidate; sometimes it's because they have been paid to do so. Of course, sometimes it's freely to express their political sentiments, as a test would like them to say; but other times, the question has no meaning at all, because people in much of the world don't vote and never will in their lifetimes.

A test of comprehension is, in large part, a test not of what people know to be true but of what they know a test scorer wants to hear. To the extent that you aim to measure people's understanding of the testing game, such a test is quite an appropriate measure. And it may well correlate with people's understanding of the same game in school. But it's no measure of successful intelligence, especially for people who were not brought up to understand testing games. Oddly enough, this test, which seems so culture-bound, isn't really tied to the culture in which people live. It's bound to a Dick, Jane, and Sally fantasy of what that culture wants to believe of itself.

3. Absurdities.   In this test, the individual is shown pictures in which there is an incongruity, and the task is to point it out. For example, the individual might have to recognize that ice hockey players do not skate on lakes into which swimmers in bathing suits are diving. But how much is a child from a tropical climate going to know about ice hockey? Would you recognize an incongruity in a picture about a game such as rugby or cricket, neither of which is even tropical? How about Go? In order to recognize an absurdity, one has to be familiar enough with the content of the picture to recognize what even possibly might be wrong.

4. Verbal Relations.   Here, the individual has to say what the first three words in a set have in common that a fourth word does not. For example, what do an apple, a banana, and an orange have in common that a cup does not? Sounds pretty easy, but it helps if you come from an environment where all these fruits are available, so you know what they are. Do you know what a guayaba is? There are countries in the world where even very young children would know without hesitation. Often, tests that are supposed to be of verbal

reasoning end up being tests of vocabulary. Both my children took the Preliminary Scholastic Assessment Test, and both had the same comment. The verbal analogies, which are supposed to measure verbal reasoning, were hard not because they couldn't figure out the analogies but because they didn't know what all the words meant.

Thus, what sometimes happens is that a test which is supposed to measure one thing (verbal reasoning) largely measures another thing (in this case, vocabulary). Try solving the SAT-type analogy MITI-GATE : ASSUAGE :: EXACERBATE : (a) improve, (b) worsen, (c) abuse, (d) aid, (e) hinder, if you don't know what the words mean.

What is particularly pernicious about tests such as these is that they lead those who interpret the scores to wrong conclusions. In the above example, one is likely to conclude that someone who doesn't know the meanings of very low frequency words is suffering from some kind of deficit in reasoning ability. I think it would be nice if everyone knew that both *mitigate* and *assuage* can mean "alleviate." Certainly, anyone who plans a career in literary scholarship should know what these words mean. At the same time, I suspect that many people could get through their lives just fine, and even with enormous success, not knowing the meaning of either of them.

5-6. Pattern Analysis and Copying.   In pattern analysis tests, the individual reproduces two-dimensional, black-and-white patterns with blocks in order to compose various geometric shapes. In copying, the individual must reproduce geometric line drawings.

These two subtests show, perhaps more clearly than any of the others, the limitation of the standard view of intelligence. The name "copying" says a lot. Basically, the individual is rewarded for copying someone else's work. What kind of notion of intelligence is that? It's like giving credit for superb artistic ability to the people who sit in museums and spend their days copying the works of the great masters. At the same time, is it any wonder that tests such as the Stanford-Binet predict school performance, which in many instances consists of copying down and spitting back what the teacher says? You do it well and you get an A. You mess up—possibly because you're not motivated by such mechanical tasks—and your intelligence is in question. Personally, I've felt that one of the advantages of being an adult over being a child is that I'm no longer expected to fill in coloring books with the "correct" colors, staying ever so carefully within the lines. If we are to believe in this test, then coloring books provide excellent measures of intelligence.

7. Matrices.   In this subtest, the individual, presented with figural matrices of which one portion is missing, has to select the best of several alternatives for what should go in the missing space. Matrices have a long history in the IQ-testing business. Indeed, Raven Progressive Matrices, consisting exclusively of figural matrix problems, has been held up by some as one of the purest measures of general intelligence; it is considered a paragon of culture fairness, because it has no words and seems to its proponents to transcend cultural content. But whatever else it may be, it's not culture fair.

You now have a sense of the kinds of items that may appear on an individually administered intelligence test. Consider some further issues in terms of how these tests are scored and the results interpreted.

In the Stanford-Binet standardization sample—the sample used to derive a system of conversion between number of responses scored correct and IQ—there was a range of twenty-two years between the youngest and oldest individuals tested, which is quite a span. This standardization sample serves as the comparison group for determining the scores of people who take the test. How many people would you guess were tested in order to establish the translation between the number of items you answer correctly (called a raw score) and your actual score on the test (the so-called intelligence quotient, about which more will be said later)? We could start with the U.S. population, currently roughly 250 million. Would you guess that the standardization sample consisted of 500,000, or maybe 50,000? How about 5,000? Actually, the number was 5,013, not a lot of people when you consider that important decisions about people's lives will depend on the accuracy of these scores. And remember that the 5,000 or so spanned twenty-two years of life, so you're talking about an average of fewer than 250 per year of age!

A span of twenty-two years is impressive from one point of view but decidedly unimpressive from another. It highlights the fact that these tests are of academic abilities. The sampling of people corresponded exactly to the ages when people in the United States spend their time in school. But people generally move on after age twenty-two or so, entering the world of work. The abilities that will lead to success change, but the tests don't. So we have a test that is not only constructed for, but standardized on, a highly age-biased sample of the population. The stark reality of the situation comes to the fore when, occasionally, people decide to go back to school and find themselves taking tests that represent the reality of an adolescent rather than an adult. They waste their time studying geometric and other techniques they have not used in many years and are unlikely to use ever again, except on the tests.

Although an attempt was made to make the sample representative of the (age-biased) U.S. population, the effort was not successful. One group was oversampled—that is, there were too many of them, relative to their prevalence in the U.S. population. Just what group was oversampled? The same group that is almost always oversampled in psychological studies, especially of intelligence—people from higher level socioeconomic backgrounds. So statistical corrections were used to compensate for this oversampling. But such corrections are guesses—again, not a procedure that is likely to give you great confidence in the accuracy of the final scores.

Comparisons with other tests, including an older version of the Stanford-Binet, show that although roughly comparable, scores for the gifted and the mentally retarded may be somewhat lower than scores both on the older version of the test and on the main competitor test, the Wechsler. Given that scores at the low end are used to assign a diagnosis of "mentally retarded" and at the high end to assign a label of "intellectually gifted," this systematic noncomparability of scores may again rob one of the confidence one would like to have in a test with life-relevant implications.

There are other problems with the test. One is that different kinds of subtests (tasks) are given at different ages, so it is hard to know whether a score at one age is comparable to a score at another age. Furthermore, the range of possible scores is different at different ages and also for different subtests and sets of subtests, making it difficult to compare scores not only across ages but across kinds of abilities (e.g., to determine a person's pattern of strengths and weaknesses).

Perhaps the most serious problem with the test is that statistical analyses (called *factor analyses*) of the structure of the test do not support the way the test is structured to give partial scores. In other words, the scores do not correspond to the ways statistical analyses reveal people actually think. Thus, one can end up with a series of scores that tell you nothing in particular about a person's thought processes. For example, what exactly does a highly spatial person do well?

The Wechsler Scales represent an alternative to the Stanford-Binet and, indeed, are the most widely used intelligence scales. They are based on the same kinds of notions about intelligence as the Stanford-Binet. There are three levels of the Wechsler: the Wechsler Adult Intelligence Scale—Revised (WAIS-R), the third edition of the Wechsler Intelligence Scale for Children (WISC-III), and the Wechsler Preschool and Primary Scale of Intelligence (WPSSI).

The Wechsler tests yield three scores: a verbal, a performance, and an overall score. The verbal score is based on tests such as *vocabulary* as well as *verbal similarities,* in which the test taker has to say how two things are similar. The performance score is based on tests such as *picture completion,* which requires identification of a missing part in a picture of an object, and *picture arrangement,* which requires rearrangement of a scrambled set of cartoonlike pictures into an order that tells a coherent story. The overall score combines the verbal and the performance scores.

The Wechsler, like the Stanford-Binet, has problems in terms of its content. For example, in verbal similarities, people get more credit for saying how two things are similar categorically (e.g., they are both members of Class X) than for saying how they are similar functionally (e.g., the first uses the second), although the realization that the first type of answer is in some sense "better" than the second represents not so much cognitive development as understanding of the testing process. Someone might be able to discern a categorical relation but not realize it is the preferred response on the test. Similarly, a test such as picture completion assumes knowledge of the content of the pictures, and picture arrangement will very likely be easier for those who are used to following temporally ordered sequences of pictures, as in cartoons.

How Intelligence Tests
Are Constructed

How do writers and publishers of intelligence tests go about constructing these measures? There are two fundamental approaches to designing tests, although one is much more widely used than the other.

The Empirical Approach

In this approach, a series of observations is made of people who succeed in a particular context—such as school—and questions are designed to separate the people who are most likely to succeed from those who are least likely to succeed. Or even more simply, one could choose items that older children are more likely to answer correctly than younger ones. This is essentially what Binet did. He chose items that would distinguish older from younger children. This approach may sound quite sensible. After all, children generally get smarter as they grow older. There are some important problems with the approach, however, problems that have led us to the kinds of dilemmas we currently face with intelligence testing.

The first difficulty is that the samples on the basis of which the tests are developed are, in fact, children. Recall that the tests were originally used, and still are largely used, to distinguish bright children from less-bright children. The result often is tests that are much more appropriate for children than for adults. That creates a dilemma. Children may spend a fair amount of their time doing mathematical word problems, for example, but many adults have not done such problems in years. When older people apply for college or graduate school, they are expected to take tests such as the SAT or the GRE, which require them to remember principles of algebra and geometry that they may have had no use for in decades. Clearly, such tests are not measuring the same thing for mature adults as they are for young people in or fresh out of school. Little wonder that older adults often do not do well on such tests.

Thus, the tests are developed with the kinds of items that may well be appropriate for the material students study in school but not for that which adults confront in their daily lives. They should be referred to as measuring *academic intelligence.* Furthermore, the schooling on which they are based is Western schooling, which many children in the world do not receive. Even in the United States, students may receive alternative kinds of schooling, as, for example, young religious Jews who go to yeshivas that emphasize Talmudic argumentation rather than the Western literary canon.

A second, related dilemma is the very act of testing. When they start school, children may be unfamiliar with tests. I personally take with a grain of salt test scores for children below the fourth-grade level (roughly nine or ten years of age), because younger children are often not familiar with the testing medium. I still remember my first test with separate answer sheets, taken when I was in third grade. The Iowa Tests of Basic Skills happened to be an achievement test. But what I recall most vividly is getting to the last problem in one subtest and discovering, to my dismay, that I was on the second-to-last answer space. Somewhere along the line, my answers had become misaligned with the test problems, but the teacher was never going to know that. All she would know was that I seemed to be at a very low level on knowledge of the content of whatever that subtest measured.

As children make their way through school, of course, they get used to taking tests. So the testing medium itself at least becomes more familiar. But people who do not get Western schooling may never have encountered tests of these kinds. And middle-aged and older adults, in the Western world or wherever, may not have taken a test in many, many years. For them, the whole testing experience may be a source of considerable consternation and even anxiety. Again, one cannot interpret their test scores in the same way one would those of young people.

Research shows that variables pertaining to the tester can matter as well. For example, black children may be at a disadvantage when confronted with a typical intelligence-testing situation. Some less-obvious issues may enter in also. Many years ago, I proctored an examination when I worked over the summer at the Psychological Corporation, one of the big test publishers, which was then in New York. The company had decided that if it wanted the test to be utterly standardized for all the people taking it, the secret was to administer it via a tape-recorded transcription. In this way, everyone would hear exactly the same voice presenting problems at the same rate and in the same way. In theory, it all sounded just fine. In practice, though, it was a very different ball of wax.

For example, one might have expected that the voice on the tape would have been that of a professional announcer, who spoke articulately and clearly, and perhaps with the kind of "vanilla" midwestern accent that is most easily understood across the country. But for whatever reason, the president of the company had decided that he wanted to be the one to administer the test. A trained announcer he wasn't. But more significantly, his strong Texas drawl left many of the New Yorkers taking the test absolutely mystified. He might have been understood just fine in Houston, but in New York, it was a challenge just to figure out what he was saying.

Even worse, the idea that everyone would follow along with the tape recording was a joke. I watched as substantial numbers of people got lost and found themselves confused about just where in the test they were. They would be at one point, his mechanically transmitted voice at another. But when the employers who were considering hiring these people got their test scores, they would see a neat, clean computer printout, which gave the impression that everything during the testing had been just so.

A final disadvantage to the empirical approach to constructing tests is that test makers are never forced to confront the issue of just what intelligence is. They use what works—what distinguishes, say, the older from the younger kids. But older kids are taller, on average, than younger ones, as well as heavier. Test publishers will not get out a ruler or a scale as ways of measuring intelligence; height and weight just don't look like measures of intelligence. But in principle as opposed to practice, there often isn't a whole lot more reason to include what is actually found in the tests than there is to include height and weight. Without a theory of intelligence, there is no specification of what intelligence is, unless we resort to the weak "intelligence is what the tests test," the operational definition proposed by a now deceased professor at Harvard named, appropriately enough, Boring.

The Theory-Based Approach

The second approach to constructing tests is to start with a theory of intelligence and then to construct a test based on that theory. The advantage, of course, is that you start with a clear conception of what you mean by intelligence. Consumers of tests—the psychologists or schools or employers who buy them—can then decide whether they like the theory and, based on their decision, whether they want to buy the tests. In many respects, this is a much more honest approach to testing. The test publishers say what they mean by intelligence, and the consumers can take it or leave it. It's truth in labeling: You're told what you are getting.

But only a very few intelligence tests are constructed on the basis of a theory of intelligence. Why? Because it forces test publishers to commit to some conception of intelligence. They usually don't want to do so, either because they don't really have any such conception or because they want to maximize their market share. They figure, as did food producers before truth-in-labeling laws, that the less people know about just what they are getting, the less likely they are to be offended. Now, if you don't like high-fat foods, you can decide not to buy them. Before, you didn't know the fat content, so you were less apt to reject an item on that basis. But with tests, since there is often no real theoretical basis for them, you don't know quite what you are getting.

How Intelligence Tests Are Evaluated

Of course, consumers of tests are not total idiots, and they want information about the tests they may buy so they can engage in at least some kind of reasonable decision process—or appear to. What are the key kinds of information about tests that they, and you, need to know?

Validity

The first key kind of information, which will be discussed throughout this book, is often called *criterion validity*. The question here is the extent to which a test score relates to whatever it is supposed to relate to. Does it measure what it is supposed to measure? For example, intelligence tests are usually validated against school grades for students in school, or they may be validated against performance evaluations in job-training programs.

So-called technical manuals for tests may give large numbers of statistics relevant to the criterion validity of the tests. There is a problem, though. How much are we, or should we be, concerned about school grades? Are they really what we care about in terms of what makes one person more intelligent than another? Or are scores on standardized achievement tests what we should care about? My son has started a new newspaper at his school, writes columns for the existing school newspaper, flies a plane, and translates descriptions of medical problems into English for Spanish-speaking patients at a local hospital. For a seventeen-year-old kid, these are not bad accomplishments. None of them, however, will show up in the kinds of criteria that are used to validate intelligence tests. At the adult level, do we really care what people's grades were? Should potential candidates for jobs as captains of industry be evaluated on their grades in school? I doubt it.

It's a sad commentary, I believe, that we view ability-test scores as the hard data—the important data—and extracurricular activities as, well, extracurricular. And because of our comfort with quantification, we are often reduced to counting rather than seriously evaluating such activities. As a result, the student who joins three after-school clubs may be better off than the student who conceives of, organizes, and runs just one club. The best predictor of future successful intelligence is past successful intelligence. Such a predictor is clearly to be found in success in real-world activities that develop over a significant period of time, but not in test-world activities that take place over three hours.

For years, I had been saying that the tests don't measure what we really care about in performance, whether in school or on the job. In particular, I argued that at the graduate level, where we are training professionals, tests don't measure the skills that really matter for success in occupations, whatever they might be. I finally decided to put my money where my mouth was. Together with Wendy Williams, I did a study of just what it is that the Graduate Record Examination predicts at the graduate level. We looked at twelve years of matriculants (166 students) in our graduate program in psychology and compared the predictions of the GRE to first- and second-year grades in graduate school, but also, and more important, to professors' evaluations of students' (a) analytical abilities, (b) creative abilities, (c) practical abilities, (d) research abilities, (e) teaching abilities, and

(f) dissertations. Of course, in graduate school, these latter variables are considered much more important than grades.

What were the results? Considering both men and women (who performed at the same levels on the tests and in the program), we found that the GREs consistently predicted grades in the first year of the program, and that was it. And the level of prediction was nothing to write home about. For the GRE verbal, the overall correlation was .18 (on a 0 = low to 1 = high scale), which was barely meaningful statistically. For the quantitative, the correlation of .14 wasn't even statistically meaningful. For the analytic, the correlation was .17, again barely meaningful statistically. The best correlation, unsurprisingly, was for the advanced achievement test in psychology: .37. Achievement on the test was the best predictor of achievement in the program. The test didn't predict any of the more important criteria. It didn't even predict second-year grades. Little wonder that validity information provided by the publisher so heavily emphasizes first-year grades!

When we broke down results by gender, we found an interesting difference. One of the subtests, the analytical one, modestly but significantly predicted some of the more meaningful criteria, but only for men. For example, the correlation for men of the GRE analytical score with professors' ratings of students' analytical ability was .31. For women, it was a mere .05. In fact, the test didn't predict at all for women. Thus, combining men and women would give a deceptive picture of the success of the test in predicting graduate success. Although men's and women's performance in the program is equivalent, the antecedents of good performance appear not to be identical across the genders. Just what the differences are we do not yet know.

There are several lessons to be learned from this study, we believe. First, tests mostly predict grades, and often grades only pretty close to when the tests were given. There's nothing wrong with predicting grades—they do matter, after all, because we make them matter—but there is a lot more to life than grades. Second, tests do not predict equally well for all groups, something we may forget when we just look at a test score without considering whom it is for. Women face various challenges that men don't face, and indeed, researchers have found that women's views of themselves as unable to do certain tasks can lead to their actually performing more poorly on those tasks. When you have an expectation of failure, failure may well be what you get.

We were not terribly surprised by the results of our GRE study, nor have we been surprised by the reaction to the data in various groups to which we have presented them. Those who start off skeptical of tests nod their heads in assent when they hear the results. But those who are hard-core believers in the tests typically greet them with skepticism. They will say, for example, that in order really to know how well the test works, we would have to look at how well people who were rejected would have done in the program.

At some level, they are right. It would be nice to know how people who were rejected would have done. I think a whole lot of them actually would have done quite admirably. But of course, we can't do that study, precisely because these other individuals were not admitted to the program, often because of low test scores. So the skeptics will not be convinced until we do a study that is impossible to do. We could do something close. For one year or several, we could admit people without regard to their test scores and see how those admitted on other grounds perform. In this way, there would be no bias in the admitted sample with respect to their having been admitted on the basis of test scores. Indeed, ideally for this experiment, we would just admit people at random. But of course, no one has wanted to let the test scores go for a year or two, and faculty certainly have no interest in random admissions. Thus, the system remains in place, and people go on in their beliefs, which they will probably never allow to be disproved.

Data such as those of the GRE study point out the need for us to have validity information that goes beyond the narrow sorts that the tests' technical manuals typically give. We need broader criteria, and also we need to know the validity of tests for various groups and in various kinds of situations. We may assume that a test works for one group because it works for another, when in fact the test doesn't work very well at all for the second group.

Reliability

There is another kind of measure that test publishers and consumers are particularly interested in when they evaluate tests. Called *reliability*, it is the extent to which a test consistently measures whatever it is supposed to measure. In other words, if you take the test once and then take it again, will you get the same score?

Most of the tests that are widely given are fairly reliable, because if they weren't, they wouldn't be widely given. But we are talking averages here. There are some people whose scores fluctuate moderately, and others whose scores fluctuate even wildly. For example, many people can improve their scores on tests such as the SAT or the GRE or any of the similar admissions tests by using a book to study from or by taking a course to prepare for the test.

The availability of such books and courses, and the fact that, on average, they result in nontrivial score improvements, raise questions of equity. What about the people who don't know about the courses, or can't afford them, or don't have time to take them? Of course, test publishers will hasten to point out that the gains are not huge. On average, they are not. But for some people they are, and more important, when you are talking about millions of decisions in a given year for millions of test scores, even quite small differences will, on average, affect outcomes of those decisions. For some people, the book or the course will make a difference, and the fact that such opportunities are differentially available and utilized results in scores having different meanings for different people. So the overall reliability of the test scores can mask important effects that occur for given individuals.

Test publishers also like tests in which items within a given subtest all measure more or less the same thing. They even report statistics that show the extent to which the various items within a given subtest are uniform in what they measure. Although this consistency is viewed as a desirable property, it has costs. The more items you have measuring the same thing, the less range there is in what you measure. Thus, consistency is often achieved at the expense of breadth of measurement. Small wonder that our tests are as narrow as they are; and they are, in fact, narrow! We have consistently good measurement of inert intelligence. So how do we use these measures?

How Tests Are Used

Tests are used in ways that illustrate the Heisenberg Principle: They affect the very things they are supposed to be evaluating. For example, in our society, people at the top of the heap—lawyers, doctors, business executives, college professors—tend to have higher IQs than do those at the bottom of the heap—day laborers, house cleaners, street sweepers, and the like. So IQ is associated with occupational success, but does it cause it?

The dangers of confusing causation and correlation are easy enough to see. We know, for example, that most people in Nigeria are black and that most people in Norway are white. It would be foolhardy to conclude, however, that living in Nigeria causes you to be black or that living in Norway causes you to be white. So much for confusing correlation and causation. There is a correlation, but as always, there are at least three possible causal explanations. Suppose there is a correlation between two things, such as measured intelligence and job placement. But for generality, let's call them Factor X and Factor Y. It may be that Factor X causes Factor Y; it may be that Factor Y causes Factor X; or it may be that some higher-order factor causes both of them.

Thus, the correlation between IQ and job placement could be due to three kinds of mechanisms. High IQ might indeed cause better job placement, which is plausible. Or better job placement may cause high IQ, which, it turns out, is true. Being in a better job enables you to practice your intellectual skills, which in turn results in higher intelligence and thus higher IQ. Or it may be that both high IQ and good job placement are dependent on some other factor or factors. But what might such a factor or factors be?

Consider the situation in the United States. In order to get into law school, you have to take the law boards (LSAT); to get into business school, you have to take the business boards (GMAT); to get into medical school, you have to take the medical boards (MCAT); to get into graduate school, you have to take the graduate boards (GRE or MAT). Graduate education requires you to take a test, and admission to competitive programs requires high scores. Competitive colleges also require such tests, as do competitive private schools.

So what is the relation between these facts and the correlation between IQ and job placement? Conventional tests of intelligence are as related to these various admissions tests as they are to each other —which is to say that for all the differences in name, they measure practically identical skills. Using slightly different names and test content may be good business but makes relatively little difference in terms of results. People who tend to do well on one of the tests tend to do well on all of them.

Suppose that some people, for one reason or another, don't test well. Maybe they are creatively smart but not analytically smart. Maybe they are practically smart—they have a lot of common sense —but it doesn't translate into abstract, academic skills. Maybe they are test-anxious, as I used to be. Maybe they grew up speaking Spanish or French or Vietnamese, and haven't learned English well. Maybe their native language was English, but their parents both had to work to make a living and didn't have time either to read to them or to give them much verbal exposure in the household. Whatever the reason, they simply don't test well.

If they want to go to a competitive graduate school—the kind that provides a ticket up the occupational ladder—they are pretty much out of luck, because all of the schools, within a given subject but even across subjects, require basically the same test. So such people will find themselves systematically excluded from many different kinds of educational opportunities. Ultimately, on average, they are likely to drift down the occupational ladder. Compare such individuals to people who do well on such tests. Maybe they aren't really all that talented in a lot of ways, but taking tests is definitely one of their talents, and high test scores will be a definite plus in admission to the graduate programs of their choice. They may not be admitted to all the programs to which they apply, but they are likely to get into at least some. Test scores become the ticket to occupational level.

As a result, it is scarcely surprising that those at the top of the occupational ladder have high test scores. They couldn't have gotten into the access routes to high-level occupations if they hadn't pulled off high test scores. In effect, *we create the correlation between IQ and job level.*

It is important to realize that it wasn't always this way, nor is it this way in most of the world today. If you go back to the 1950s, you will find average SAT scores were much lower than they were a decade later. What happened? Did the population suddenly become much smarter? Obviously not. Rather, many colleges changed their criteria for admission, emphasizing test scores more and social class less. From this point of view, reliance on test scores gave individuals a better, not a worse, chance of being admitted for their intellectual qualifications. In other countries, many other factors still influence who is given access to higher education, including social class.

Consider an analogy. Suppose that we decide, as a society, that we just don't care that much about test scores, because when people take tests, their scores are so variable. You can take the SAT one day and get 500, then take it again the next day and get, say, 570. So we decide instead to go with something we can measure much more consistently—height. Henceforth, admission to college and graduate school will be determined on the basis of height. To get into Harvard, maybe you have to be six feet four. To get into Yale, maybe you only have to be six feet three (but good-looking). And on we go, until we get to Podunk, which requires you to be only four feet three. Of course, to get into a competitive medical school or law school, you will have to be even taller, maybe six feet seven. This may sound totally ridiculous, but actually it's not. In fact, people at the top of the occupational ladder do tend to be taller than those at the bottom. We do count height, whether we admit it or not.

Anyway, twenty-five years after starting to use height as the main variable for making admissions decisions, you decide to compare the average IQs of people in different occupations—lawyers, doctors, and CEOs, on the one hand, versus day laborers, cleaning people, and assembly-line workers on the other. What do you find? You find that the higher you are on the occupational ladder, the taller you are. Have you shown that height is somehow advantageous to good work in any of the higher-level occupations? No. What you have shown is that you used height as a basis for deciding what jobs people will—and will not—be allowed to pursue.

I am not saying that IQ is unrelated to job success. It is related, although weakly. What I'm saying is that we should not conclude, as do Herrnstein and Murray in their controversial book *The Bell Curve,* that some invisible guiding hand—some force of nature—is responsible for the cream rising to the top and the dregs falling to the bottom. Rather, we need to recognize that we will get as a society what we create. It wasn't nature that decided whom to value; it was society.

IQ matters, but not much. IQ-based measures typically account for less than 10 percent of the variation among those people who are more and those who are less successful according to societal standards. That means that IQ leaves more than 90 percent of the variation among individuals unexplained—scarcely a basis for claiming that IQ is what really matters. But how about differences between groups?

Group Differences in IQ and Intelligence

One thing is not in doubt. In the United States, different racial and ethnic groups have different average IQs. The fact of such a difference is not, in itself, evidence of a bias in the tests. Bias is not a function of differences in scores between groups. It is a function of prediction. A difference between groups would be evidence of bias only if whatever the tests are designed to predict did not show similar differences.

The literature on test bias has been reviewed in great detail and ad nauseam. And the general conclusion from this literature is that tests are not biased, at least not in the traditional sense. We need to think about what, exactly, this finding means.

What it means is that if Group A does worse than Group B on a test of intelligence, then typically it will also do worse—to about the same relative degree—on whatever performance the tests are used to predict, if the tests do indeed predict this entity. Thus, if Group A does worse on conventional intelligence tests than does Group B, then Group A is likely to do worse as well in, say, school achievement. For example, blacks score about one standard deviation (15 IQ points) below whites in the United States, on average. They also achieve at lower levels in school. Voilà, according to Arthur Jensen, Richard Herrnstein and Charles Murray, and others of the intellectual right: The tests are unbiased. Japanese and other Asian Americans tend to do somewhat better than whites on many tests and also tend to do somewhat better in school. Voilà, no bias. But wait a minute.

Are differences between racial groups inherited? Herrnstein and Murray imply they are.[5] The data, however, just don't support their conclusion. Herrnstein and Murray, as well as others, point to the heritability of intelligence as suggesting heritability of between-group differences. In fact, the data available are what are called *within-groups* heritability estimates. They tell us about sources of transmission of intelligence within, not between, groups. Thus, a study of predominantly white twins tells us about sources of variation between individuals who are white twins, not about sources of variation between groups of individuals, some of whom are white and some of whom are black.

The difference is not just a matter of statistical fine points. To use a frequently cited example, one that Herrnstein and Murray themselves use, suppose we have a large handful of corn seeds that show the normal variations in the corn. We plant half the seeds in corn-fields in Iowa and the other half in barren land in the Mojave Desert. Although the attributes of the corn will be highly heritable, the differences in development between the two sets of corn seeds will be due wholly to the environment. How does this logic apply to black-white differences?

Even if intelligence is moderately heritable, such heritability as determined within groups doesn't tell us anything about causes of differences between groups. That's the point of the corn example. Moreover, when we compare groups, we have to be clear about the groups we are comparing. For example, in the United States, it is downright silly to talk about pure races. African Americans represent, for the most part, interbreeding between predominantly black individuals of African descent and predominantly white individuals of European and other descent. The racial groups used in psychological investigations are socially, not biologically, constituted. In other words, people are characterized as being of a race because of what they say, not because of how they were born.

There is evidence suggesting that, in fact, black-white differences are predominantly environmental rather than genetic in nature. For example, children of several hundred German children fathered by black GIs in World War II had average IQs within a half point of those fathered by white GIs. Moreover, children of black-white unions have IQs that are higher if the mother is white, consistent with socialization rather than genetic effects.

Another thing: Richard Nisbett, a psychologist at the University of Michigan, has reviewed the literature and has found seven published studies that compare genetic versus environmental origins of differences in black-white IQs. These studies, unlike the twin studies, directly seek to find the source of the differences between blacks and whites. Six of the studies fail to find any evidence for genetic effects. A 1976 study by Scarr and Weinberg is equivocal. It's just not clear how the results should be interpreted, although its authors themselves interpret the results as failing to support a genetic explanation. Interestingly but depressingly, Herrnstein and Murray discuss only the one equivocal study at any length and, predictably, their interpretation of the results is opposite to that of the authors of the study. Here and elsewhere, evidence that fails to support their hypotheses is largely ignored, and evidence that is open to alternative interpretations is interpreted to fit their sociopolitical agenda.

Is IQ what is behind group differences in various kinds of success in society? Herrnstein and Murray certainly think so. Their whole book is aimed at making this point. They are not alone. Jensen and others believe the same. But curiously, Herrnstein and Murray's own data fail to support this claim. In one set of analyses, they find that compared to whites, blacks of the *same* average IQ are twice as likely to be living in poverty, five times more likely to be born out of wedlock, three times more likely to be on welfare, more than twice as likely to have lived in poverty during the first three years of their lives, and twice as likely to have had low birth weight. These findings fail to support a view of IQ as causing differences in these various aspects of adaptation, because the IQs of the two groups were equated.

Since the beginning of the century, alarmists have pointed to group differences in IQ and have warned that these differences are most threatening not because they exist but because the differential reproduction rates of those in the various groups inevitably will result in a decline in the level of our intelligence as a nation. If, as these individuals point out, people who are lower on the socioeconomic as well as IQ scales reproduce faster, then, whether intelligence is genetic or environmental, IQs will go down, because the bad genes and the bad environments provided by the bad parents with low IQs will result in a downward drift.

This hypothesis is accepted by the alarmists despite the fact that over the past thirty years or so IQs have risen very dramatically, to the tune of about a full standard deviation (about 15 points of IQ). The alarmists have a great deal of difficulty dealing with this "Flynn effect"—named for its discoverer, James Flynn[6]—and never satisfactorily resolve it. The Flynn effect is not limited to the United States. It has occurred in many countries throughout the world. Indeed, what would get someone an IQ of about 85 today would have gotten the same person an average score—about 100—just a couple of generations ago.

There have been many speculations, but no resolution, as to the cause of the Flynn effect. Better education, better nutrition, more schooling—all are possibilities, but we just don't know. What we do know is that contrary to the prediction of downward drift, abilities have been, on average, rising.

However, we do have a problem of another kind, and it is a sort of downward drift. At the same time that IQs have been rising, scores on various kinds of tests used for college admissions have been declining. Of course, these tests measure only a part of a person's abilities. But the signs are there of decreasing academic skills. Many professors, including myself, have noted a downward drift in students' verbal skills over the years. The drift was so substantial that after many years of maintaining the same norms on the SATs, the Educational Testing Service finally renormed the test to set the averages at 500, the middle score.

The low scores are not due, as one might think, to declining skills of those at the bottom. Although there have been more low scores, this particular trend is due largely to differences in the populations of children taking the tests. Many more students now take the tests than took them during the 1950s or 1960s or even 1970s, when scores were higher. Before, only the better students took the tests; now students of all stripes do. The real problem is the decline in high scores. Until the test was renormed, what was most notable was the decline of scores in the 700s and 600s—that is, near the high end of the scale. Why are scores at the high end declining? I think there are three reasons.

The first is our national preoccupation with the disadvantaged. Those at the low end of the abilities scales deserve special services, but so do those at the high end. Our national priorities are revealed by the fact that 99.9 percent of the special-education budget goes to the low end. And that's plain stupid. Our gifted kids—and I mean gifted in the sense of all the talents that constitute intelligence, not just IQ—are probably our most precious national resource. They are our major hope in an increasingly competitive world. At the elementary and secondary levels, we pay far less attention to them than we do to those who have various difficulties. Gifted kids, it is thought, can fend for themselves. After all, who needs services less than they do? Wrong. They need services as much as those at the lower end. The kind of schooling they get often bores them and makes them hate school. One of my own kids, by no means a math genius, spent about two-thirds of a year in middle school reviewing mathematics he already knew. That's a waste of time and a disgrace. In turn, these kids never learn how best to utilize the gifts they have.

Second, we are dumbing down our textbooks, a point made by Sally Reis of the University of Connecticut in a study supported by the U.S. Department of Education. Textbooks at a given grade level are about three levels lower now than they were when I was in secondary school, thirty years ago. Elementary texts are also at a lower grade level. As a textbook author, I find I am never under pressure to raise the level of what I am writing. The pressure is always to lower the level.

It is easy to blame the publishers. Why are they doing this to our kids? The problem is not with the publishers, however, but with the schools. The publishers publish what the schools buy. If the schools want high-level texts, that's what the publishers will produce. If the schools want pretty colored pictures, that's what the publishers will produce. The publishers are in business to make money, and they give customers what they demand.

We talk in this country about high standards, and we have produced governmental and foundation reports ad infinitum calling for their need. But we are all talk, no action. When publishers produce texts at a relatively high level, the texts don't sell. The big market is downmarket, and everyone in the publishing industry knows it. When school districts buy—even when college professors buy—they buy easy, so that their students don't get too upset. But their students don't get much of a challenge either.

Our hypocrisy is not limited to education. I have visited perhaps two dozen countries, and in my experience there is no country that has more overweight people than the United States. What's our solution? We raise the levels of weight regarded as acceptable at a given age. Meanwhile, more people die of heart disease than ever before. What did clothing manufacturers do recently when they discovered that small sizes went begging and that more and more women were buying large sizes and becoming depressed in the process? They changed the sizing so that women could buy lower size numbers and feel better about themselves. We can change the way we label things, but that obviously doesn't change the things themselves, or the problem. We can call a text "sixth-grade level," but the true reading level is what it is, and the level is on the downswing, at all grades.

In *The Learning Gap,* Harold Stevenson of the University of Michigan and James Stigler of UCLA have pointed out the paradox. Comparing Japanese and American parents, they found that parents in this country are more satisfied with the achievements of their children than are Japanese parents, despite the considerably lower achievements of their children. American parents believe things are going quite well—that all is well with our schools and there is a conspiracy to make the schools look bad. And our waistlines are fine too. Our national capacity for self-delusion is a marvel. Unfortunately, travel anywhere else, and no one is deceived. Unless we start challenging kids' minds, we can renorm our tests however often we want, just as we can pretend our kids are reading at grade level when they are reading fluff. The cost of our self-deception is a drop in our national competitiveness. It's a stiff price to pay, and it's getting stiffer. We need to be raising levels of intelligence, not lowering them.

Modifiability of Intelligence

Intelligence and even IQ are modifiable. At one time, it was believed that intelligence is fixed—that we are stuck forever with whatever level of intelligence we may have at birth. Today, many and perhaps most researchers in the field of intelligence believe that it is malleable —that it can be shaped and even increased through various kinds of interventions.[7]

For example, the Head Start program was initiated in the 1960s as a way of providing preschoolers with an edge on intellectual abilities and accomplishments when they started school. Long-term follow-ups have indicated that by midadolescence, children who participated were more than a grade ahead of matched controls who were not in the program.[8] Children in the program also scored higher on a variety of tests of scholastic achievement and were less likely to need remedial attention and show behavioral problems. Although such measures are not truly measures of intelligence, they show strong positive correlations with intelligence tests of the conventional kind. A number of newer programs have also shown some successes in environments outside the family home. The Abecedarian Project of Ramey and Campbell (1984, 1992), initiated in North Carolina, is a notable example. It has succeeded in raising intellectual abilities of schoolchildren in a number of different instances.

Work done by Robert Bradley and Bettye Caldwell has shown the importance of the home environment in regard to the development of intelligence in young children. These researchers found that several factors in the early (preschool) home environment may be linked to high IQ scores: emotional and verbal responsivity of the primary caregiver and the caregiver's involvement with the child; avoidance of arbitrary restrictions and punishment; organization of the physical environment and activity schedule; provision of appropriate play materials; and opportunities for variety in daily stimulation. Further, Bradley and Caldwell found that these factors more effectively predicted IQ scores than did socioeconomic status or family-structure variables, such as number of children.

Home environment is most important in cases of severe deprivation. For example, Wayne Dennis, an American psychologist working in Iran, showed that children from certain Iranian orphanages who were not adopted by the age of two became, for the most part, mentally retarded. Those who were adopted were not retarded. There was no particular intervention; there were just differences in intellectual stimulation and the nurturance of the respective environments. We are talking about major differences here, averaging 50 IQ points. As you can see, when there is enough range in the quality of the environment, environment can be very powerful. In effect, even a decent environment becomes a powerful means for increasing IQ, and probably other aspects of intelligence as well.

One of the most impressive of the intellectual-skills training programs has been Project Odyssey, which was instituted in Venezuela during a period when there was a Ministry for the Development of Intelligence, a unique enterprise in human history, in which an entire national government bureau was devoted to the improvement of human intellect.[9] The program covered a wide variety of analytical and creative skills and was carefully evaluated. Indeed, its evaluation was a model for how to evaluate such programs, because it used such a wide variety of cognitive measures to determine the program's success. The results were published in one of psychology's most prestigious journals.

I mention this program especially because of the authors of the careful evaluation—namely, Richard Herrnstein and his colleagues (Ray Nickerson, Margarita deSanchez, and John Swets). The study was the outcome of Project Intelligence, whose aim was to develop the intellectual skills of Venezuelan schoolchildren. Herrnstein was the same man who later, in *The Bell Curve,* would say that attempts to increase intelligence have been a resounding failure—an example of overblown claims that have never materialized in concrete results. At one level, it is puzzling how a coauthor of a successful program and the senior author of its evaluation would later conclude that such programs are doomed to failure.

At another level, it is not surprising. Many fields of science have such powerful political overtones that discussions about them that purport to be scientific are often really political. The study of intelligence is almost certainly one of these fields, especially when we come to issues of modifiability and group differences. The political arguments come from both sides, right and left, and the danger of politicization is that the scientific issues get lost in the noise.

We need to distinguish genuine teaching of intellectual skills from routine test preparation. For example, there are a number of books and courses available that may increase scores on tests, because they provide practice in the types of items found on particular tests, but do not necessarily produce generalizable gains in intelligence. This is not to knock such books or courses. My own children are of the age when they will soon be taking the SAT. I bought them both a book and will be delighted if they want to take a course. My goal is not to improve their intelligence but to improve their test scores so they can get into the college of their choice. And on average, such courses do result in small to moderate gains on standardized tests.[10] Successfully intelligent people don't necessarily ace these tests, but they recognize that decent scores are needed to pass through the educational system. And so they do what they can to maximize their scores, not because of what the tests measure but because of the (false) importance assigned by society to scores on these tests.

At the same time, there is an issue of equity with such books and courses. Not everyone can afford the time or the money for them. And the people who can't find themselves at a disadvantage, on average, in comparison with those who can. Moreover, people with the time and money are unlikely to be randomly distributed across the population. Rather, they are likely to be people in the middle-to-upper-middle socioeconomic classes. Once again, the tests work in favor, on average, of those who are better off to begin with.

This common finding—with regard to both tests and other measures of success in society—is sometimes called the Matthew Effect. In the Bible, Matthew pointed out that the rich tend to get richer and the poor poorer. And he was not referring only to money. Matthew Effects tend to result in increasing polarization in the resources of society—which we are seeing right now in the United States as well as in other countries—and also in increasing misunderstandings between the haves and the have-nots.

Curiously, schools, at least at the high-school level, are increasingly becoming glorified classrooms for test-preparation courses. One Parents' Day, I attended my daughter's English class and observed the students memorizing and then repeating back definitions of difficult English vocabulary words. The class was a thinly disguised preparation for the SAT. It's hard to blame the schools exclusively: They are under pressure from parents as well as district personnel to improve test scores. But students often forget the vocabulary soon after they memorize it, because it is never well integrated into their minds. They never really learn how to use the words and to relate them to what they already know.

We did a study that looked at an alternative approach to improving vocabulary-related skills.[11] Rather than having children memorize vocabulary words, we taught students in instructed groups how to learn the meanings of words from their context. They would see a new word in a natural context, and they'd be instructed in using context clues to figure out the meaning. Thus, if they read that "the mother looked at her child through the oam of the bubbling stew," they would be taught how to figure out that *oam* probably means steam or possibly smoke. In this case, oam is something that arises from a bubbling stew and is transparent or translucent, making steam and smoke likely meanings.

Our study had two control groups. One group got practice but not instruction on figuring out the meanings of words from context—the kind of practice the children would probably get from a test-preparation book. The other group got nothing—no treatment at all. We then compared the performance of the instructed groups to the performance of the two control groups. We found that all of the instructed groups increased significantly more than did either of the control groups from pretest to posttest on measures of the ability to figure out meanings of words from context. The two control groups did not differ from each other. In other words, practice alone is not particularly effective.

People need instruction on how to figure out the meanings of the words. Long after such children have finished school, they will have skills that they can apply to the learning of new vocabulary, rather than a memorized list of vocabulary words that they will quickly forget. If you want to develop intelligence, you need to teach people to think with content, not just to memorize. And the available evidence suggests that we can, in fact, teach people to think better.[12] But as long as we continue to rely on the IQ and a wide range of other tests as the sole measures of intelligence, we will deprive many of our children of the instruction and the opportunities that are necessary if they are actually to become more intelligent.

CHAPTER THREE

What IQ Doesn't Tell Us

As I have said, we would all stand to gain if we used tests that are based on theories of what intelligence is. What, then, is intelligence? Sooner or later, if you want to understand intelligence, you have to answer that question, although people in the business of testing intelligence have done a truly marvelous job of failing seriously to do so.

Expert Definitions

In 1921, fourteen famous psychologists were asked by the editors of the *Journal of Educational Psychology* to give their views on what intelligence is. Although their responses varied, two common themes ran through many of them. Intelligence is (1) the capacity to learn from experience, and (2) the ability to adapt to the surrounding environment. These common themes are important. Capacity to learn from experience implies, for example, that smart people can and do make mistakes. In fact, smart people are not those who don't make mistakes but rather those who learn from mistakes and don't keep making the same ones again and again.

If only our schools would realize this—if only we and our children did! Research has looked at children's conceptions of intelligence, and it turns out that children tend to fall into two groups.[1] Those called *entity theorists* believe that intelligence is more or less a fixed entity that you have a certain amount of and that you will always have in the same, fixed degree. The way you show that you have intelligence is to come off as "smart." You give correct answers in school or elsewhere, and you are careful not to make mistakes. The problem with this view is that kids can cut themselves off from learning. They are so concerned with appearances that often they will not take on tasks that are challenging or respond when they are unsure of the correct answer. In contrast, children who are *incremental theorists* believe that as you learn, your intelligence increases. Thus, you need to learn as much as you can, and making mistakes is a part of the process of learning. Unsurprisingly, incremental theorists are in a better position to learn and improve their skills than are entity theorists.

The second ability identified by the theorists, the ability to adapt to the surrounding environment, is also important. Adaptation to the environment means that being smart goes beyond getting high scores on tests or good grades in school. It includes how you handle a job, how you get along with other people, and how you manage your life in general.

It's interesting to note that the experts' definitions of intelligence in terms of learning from experience and adapting to the environment are very much in the spirit of successful rather than inert intelligence. Unfortunately, the tests we use to measure intelligence are not in that spirit. They don't measure, for example, who learns from experience or who adapts to the environment. Rather, they focus on academic learning and adaptation, important in their own right but certainly not central to the game of life, especially after students move beyond school into the world of work. Little wonder that a salesperson once said to me that it is the fate of A students to be managed by B students.

Sixty-five years after the initial journal symposium, twenty-four different experts were asked to give their views on the nature of intelligence.[2] Once again, the experts noted the themes of learning from experience and adapting to the environment. However, contemporary experts put more emphasis than did earlier ones on the role of *metacognition*—people's understanding and control of their own thinking processes (such as during problem solving, reasoning, and decision making). Contemporary experts also more heavily emphasized the role of culture, pointing out that what is considered intelligent in one culture may be considered stupid in another.

As for more explicit theories of what intelligence might be, there is nothing even approaching a consensus among the experts, even as to how it should be studied. One of the great myths perpetrated by those who do testing is that psychologists agree that the testing-based, or psychometric, approach tells us what intelligence is. But consider now the actual diversity of approaches psychologists use. Only some of the psychometric theories, the first ones considered, focus on IQ. And even most of those recognize the limitations of a single IQ.

The Psychometrics of Intelligence

Intelligence testing has its origins in a psychometric—that is, measurement—model, the idea being that through tests we can obtain some kind of map of the mind. During the first half of the twentieth century, the model of intelligence as something to be mapped dominated theory and research. Psychologists studying intelligence in this way were both explorers and cartographers, seeking to chart the innermost regions of the mind. And like any other explorers, they needed tools. In the research on intelligence, the indispensable tool appeared to be *factor analysis,* a statistical method and model for separating a construct—intelligence, in this case—into a number of distinct hypothetical abilities that the researchers believed formed the basis of individual differences in test performance. The specific factors derived, of course, still would depend on the specific questions being asked and the tasks being evaluated.

The g Factor

Charles Spearman is usually credited with inventing factor analysis.[3] Using factor-analytic studies, he concluded that intelligence could be understood in terms of both a single general factor *(g)*, which pervaded performance on all tests of mental ability, and a set of specific factors *(s)*, each of which was involved in performance on only a single type of mental-ability test (e.g., arithmetic computations). In Spearman's view, the specific factors were of only casual interest due to their narrow applicability. The general factor, however, provided the key to understanding intelligence. Spearman believed that *g* is derived from individual differences in mental energy.

Spearman could be excused for what might sound like a simplistic theory of intelligence. After all, he had just invented factor analysis and didn't yet know a whole lot about it. Moreover, in the early 1900s, factor analyses all had to be done by hand. Today, though, people should know better. We now understand that if you do a factor analysis and just accept as givens the results that come directly out of the analysis, you will always get a general factor, because it is in the nature of the statistical procedure. What factor analysis does is to take first the strongest source of individual differences and lump all that information in the first factor; then it takes the second-strongest source of individual differences and lumps that information in the second factor; and so on. So the first factor will be the most general one. It may be stronger or weaker, but it will be there.

A factor analysis gives you a map. But here's the rub: The initial solution from a factor analysis is that solution, among all the potentially infinite solutions possible, which maximizes the extent to which you will identify a "general factor." Thus, people who like the idea of intelligence being a single thing—a *g* or an IQ—love to use the initial solutions that come out of factor analyses. But there are an infinite number of coordinate systems for identifying abilities. Not surprisingly, people who argue for the single-ability view choose exactly that system of all the infinite ones possible which best fits their theory.

Bonds

Even if you accept the notion of a general factor of intelligence, it doesn't mean that intelligence is just a single thing, because tests may measure many different things. Suppose that every single subtest that you use (e.g., vocabulary, verbal similarities, arithmetic problems, picture completions, or whatever) requires a certain array of skills— maybe reading stimuli, understanding what the stimuli say, responding to the stimuli in writing, working quickly, and the like. Then all of these many things that are required by all the subtests will appear as a single thing in the general factor of the factor analysis. Thus, you will get a general factor solely as a result of the statistical method being used. But you will also get one because the method doesn't make any distinctions at all among abilities that are required of all the subtests in a given test battery. So, according to British psychologist Godfrey Thomson, g is probably largely artifactual. It represents a very large number of what Thomson referred to as "bonds," or what you might view as the many skills underlying intelligence.

Primary Mental Abilities

Maybe the general factor is just a statistical artifact, a chimera of the imagination. Some researchers have argued just that, and that the core of intelligence resides not in one single factor but in several factors—seven in a theory proposed in 1938 by Louis Thurstone, a psychologist at the University of Chicago. Thurstone used a different coordinate system from Spearman's g-factor analysis and suggested that the seven factors are (1) *verbal comprehension,* measured by vocabulary tests; (2) *verbal fluency,* measured by tests requiring the test taker to think of as many words as possible that begin with a given letter, in a limited amount of time; (3) *inductive reasoning,* measured by tests such as analogies and number-series completion tasks (what number comes next in the following series: 2, 5, 9,

15, . . . ?); (4) *spatial visualization,* measured by tests requiring mental rotation of pictures of objects; (5) *number,* measured by computation and simple mathematical problem-solving tests; (6) *memory,* measured by picture and word-recall tests; and (7) *perceptual speed,* measured by tests that require the test taker to recognize small differences in pictures, or to cross out the *a*'s in strings of various letters.

Thurstone used group-administered rather than individually administered tests like the Stanford-Binet or Wechsler. Group tests, however, have at least as many problems associated with them as do individual tests. For one thing, they tend to be even more heavily speed oriented, valuing people who are quick but not necessarily deep. Often, they measure the constructs of interest in a somewhat trivial way. For example, the ability to memorize lists of words is probably not the most meaningful test of memory. Even when you look at memorization in the impoverished way it is sometimes done in school courses, at least students have to memorize material with some meaningful connections, not just unrelated strings of words. Number tests often put a premium on computational skills, which, with calculators and computers, are probably becoming less and less important to intelligence in everyday life. And a test such as number series assumes that there is, in fact, a unique answer to a number series.

Consider the difficulty with number series as illustrated by the so-called 2, 4, 6 problem.[4] You say to someone: Look, I have a rule in mind for a sequence of numbers. The first three numbers in the sequence are 2, 4, and 6. You have to guess the rule behind the sequence, and the way you can do it is by giving me a number, and I will tell you whether it is in the sequence. The problem illustrates *confirmation bias:* People give numbers to confirm their initial hypothesis. As most people believe that the rule is increasing even numbers, they will give probes like 8, 10, 12, 22, and so on. They much more rarely give probes that might disprove their hypothesis, like 3, 7, or 18½. In fact, the sequence you had in mind was increasing integers. Thus, any integer greater than 6 would be possible for the next number. But if you were to see this problem on an IQ test, you had better give 8 as the next number, or you will, for sure, be marked wrong. In fact, you can always generate a mathematical function that will produce any number at all as the next one in the sequence.[5]

The Structure of Intellect

At the opposite extreme from Spearman's single g-factor model is a model proposed by J. P. Guilford, formerly a psychologist at the University of Southern California. His structure-of-intellect (SOI) model includes more than 120 factors of the mind. According to Guilford, intelligence can be understood in terms of a cube that represents the intersection of three dimensions: operations, contents, and products. Operations are simply mental processes, such as memory, cognition (defined by Guilford as understanding), and convergent production (reaching a single "correct" answer to a problem that requires a unique response). Contents are the kinds of terms that appear in a problem, such as semantic (words), symbolic (e.g., numbers), behavioral (what people do), and visual (pictures). Products are the kinds of responses required, such as units (e.g., single words, numbers, or pictures), classes (e.g., hierarchies), or relations (e.g., John is taller than Mary). In a recent version of the theory, Guilford proposed as many as 150 factors.[6]

Some psychologists believe that the number of factors has made the SOI model too complex and unwieldy. Who could really measure 150 factors? Moreover, it turns out that there are serious problems in the way Guilford went about identifying his factors, once again illustrating how psychologists can hide trash behind the veil of statistics.

One problem with his theory was that Guilford analyzed his data in a way that made his model look better than it really was. Today, psychologists recognize that Guilford's data really did not fit his model very well at all. Guilford was not being deceptive. He just did not realize the flaws in the specialized methods he was using. So don't accept what people say just because they have impressive statistics. You have to make sure that the statistics really say what you are being told they say.

A more parsimonious way of handling a number of factors of the mind is through a hierarchical model of intelligence. One such model proposes that general intelligence comprises two major subfactors: fluid intelligence and crystallized intelligence.[7] *Fluid intelligence* requires understanding of abstract and often novel relations, as required in inductive-reasoning tests (where one reasons from the specific to the general), such as number series completions and analogies. *Crystallized intelligence* represents the accumulation of knowledge and is measured, for example, by vocabulary tests and general-information tests. Subsumed within these two major subfactors are other, more specific subfactors.

All models of intelligence represent theoreticians' attempts to simplify and to understand the underpinnings of intelligence. But in simplifying, there are always issues that are insufficiently dealt with. I have already mentioned one such issue in the psychometric models. Factor analysis, the primary method for identifying various psychometric theories, allows an infinite number of different axes. Imagine, if you will, lines of longitude and latitude, and you realize that they are arbitrary. You could rotate them in any direction to change the coordinate system in a coordinate space. For example, they could be at diagonals to each other. The axes don't even have to be perpendicular (at right angles) to each other but could be at any angle, such as 30 degrees, 60 degrees, or whatever. No one set of axes is right or wrong, or mathematically better or worse than any other. Each different rotation of the axes gives us a somewhat different psychometric theory of intelligence. What this means is that the different psychometric theories of intelligence, based on the different psychometric rotations, cannot be characterized as fitting the data better or worse. A bit of a mess! All these different theories largely represent nothing more than different transformations of the same data. They can't be distinguished mathematically from each other.

Another problem with the psychometric theories is that the abilities specified by the theories are identified by means of individual differences across people. If everyone scored the same, you could not identify any abilities at all. In other words, suppose one hundred people take an intelligence test, and all receive exactly the same scores, or even close to the same scores. The method of factor analysis would not be able to uncover any abilities whatsoever.

But the identification of abilities should not depend on individual differences. For example, suppose we are interested in the ability to speak, and we test thirty children in a classroom for whether or not they can speak. All can. We would not want to infer that speaking is not an ability because there are no individual differences. But factor analysis would be powerless to identify speaking as an ability, because of the absence of individual differences.

Most psychometric theories, with a few exceptions, also have little or nothing to say about the *processes* of intelligence. Why would we care about processes of intelligence? Here are a couple of reasons why we should care. Suppose we give kids—or adults, for that matter—a test of verbal analogies. For example, a verbal analogy is: "Four score and seven years ago" : Lincoln :: "I'm not a crook" : (a) Washington, (b) Capone, (c) Harding, (d) Nixon, (e) Agnew. For someone my age (forty-six) who grew up in the United States, this analogy is a relatively easy one. Most people of my generation will remember Nixon's faltering "I'm not a crook" line, which he uttered shortly before resigning as President. But many younger people will not know this line, having grown up after the Nixon presidency. So what does that say about verbal analogies, and why is it important?

Verbal analogies are supposed to measure verbal reasoning skills. But analogies tests really largely measure knowledge. You may believe that analogies like this one don't appear on the tests. But if you have ever taken the Miller Analogies Test, you will find that to do well, you have to know about things like mathematics formulas, physics formulas, historical figures, fine wines, and the like. On the SAT, to solve the verbal analogies, you have to have an extensive vocabulary.

One study related analogies on the Miller Analogies Test to various subtests of the Wechsler Adult Intelligence Scale.[8] It was found that the strongest relation between the two was not with the verbal similarities scale, which is supposed to measure verbal reasoning on the Wechsler, but with the Wechsler vocabulary scale. The second-strongest relation was with the general-information scale. In other words, tests that are supposed to measure verbal reasoning are, in large part, measures of vocabulary and general information.

This fact is problematical because those interpreting the tests are likely to draw wrong inferences. An Asian American or a Hispanic American or anyone else whose native language is not English, or who grew up with relatively less exposure to the American language and mainstream culture, is clearly going to be at a disadvantage on these tests, regardless of how strong the person's verbal reasoning skills may be. Little wonder that white, middle-to-upper-middle-class people are at an advantage on these tests. The tests are almost tailor made for them, but not even for all of them, because their backgrounds too will differ. That being the case, those seeing the test scores of such people are likely to think they are pretty dumb. Had we been able to disentangle the processes of verbal reasoning from the knowledge of vocabulary, we would have been a whole lot better off in terms of accurately interpreting the results of the test.

There is a piece of conventional wisdom in some academic circles that extremely high scores on the Miller Analogies Test are a negative predictor of success, even in graduate school. I have never actually seen a study testing this hypothesis, so it may be mythology. Were it true, though, it wouldn't surprise me. The kind of person who is a repository of trivia is often not the kind of person who functions best in even the academic world, which rewards big and powerful ideas. The kind of trivia recall that can pay off so well in school, in Trivial Pursuit, or on quiz shows is relatively useless outside these and a few other limited settings.

It is absolutely pathetic that high-school and college competitions on television, such as *College Bowl*, reward the kind of mindless recall of trivia that will later produce a thinker who is good for practically nothing except such games. The National Geography Bee, the National Spelling Bee, and other such contests are similar examples of the mindlessness for which we reward our children. How impressive when children can spell a word they will probably never once encounter or use in their entire lives! And then we complain that our children don't think well. What's worse is that we're surprised. Not only don't we measure thinking processes, we usually don't teach or reward them either.

Take another example of where it would be useful to be able to separate processes—in this case, one kind of process from another: the measurement of spatial ability. Spatial ability is what you need to fit the suitcases into the trunk of your car. For whatever reason, car trunks show strong preferences for some people and seem to expand to allow all the suitcases to fit in. For other people, myself included, they shrink and all the suitcases just don't fit. Car trunks don't seem to like me.

Admittedly, my spatial ability isn't the best. And predictably, when I was young, I did terribly on tests of spatial ability, because I just couldn't visualize how the different shapes might be rotated, or the paper might be folded, or whatever the test required me to do. I may have sold myself a bill of goods that I couldn't do these problems, and soon fulfilled my own prophecy.

By the time I was in high school, though, a strange thing had happened. My scores on tests of spatial ability improved radically. No longer was I a bottom-of-the-barrel, down-in-the-dumps failure in the art of visualization. Or so it seemed. Had my spatial ability improved? Not really. It was no better than it had been years before. But I had come to realize that many spatial-ability problems on these tests can be solved verbally rather than visually. In other words, instead of trying to visualize what, say, a set of forms would look like in another spatial position, I tried to talk the problems through to myself. I would describe the figures verbally and then try to match that description with the answer options. I didn't get every answer correct, but I got enough correct answers to move up from being a dunderhead on these tests to being somewhat above average.

The better scores were nice for me, but they might have had unfortunate consequences. Suppose I was trying to decide on a career, or a counselor was trying to help me decide, and one of us took my relatively high scores in spatial ability at face value. I might have ended up in a career that was wholly inappropriate for me—air traffic controller, for example. Air traffic controllers need very high levels of spatial ability; otherwise, they are in trouble, and so are the millions of people flying on the planes they monitor. Suppose I had decided to be an air traffic controller, took a spatial-ability test for the job, and passed. It would have done no one any favor if I were there talking to myself about what would happen as the two little blips on the screen raced toward each other.

That is another good example of why conventional ability tests are unlikely ever to be of much value as measures of successful intelligence. Ask yourself what abilities are needed to be successful as an air traffic controller or in other complex jobs, and if you answer your own question honestly, you will see that conventional inert abilities play a relatively small part in success. Spatial ability is important. But so are planning, monitoring, vigilance, concentration, flexibility, and a whole array of other abilities. I wouldn't want my life in the hands of someone whose main claim to fame as an air traffic controller was a high score on a conventional multiple-choice test.

So we need some kind of theory and measurement that can give us not only an overall IQ or SAT score or whatever, but scores for the mental processes that go into solving problems on these tests. That's what theories and studies of information processing and intelligence do.

Information Processing and Intelligence

The idea behind information-processing work is to specify the mental processes underlying intelligence. In this work, the mind is viewed much like the software on a computer, accepting inputs, transforming and processing the information, and later producing outputs. There have been different computational approaches to understanding intelligence. One of them emphasizes simple information processing. You sit yourself down in front of a device that presents two arrays: one of little lightbulbs, the other of little buttons. Each button connects to one light. Your finger is on a "home" key right in front of you. As soon as you see one of the lights flash on, you have to put it out by pressing the button in front of the light. The psychologist measures two response times: the time it takes you to remove your finger from the home button, and the time it takes you to push the button in front of the light.

What does such a simple task have to do with intelligence? A series of studies has found correlations between both of the response-time measures and scores on intelligence tests.[9] Which of the two measures —the time to remove your finger from the home button, or the time to push down the button corresponding to the light—do you think shows the higher correlation? The answer is the time to remove your finger from the home button. Why? Because this response time seems to package within it the mental processing you do to decide where to move your finger, whereas the second response seems more to measure simply how quickly you can zip over to the right button. How high are the correlations? On a 0 to 1 scale, where 0 indicates no relation and 1 indicates a perfect relation, the magnitude of correlation is typically about .3. It's not high, but it's not zero either.

What are we to make of what seems like a rather mysterious correlation between scores on a simple task and scores on fairly hard IQ-test items? It depends on whom you ask. One point of view holds that the choice-reaction time task—as it is sometimes called— somehow measures how quickly nerve cells within the human body can transmit information.[10] In this view, the faster information is transmitted, the smarter a person is. Pretty impressive? Also a pretty big stretch. But there are other, less interesting and, I believe, more plausible explanations for what is going on.

For one thing, IQ tests and tests like them are timed. And the choice-reaction time task is also timed. People who respond faster on one kind of task are likely to respond faster on another. So some of the correlations may reflect simply speed of processing. People who are fast . . . are fast. They're not necessarily deep or perceptive or shrewd or much else.

For another thing, the more forced-choice options the participant has on these response-time tasks—the more lights there are—the higher the correlation between scores on his task and IQ. But as you add choices, you make the choice-reaction time task more complex. So it may be that what looks like quite a simple task actually isn't that simple. Of course, I'm not saying that the task is remarkably complex either, but then, the correlation with IQ isn't that high.

For yet another thing, almost everything that requires any cognitive processing at all correlates .3 with IQ.[11] Tests tend to correlate with other tests of the same kind. People who do well on one cognitive test tend to do pretty well on other cognitive tests. There's nothing mysterious here. People who get along well with some people tend to get along well with others; people who have good night vision under some circumstances tend to have it under other circumstances. So the fact that .3 correlations are obtained really doesn't mean that much, and certainly doesn't mean that the test is somehow measuring speed of conduction in the nerve cells.

One of the things you may have noticed—and if you have, you are noticing correctly—is that people in the intelligence business aren't so different from those in any other business. They tend to interpret the available data in the most favorable light possible for their own beliefs. Real estate agents like to look for signs that housing sales are on the upswing; stockbrokers like to look for signs that stocks are about to shoot up. And intelligence researchers like to look for signs that their pet theories are supported by their data. Whatever their reputation, scientists are nothing if not human. And of course, they are as eager as the next person to hide behind a cloak of objectivity. Sometimes, they're wearing no cloak.

Other information-processing theorists have looked at other tasks. For example, quick, do "A" and "A" have the same letter name? How about "A" and "a"? A series of studies showed that your response time in answering questions like the second one, minus your response time in answering questions like the first one, turns out to be a predictor of scores on intelligence tests, especially verbal intelligence tests—the one that use words in the test problems.[12] These studies suggested that a crucial aspect of intelligence is speed of retrieving verbal information from memory.

Look at it this way. As you read this text, you have to match each letter and each word against a representation in memory. If you can't make a match, you can't read the text. This inability to read can be disadvantageous not only to yourself but to others. On an airplane I recently took from Los Angeles to Washington, D.C., there was a card in front of me saying, "If you are sitting in an exit row and you cannot read this card, . . . please tell a crew member." That makes about as much sense as asking a person out loud whether he or she is deaf. Fortunately, the plane didn't crash.

Perhaps people who can make quick matches are at an advantage compared to those who can't, because over the course of reading millions of words in their lifetimes, they will be doing more processing of information per unit time and thus will be in a better position to learn more than will people who don't process information so quickly. So it makes sense that they would have higher levels of intelligence, although again, the relationship is pretty weak.

The fact that very simple tasks correlate with IQ is seen by many information-processing psychologists as speaking well for the tasks. The game is to get as high a correlation with IQ as possible. I look at it from exactly the opposite perspective—as speaking poorly for IQ. You have to ask just how consequential a measure is that relates to how quickly a person can push buttons when lights go on. I'm not saying that quick reflexes and rapid solutions to very simple problems are never important. But they just aren't what's really central to intelligence. In fact, there are many situations in which people respond too quickly and regret it later. I believe the message here is that when we measure IQ, we are measuring an aspect of intelligence, but almost certainly not one of the more important aspects.

Many high-IQ people seem to be characterized by what might be called *dysrationalia*.[13] They have high test scores but don't seem to think very well. For example, a lot of so-called smart people can be taken in by political slogans, false advertising, or any garden-variety senseless argument they happen to hear. Perhaps, then, they have a disability when it comes to thinking rationally.

Psychologists should not be congratulating themselves for finding correlations between trivial tasks and IQ scores. Instead, they should be asking whether these correlations, modest though they may be, don't indicate that there is something wrong with the whole enterprise. I have found that people's ability to solve everyday reasoning problems doesn't much correlate with IQ. It's not because everyday reasoning problems measure something "other than" intelligence but because IQ measures only a very small aspect of intelligence. But do any of these measures tell us anything about what really goes on inside the head, at the level of brain functioning? Some investigators have sought to find out.

Biology and Intelligence

Intelligence can also be studied with biologically based methods. The idea is usually to relate scores on IQ tests to aspects of brain functioning. Different methods have been used, but right away, you can see a problem. The biological measures are validated against IQ test scores, which are themselves suspect. So we can end up validating a measure we do not well understand against a measure we think we understand but don't.

One set of methods is based on electrical activity of the brain. This activity can be measured by attaching electrodes to the brain to obtain an electroencephalogram, or EEG. For EEGs, electrodes establish contact between the brain and a source that sums and records brain activity over large areas containing many neurons. Usually, electrodes are attached directly to the scalp; sometimes, however, microelectrodes are inserted into the brain. The former technique is used with humans, the latter only with animals. In either case, the minute quantifiable fluctuations of electrical activity are what are important. Sometimes, EEGs are averaged, yielding what are called *evoked potentials* (EPs). These measures are more stable, precisely because they are averages and thus not susceptible to the sometimes wild fluctuations one can get with individual brain waves.

We now know that complex patterns of electrical activity in the brain, prompted by specific stimuli, can correlate with scores on IQ tests.[14] In this kind of work, brain activity is measured by the use of evoked potentials. Several further studies have suggested that speed of conduction of electrochemical nerve impulses in the body is positively correlated with that aspect of intelligence measured by conventional intelligence tests.[15] In general, investigators in the field believe that higher degrees of academic intelligence are associated with greater degrees of neural efficiency.

Additional support for the idea of a relation between intelligence and neural efficiency comes from studies of how the brain metabolizes glucose, a simple sugar required for brain activity. Research has shown that higher academic intelligence correlates with reduced levels of glucose metabolism during problem-solving tasks.[16] In other words, people with smarter brains consume less glucose while engaged in problem solving. It has also been found that cerebral efficiency increases as a result of learning in a relatively complex task involving spatial manipulations, such as the computer game Tetris. After practice, more academically intelligent participants show lower brain metabolism of glucose overall; but in specific areas of the brain, glucose metabolism is higher, suggesting that the brighter participants have learned how to use their brains in an efficient way, so that processing of information can be localized to a relatively small part of the brain.

The research in this field is certainly impressive and suggests a connection between intelligence and information processing in the brain. At the same time, how could there not be? Even psychologists who eschew the study of the brain would probably admit that there must be some kind of connection. But in interpreting the research of the behavioral neuroscientists, as they are called, there are three important factors to keep in mind.

First, the results need to be interpreted with great caution. There is a history of research in this field wherein some startling finding emerges and, later, no one is able to repeat it. This history seems not to be totally behind us. For example, in 1994, two investigators in this field attempted to replicate their 1992 results regarding the correlation between speed of neural conduction and intelligence, and failed.[17] Some of the results of the 1980s providing spectacularly high correlations between EEG and intelligence have also not been replicated.[18] These results were based on small numbers of cases, and the samples were rather atypical, for example, in including disproportionately large numbers of people with very low and very high IQs.

Second, one cannot immediately assume that biological phenomena are causes, rather than effects, of individual differences in intelligence. We know, for example, that learning causes structural changes in the brain.[19] As you learn new information, your brain builds new neurons and new connections between existing neurons. These connections result from cognitive processes of learning—they don't cause them. We thus need to be open to the possibility that increases in intelligence might lead to biological changes in the brain. In other words, as we learn better how to perform various tasks, our neural processing, at least for those tasks, speeds up.

Third, biological theories deal with one important level of intelligence, but not the only level. Think of a car that stalls when you try to start it in the morning. There are many levels at which you could try to understand why it stalled or what the relevant consequences would be. You could understand what happened at the level of interactions of molecules entering into electrochemical reactions, or at the level of parts of the car that might not be functioning (e.g., the battery or the starter), or at the level of what you might not be able to do during the day if you are unable to start the car. There is no one "right" level at which to understand why a car stalled. The optimal level will typically depend on your purpose in analyzing the failure of the car to start. If you are taking a course in chemistry, the electrochemical level of analysis may be just right. If you need to figure out whether to try to jump-start the battery, the level of parts of the car is probably right. If you are trying to figure out whom to call to cancel appointments you made that morning, the level of interpersonal relationships is pertinent. There are many, many levels at which any event can be understood, but there is no one right level for all purposes. Rather, one has to decide what level is right given the circumstances.

The same, of course, applies to the biological understanding of intelligence. Of course we want to understand the electrochemical reactions that take place in the brain. But these reactions are not the only level at which we can or should understand intelligence. And almost certainly, they are not the level at which we are going to understand successful intelligence. If, for example, we want to understand what we can do to help an employee be more productive or a child learn better, we might be more successful if we tried to understand the employee's time management or the child's cognitive learning strategies rather than the electrochemical reactions in their brains. We might also want to understand the organizational and even the cultural context in which the employee is working or the child is learning.

Intelligence and Culture

Research has shown that different cultures have different conceptions of intelligence. What one culture considers smart, another may consider stupid, and vice versa. The behavior that leads to success in one environment can lead to failure in another. Often, we can get a sense of the differences in cultures through the kinds of jokes they tell about their own cultural customs.

Here's a joke I heard when I was in Spain to talk to a group of professors. An overnight-delivery man arrives at a university with a special package for Professor Torres. Upon inquiring of the departmental secretary, he learns that Professor Torres isn't in at the moment but is expected shortly. The delivery man sits down to wait for the professor. He waits an hour, two hours, a day, a week, a month, a year, two years, saying nothing to disturb anybody. Finally, after three years, the department appoints him as a professor.

Everyone loved the joke and knew exactly what it meant. To get to the top in a Spanish university, you hear nothing, say nothing, and above all never complain about anything to anyone. If you don't make waves—if you don't offend anyone—you're set for life. That apparently is the smart move in Spain. The system in the United States is very different. With the emphasis on publications and making a name for yourself, you can't afford *not* to say anything. The differences in jokes among cultures are mirrored by differences in what is considered intelligent as revealed by more formal studies.

The language, legacies, needs, and beliefs of a society combine to form a culturally appropriate conception of intelligence. In the case of a non-Western society, this may be equivalent to the Western concept in some regards but not in others. For example, consider the Zambian Chi-Chewas' concept of *nzelu,* which is similar to the Western concept of intelligence but differs from it in important ways.[20] Whereas the Western concept of intelligence has a cognitive orientation, *nzelu* appears to include the dimensions of wisdom, cleverness, and responsibility within the Zambian cultural context. Thus, as compared with Western children, Zambian children learn to value a broader notion of intelligence and may be expected to demonstrate a broader range of behaviors that would be defined as intelligent within their culture.[21]

The mental abilities required for successful intelligence almost certainly differ from one culture to another. This is why I am uncomfortable with any theory that attempts to specify a fixed set of mental abilities as though they are universally important. The abilities required for reading and writing—so important in our culture—don't matter a whole lot in preliterate societies. But the ability to make very fine distinctions in visual patterns, which is not of great value in our culture, might make the difference between life and death when one is about to be attacked by a camouflaged predator blending in with the background.

A study of the IQs of an immigrant population of Italian Americans provides a closer-to-home example regarding the effects of cultural differences on intelligence, particularly on intelligence tests.[22] Less than a century ago, first-generation Italian-American children showed a median IQ of 87 (low average), even when nonverbal measures were used and when so-called mainstream American attitudes were considered. Some social commentators as well as psychological researchers at the time pointed to heredity and other nonenvironmental factors as the basis for the low IQs—much as they do today for other minority groups.

For example, Henry Goddard, a leading researcher of the day, pronounced that 79 percent of immigrant Italians were "feebleminded" (he also stated that about 80 percent of immigrant Hungarians and Russians were similarly unendowed with intelligence).[23] Goddard further asserted that moral decadence was associated with this deficit in intelligence and recommended that intelligence tests be administered to all immigrants and that all those he deemed to be substandard be selectively excluded from entering the United States. Stephen Ceci has noted, however, that subsequent generations of Italian Americans have shown slightly above average IQs; other immigrant groups that Goddard denigrated have shown similar substantial increases in IQ.[24] Even the most fervent hereditarians would be unlikely to attribute such gains in so few generations to heredity. Cultural assimilation, including integrated education, provides a much more plausible explanation.

Perhaps it now can be clear why it is so difficult, and arguably impossible, to come up with tests that can truly be called *culture fair* —that is, equally appropriate and fair for members of all cultures. If members of different cultures have different ideas of what it means to be intelligent, then at the very least, such tests should be devised by members of those cultures.

Yet some authors and publishers of intelligence tests have invoked the term *culture fair* because, in their view, using only geometric figures renders the test both nonverbal (and thus uninfluenced by language) and nonpreferential to one culture over another.[25] The

Raven Progressive Matrices test, which also relies exclusively on geometric forms, has similarly been viewed by some psychologists as culture fair.

But do people in all cultures have equal exposure to geometric forms? Obviously not. Even those who believe that tests such as the Raven are culture fair now admit that there are greater differences between cultures on geometrically based tests than there are on verbal ones.[26] Students who have not had a Western education, and who have not learned geometric concepts in school, right up through whole courses on geometry, are obviously going to be at a disadvantage on tests that require reasoning with geometric constructions. These constructions, which make sense and are familiar to Western students, may make little sense to children and even adults who have not had Western schooling.

The differences in cultures, however, are not limited to concepts of geometry. Consider, for example, the concept of mental quickness. In mainstream American culture, quickness is usually associated with intelligence. To say someone is "quick" is to say that the person is intelligent, and indeed, most group tests of intelligence are quite strictly timed, as many of us have found out the hard way. When, as a senior in college, I took the Graduate Record Examination, I found myself in the uncomfortable position of not having completed all the items on the first verbal section when time was called. And by this point in my life, I was no novice. I had worked one summer at the Psychological Corporation, a major test publisher, another summer at Educational Testing Service, publishers of the very test I was taking, and I had by then even devised my own test of intelligence. But there I was. And as I looked at the items I had not yet completed, I realized that I would be able to answer almost all or possibly even all of them correctly, if only I were given the time to do so. But of course, I wasn't being given the time.

I was left with two alternatives, neither of them very satisfactory. The first was to write off the items, have them scored as wrong, and get a lower score on the test. The second was to return to the verbal section after I had completed the mathematical section, which came next. My total time on the test would not differ. I would be taking time away from the mathematical section to work on the verbal section. But this was a test on which skipping around sections was not allowed, though it was on some tests. So I was stuck. Going back would be considered cheating. Obviously, I'm not going to say what I did. However, my score was quite good on the verbal section of the test, and on the math section too!

In many cultures of the world, quickness is not at a premium when it comes to being considered intelligent. In these cultures, people may believe that more intelligent people do not rush into things. Indeed, a leading psychometric theorist of intelligence defined intelligence as the ability to withhold an instinctive response.[27] Ironically, his own intelligence tests were among the most severely timed of all that could be found.

Many of us have encountered situations where cultural differences impact upon what is considered intelligent, whether at work or in everyday situations. For example, in the United States, we are enamored of fast food. There may be many reasons for this preference, but one of them almost certainly is not the quality or the appetizing aromas of the food. Nor is it its health-promoting value. It is, however, fast, and we value that. A typical lunch hour, after all, ranges between a half hour and an hour.

In Mediterranean countries, of course, the situation is different. There, a typical lunch hour is two and a half to three hours long. Even the stores close at lunchtime. Moreover, if you try to get through a lunch quickly, people are often annoyed or even offended. The suggestion is that you don't value their company. These countries don't lose much in the bargain; the stores and offices stay open later at night than do many stores and offices in the United States, so that the working day is about the same. But the time that American company workers would consider wasted at lunch many Mediterranean people consider an important time to spend with family and friends.

This difference in viewpoint is prevalent in much of Latin America as well. I attended a conference in Venezuela that was scheduled to begin at eight in the morning. My contingent from the United States was annoyed by the early hour, because everyone was tired from traveling all the way to Venezuela the day before. Nevertheless, wanting to make a good impression on our hosts, we arrived on time. None of the Latin Americans, who were the overwhelming majority of people at the conference, were there, and when they started arriving, at around nine, their attitude was one of incredulity that we had wasted more than an hour that could have been spent productively rather than sitting and waiting for the conference to begin. When you travel internationally, either you learn quickly that flexibility in conceptions of intelligent behavior pays off, or you become frustrated very quickly.

Of course, we need to recognize that our own conceptions of time and its relation to intelligence are more flexible, and one might even say more sensible, than they appear. If you tell someone that you have thought about it carefully for fifteen seconds and then decided to marry your current dating partner, or take a particular job, or buy a certain house, you are not likely to be commended for your intelligence. Even we in the United States know that it's not always smart to be quick or punctual. It depends on the situation. We may start our meetings on time, but how happy are dinner hosts when you arrive on time or, worse, early?

Sometimes, systems that seem foolish to us make more sense in the intellectual context of a given culture. For example, in Turkey, scores on objective tests are considerably more important than they are in the United States. In fifth grade—the last year of compulsory schooling—students who wish to go on to a private school or an elite public school are required to take a test. The result of this test, typically taken at ten years of age, will totally determine not only admission to the school but, essentially, the child's whole future. Failure to gain admission to one of these schools means either quitting school or going to a regular public school of doubtful quality.

The emphasis on testing seems wholly wrongheaded at first. Don't these people know anything about errors of measurement, and test anxiety, and the host of other factors that can affect the results of a test? How could a system be so maladaptive? The truth is, it still seems maladaptive to me, even though, inquiring further, one learns more.

In the United States, we sometimes say it is who you know rather than what you know that carries the day. Sometimes it is, and sometimes it isn't. But regarding admissions to private schools and colleges, grades, scores on tests, letters of recommendation, and the like help ensure that the system, for all its flaws, more or less depends on the qualifications of the students. But in Turkey, as in many Middle Eastern countries, who you know is a whole lot more important even than it is in the United States. Many decisions are made solely on the basis of connections.

So why the extreme reliance on a multiple-choice test? It provides an adaptive way of dealing with the problem of pull. Were it not for such a test, the measures available would, for the most part, be corrupted. Grades are affected by pull, and so are letters of recommendation, even from teachers and university professors. That's the way the system works. Heavy reliance on objective tests, then, allows qualified students without pull to have access to educational opportunities that might otherwise not be available. Multiple-choice tests are lousy measures of successful intelligence, but pull is an even worse measure.

Psychologists differ in the extent to which they believe that cultural issues ought to be taken into account in analyses of intelligence. For example, some have expressed an extreme view of cultural relativism.[28] According to this view, indigenous notions of cognitive competence should be the sole basis for any valid description and assessment of psychological phenomena such as intelligence. Radical cultural relativists believe that the Western concept of intelligence has no universal merit because intelligence is different in each culture. To the radical relativists, our goal should be to understand what constitutes intelligence in the culture at hand.

Not only the concept of intelligence but also that of testing may not apply equally well in all cultures. For example, people in Mayan cultures may perform quite poorly on tests because they don't even share our assumption about how testing is done.[29] When asked a question to which the examiner obviously has the answer, Mayans may become confused, wondering why he would ask something he already knows. They also cannot understand why, if one individual does not know the answer to a problem, he should not be able to consult other members of the family. After all, isn't the goal of a question to find an answer? What in our highly individualistic culture may seem like cheating is in their collectively oriented culture the only path that makes any real sense.

Sometimes, we are so sure of our assumptions in giving tests that we fail to consider how these assumptions might impact upon others who take our tests. I have made this mistake myself. Some years back, we did a study of abstract analogical reasoning ability, testing children in the second, fourth, and sixth grades, as well as adults, for their ability to solve picture analogies.[30] The second graders did the worst, the fourth graders did somewhat better, the sixth graders did better still, and the adults did best. No great surprise there. Indeed, we might have just gone ahead and published these fairly boring results. But I decided to look more carefully at the data and found, to my surprise, that a number of second graders had no correct answers at all—absolutely none. Given that the test items had only two choices, a chance score would have been 50 percent. Something was clearly wrong.

I then looked at the test booklets of the children who had no correct answers. All had done the same thing. They had circled as correct either the first or the second term in the stem (given part) of the problem. In other words, instead of circling answers, they had circled parts of the question. Why? Actually, it wasn't so complicated. The test had been conducted in a Hebrew day school that had English instruction in the morning and Hebrew instruction in the afternoon. Because the test was administered in the afternoon, it was a time when the students typically would have been studying Hebrew, which is read from right to left. Some of the second graders had, in fact, read right to left, with disastrous results for their scores. But had we not looked at their actual responses, we never would have known what had gone wrong. The point is that we cannot presume a whole lot when we give tests, even that the normal way to read is left to right.

We should be aware that culture and, more important, acculturation into the ways of culture in general and Western culture in particular are the keys to doing well on conventional IQ tests. Indeed, one researcher has found that the single best predictor of adult IQ is not parental IQ or income level or social class or any of the variables one might expect.[31] Instead, it is number of years of schooling, and especially Western schooling. For those who doubt that intelligence, even conventional intelligence, can be taught, this result should give pause. In a way, it is not so surprising. IQ tests often measure achievement, but that which people might have been expected to accomplish a few years before they are tested. A clean separation of intelligence and achievement is virtually impossible in conventional testing, because intelligence is measured through achieved competencies. A strictly biological view does not take these facts into account.

Although a culture-fair test is not a realistic goal, a *culture-relevant* test is. Such a test requires skills and knowledge that relate to the cultural experiences of the test takers. Culture-relevant tests assume a given culturally based definition of intelligence, involving, say, memory and other aspects of information processing, but they use content and procedures that are relevant in measuring intelligence according to the culture's underlying definition of it.

Designing culture-relevant tests requires creativity and effort but is probably not impossible. For example, a study that investigated memory abilities (one aspect of intelligence as Western culture defines it) in American and Moroccan cultures[32] found that level of recall depended on the content that was being remembered, with culture-relevant content being remembered more effectively than nonrelevant content—e.g., Moroccan rug merchants were better able to recall complex visual patterns on black-and-white photos of Oriental rugs. The results further suggested that when tests are not designed to minimize the effects of cultural differences, the key to culture-specific differences in memory may be prior knowledge and use of metamemory strategies (involving people's knowledge about their memories), rather than actual structural differences in memory— e.g., the number of words you can recall and how quickly you forget them. In short, making a test culturally relevant appears to involve much more than just removing specific linguistic barriers to understanding.

Similar context effects can be shown in children's and adults' performance on a variety of tasks.[33] The *social context* (e.g., whether a task is considered masculine or feminine), the *mental context* (e.g., whether you are checking out a house in order to buy the house or to burgle it), and the *physical context* (e.g., whether a task is presented at the beach or in a laboratory) all affect performance. For example, fourteen-year-old boys performed poorly on a task when it was couched in cupcake-baking terms but performed well when it was framed as a battery-changing task.[34] Children were able to do a video game much better when they were told it was about the flight trajectories of butterflies than when they were told the same task was about movements of abstract geometric objects. And Brazilian house maids had no difficulty with proportional reasoning when hypothetically purchasing food but had great difficulty when hypothetically purchasing medicinal herbs.[35]

This long discussion of cultural issues leads to a single conclusion. You can't fully understand intelligence, as adaptive behavior, outside its cultural context. Again, what may seem smart in one culture may seem stupid in another, and vice versa. But if we could integrate the study of culture with the study of biology, perhaps we would be further along the way to a true understanding of intelligence. Some investigators have chosen to do just that.

Combining Biology and Culture

Theories that consider cultural context are not necessarily mutually exclusive with respect to theories that consider biology. A theory of multiple intelligences attempts to take into account both biological and cultural aspects of intelligence.

According to the theory of multiple intelligences proposed in 1983 by Harvard psychologist Howard Gardner in his book *Frames of Mind,* intelligence is not really just a single, unitary construct. Nor is it sufficient just to talk about multiple abilities. Rather, this theory proposes seven distinct, relatively independent intelligences. Each of them is a separate system of functioning, although the systems can interact to produce what is seen as intelligent performance.

1. Linguistic intelligence: used in reading a book; writing a paper, novel, or poem; and understanding spoken words.

2. Logical-mathematical intelligence: used in solving mathematical problems, balancing a checkbook, doing a mathematical proof, and in logical reasoning.

3. Spatial intelligence: used in getting from one place to another, in reading a map, and in packing suitcases in the trunk of a car.

4. Musical intelligence: used in singing a song, composing a sonata, playing a trumpet, or even appreciating the structure of a piece of music.

5. Bodily kinesthetic intelligence: used in dancing, playing basketball, running a mile, or throwing a javelin.

6. Interpersonal intelligence: used in relating to other people, such as when we try to understand another person's behavior, motives, or emotions.

7. Intrapersonal intelligence: used in understanding ourselves— the basis for understanding who we are, what makes us tick, and how we can change ourselves, given the existing constraints on our abilities and our interests.

This view of the mind is modular, which means that each intelligence is viewed as emanating from a distinct portion of the brain and thus as independent of the others. The theory is intriguing and has found wide application in education.[36] It is a good example, however, of how theories can impact on society and yet generate relatively little research to verify their claims. Since its being proposed, it is not clear that there has been even a single piece of research that could be interpreted as supporting, or even as testing, the theory.[37] Thus, we have a powerful theory that has generated programs in education, but not empirical research in psychology to support its claims. It is important that such research be forthcoming, as psychology has something of a history of bestowing gifts upon the world that are later shown to lack credibility in one way or another. IQ testing, in my opinion, is one of the best examples.

Whether we agree with the theory of multiple intelligences or not, it is, I believe, fundamentally important in recognizing the multiple nature of intelligence and that theories of a single ability just do not take into account the complexity of the human mind. In my view, as a theory of single intelligence, IQ fails to do just that. My own theory attempts to go beyond IQ to understanding not just intelligence but successful intelligence in all its aspects.

PART III

Successful Intelligence Is What Counts

CHAPTER FOUR

The Three Keys
to Successful Intelligence

Jack, who considers himself smartest in his class, likes to make fun of Irvin, the boy he has identified as stupidest in the class. Jack pulls aside his friend Tom and says, "You want to see what 'stupid' means, Tom? Watch this. . . . Hey, Irvin. Here are two coins. Take whichever one you want. It's yours."

Irvin looks at the two coins, a nickel and a dime, for a while and then selects the nickel.

"Go ahead, Irv, take it, it's yours." Jack laughs.

Irvin takes the larger coin and walks away. An adult who has been watching the transaction from a distance walks up to Irvin and gently points out that the dime is worth more than the nickel, even though it is smaller, and that Irvin has just cost himself five cents.

"Oh, I know that," replies Irvin, "but if I picked the dime, Jack would never ask me to choose between the two coins again. This way, he'll keep asking me again and again. I've already collected over a dollar from him, and all I have to do is keep choosing the nickel."

This apocryphal story points out something we already intuitively know—that someone can be slow in school but think well outside it, and vice versa. The hoary question "How can someone so smart be so dumb?" reminds us that people can be good or bad thinkers, regardless of how well they may do in a school setting. I found this out the hard way.

In Search of the Keys
to Successful Intelligence

My interest in broadening our means of identifying potential high performers in life and not just in school came from an experience in my own career. Because of my wretched performance on IQ tests as a child, I became very interested in psychology. By the time I was in seventh grade, I decided I wanted to study intelligence. I did just that. In carrying out a project on the development of mental tests, I constructed my own test. I also found in my hometown library the Stanford-Binet intelligence test and decided to give it to some of my classmates.

My first subject was a girl in whom I was romantically interested. I figured I would break the ice by giving her the test. Not a good idea. The relationship not only terminated at that point, it never even got started.

My choice of the next subject—a boy I had known from Cub Scouts—was also a mistake. I thought he was a good friend, but he was a fink. He told his mother I had given him the test. She told the junior high school guidance counselor, who reported me to the head school psychologist. The whole affair came to an unpleasant conclusion when the psychologist took me out of social studies class and, after bawling me out for fifty minutes, threatened to personally burn the book containing the test if I ever brought it to school again. He suggested that if I wanted to continue studying intelligence, I should limit my subjects to rats.

Once in college, I was still eager to study intelligence and figure out why I was so stupid, because I knew that I had a low IQ. There is a not so hidden point here. Once students get low scores on aptitude tests such as an IQ test, the SAT, or the ACT, they come to think of themselves as dumb. Even if they achieve, they may view themselves as achieving in spite of their being dumb. Society may view them in the same way. They may come to be labeled overachievers, people whose achievements seem to exceed their intelligence and who ought to be pushed down to size.

Some societies don't value outstanding performance or, at least, performance that stands out. In Norway, they speak of the Law of Jante, according to which if someone's head sticks up over the heads of others, then it should be cut off to get that person down to size. This same mentality is rather common in other parts of the world and is not unknown here. Many people grow up in families or go to schools where what is valued most is *not* standing out from the crowd —at least in unconventional ways. Too often, conformity is the norm.

Pursuing my interest in psychology as a freshman at Yale, I got off to a bad start. I got a grade of C in the introductory psychology course, scarcely an indication of a bright future in the field. It was further confirmation that my IQ scores were right and I didn't have the ability. My psychology professor apparently agreed with me. Handing back a test to me one day, he commented that there was a famous Sternberg in psychology (Saul), and it appeared there wasn't about to be another. I took the message to heart and decided to switch to another major. I chose mathematics, because I thought it was useful. The choice turned out to be fortunate. After receiving a worse grade in the introductory course for math majors than I had received in the introductory psychology course, I decided to switch back to psychology. And I did well in the upper-level courses.

I have now been a psychologist for twenty-one years, and one thing of which I am certain is that I have never—not even once—had to do in the profession what I needed to do to get an A in the introductory course, as well as in some of the other courses. In particular, I've never had to memorize a book or a lecture. If I can't remember something, I just look it up. The way schools set things up, however, they reward with A's the students who are good memorizers, not just at the college level but at many other levels as well. In defense of our schools, the educational systems in many other countries are worse in this regard.

The problem is that, in psychology is in other fields, the demands of the field bear little or no resemblance to the demands of the training needed in order to enter the field. For example, my son once said to me that he hated history and wished he never had to take another history course. I said to him that I, personally, had always found history interesting and I wondered why he didn't. His response was that he hated memorizing dates. Indeed, memorizing dates, battles, and historical documents constitutes the way many history courses are taught. But historians are not experts in their fields by virtue of being walking encyclopedias of dates or names of battles or historical documents.

In general, the same thing is true in the sciences. Often, what gets an A is memorizing formulas or solving problems in textbooks and on tests. But scientists don't memorize formulas for a living, nor do they solve textbook problems. Rather, they generate problems for themselves. Indeed, to a large extent they are judged on the importance of the problems they decide to study.

I went to my son's English class one Parents' Day. They were studying the *Odyssey*. A good book—actually, a great one. The teacher read a quote, and the students had to identify who said it, or what was happening at the time. For students who loved to memorize, that was just fine. But no one who excelled in that class was showing the talents of either a writer or a literary critic. And among those who did not do well was, for all we could tell, one who had the potential talent to be the next Shakespeare. Unlikely, perhaps, but the teacher would never know, given the way the class was taught.

The danger is that we overlook many talented people in any field of study because of the way we measure intelligence, and some of the best potential psychologists, biologists, historians, or whatever may get derailed because they are made to think they don't have the talent to pursue their interests. Clearly, we need to teach in a way that recognizes, develops, and rewards the three aspects of successful intelligence that are important to pursuing a career in any field.

The Three Aspects
of Successful Intelligence

Two boys are walking in a forest. They are quite different. The first boy's teachers think he is smart, his parents think he is smart, and as a result, he thinks he is smart. He has good test scores, good grades, and other good paper credentials that will get him far in his scholastic life. Few people consider the second boy smart. His test scores are nothing great, his grades aren't so good, and his other paper credentials are, in general, marginal. At best, people would call him shrewd or street smart. As the two boys walk along in the forest, they encounter a problem—a huge, furious, hungry-looking grizzly bear, charging straight at them. The first boy, calculating that the grizzly bear will overtake them in 17.3 seconds, panics. In this state, he looks at the second boy, who is calmly taking off his hiking boots and putting on his jogging shoes.

The first boy says to the second boy, "You must be crazy. There is no way we are going to outrun that grizzly bear!"

The second boy replies, "That's true. But all I have to do is outrun you!"

Both boys in that story are smart, but they are smart in different ways. The first boy quickly analyzed the problem, but that was as far as his intelligence took him. The second boy not only spotted the problem, he came up with a creative and practical solution. He displayed successful intelligence.

To be successfully intelligent is to think well in three different ways: analytically, creatively, and practically.[1] Typically, only analytical intelligence is valued on tests and in the classroom. Yet the style of intelligence that schools most readily recognize as smart may well be less useful to many students in their adult lives than creative and practical intelligence.

The three aspects of successful intelligence are related. Analytical thinking is required to solve problems and to judge the quality of ideas. Creative intelligence is required to formulate good problems and ideas in the first place. Practical intelligence is needed to use the ideas and their analysis in an effective way in one's everyday life.

Successful intelligence is most effective when it balances all three of its analytical, creative, and practical aspects. It is more important to know when and how to use these aspects of successful intelligence than just to have them. Successfully intelligent people don't just have abilities, they reflect on when and how to use these abilities effectively.

Analytical Intelligence

Alice (a real student, but with her name changed) was the teacher's dream. She scored high on tests, performed well in class, and, in general, did everything a teacher would expect a bright student to do. As a result, Alice was always considered to be at or near the top of her class. Her high test scores were accepted as a valid indicator of her ability to do outstanding work throughout her academic career. Yet by the time she had finished graduate school in psychology, she was performing at a very modest level. About 70 to 80 percent of her classmates were doing better. People like Alice are found at all levels of schooling.

Now consider the case of Ben, told to me by my colleague Louise Spear-Swerling. Ben, at just five years of age, started school early. In October of the first grade, he tested at a third-grade level in oral reading and could decode almost any word. His general reading comprehension was also excellent. When asked to write something, he produced a coherent story a page long that included commas and quotation marks. He also requested permission to look up the spelling of some of the more difficult words in a dictionary—which he accomplished on his own when permission was granted. According to all accounts, this boy had not been in any kind of instructional program in preschool; he was simply fascinated by books and words, and he spent a lot of time on his own trying to figure out how to read and spell. Here's a child almost everybody recognized as smart.

There was just one problem. Ben's story was uninspired, and so was the rest of his writing. It was technically excellent, but dull. Asked to write creatively, Ben seemed at sea and generally repeated, with little change, plots from stories he had read in school or on his own.

The question that naturally arises is: What went wrong with Alice and may go wrong with Ben? The answer, quite simply, is that while Alice was excellent at remembering and analyzing other people's ideas, she was not very good at coming up with ideas of her own. Consequently, she faltered in advanced schooling, where (as in life) it is necessary to have original ideas. Similarly, although Ben's academic skills certainly are impressive, he will require more than just a high level of academic achievement in order to do well in advanced schooling and in adult life. If we think about schooling as preparation for the world of work, we should be concerned about whether it requires and develops creative thinking, because for Alice, and eventually for Ben, to stay competitive in most jobs, it is and will be necessary for them to come up with their own ideas.

To excel in the practice of science, for example, requires the ability to generate creative, significant ideas that make a difference to the field and, ultimately, to the world. Yet students of science are typically rewarded for their analytical, not their creative, intelligence. Biologist James Watson has commented publicly a number of times on his low IQ scores, but that IQ did not prevent him from codiscovering the structure of the DNA molecule and thereby winning a Nobel Prize. The same dynamic applies in other occupations. Consider writing or art. It is one thing to succeed in writing good stories when told what to write about, or to draw nice pictures when told what the pictures should show. It is quite another thing to come up with one's own ideas for stories or pictures.

I was recently talking to Jim Halperin, the author of one of the most creative novels I've come across in the past few years. *The Truth Machine* is about a future time when a machine is able virtually infallibly to determine the truth versus falsity of what people say. There's just one little exception, and the fate of the machine's inventor, and much of the plot, hinges on that exception. I won't give away the story. More to the point here is that this highly creative author had a SAT verbal score of 620, which is good but nothing special, and far lower than the 800 of the noncreative Alice.

Another interesting fact about Halperin is that when he was in school, he had a great deal of difficulty in courses requiring memory. Later, as a rare-coin dealer, he found that he could remember every coin he had seen and every trade he had made. Often, abilities are quite domain-specific. Someone who cannot remember things in one domain has no trouble remembering them in another. Often, people simply don't remember what doesn't interest them.

I once looked at roughly two dozen pictures of houses drawn by children. They were nice pictures, but it was clear that the teacher had told the students what to draw; it did not seem likely that twenty-four children had independently decided to draw pictures of houses. In the real world of art and writing, however, someone is not always there to tell the artist and the writer what their compositions should depict. Indeed, creative writers and artists are, almost by definition, people who come up with their own imaginative ideas. Is anyone going to predict that the child who draws a nice picture of a house will become a marvelously creative artist? I hope not. Telling students what to do is often unrealistic with respect to what will be required for later success. Teachers should curtail the habit of formulating problems for students and instead urge them to formulate problems for themselves.

One could argue that most students will not become successful scientists or writers or artists, but the situation is no different in a very pragmatic occupation like business. Many of the executives interviewed during our studies of practical intelligence complained that they could hire a top-level graduate of a business school and get someone who might be good at analyzing textbook cases of business problems but was unable to come up with innovative ideas for new business products or services—furniture designs that create more shelf space, for example, or ways to stay competitive with similar industries in other countries.[2] The point, of course, is that there are large gaps between the kind of performance needed for success in a business setting and the kind required for success in schools, even those that are supposed to be quite practical in training students for the world of business. Thus, we often end up with adults who are unable to do what is expected of them in a work setting.

This same problem afflicts the study of education itself. It is one thing to get A's in education courses and quite another to succeed when called upon to be innovative in a classroom setting. I know from experience just how challenging classroom situations can be. For example, several years ago I was giving a lecture at the University of Puerto Rico and found myself confronting a serious classroom management problem—the professors of education in the audience simply weren't listening. For whatever reasons, they had decided to tune out, and they were talking and walking around the room, generally unattentive.

I tried the standard, uncreative techniques one learns in the course of training to be a teacher. I lowered my voice in the hope that these professors would do likewise and be able to hear me. Of course, I was assuming they wanted to hear, an assumption that proved false. Instead, they appeared to be grateful that I had lowered my voice, so they could hear themselves better. I then tried asking them to be quiet, but that didn't work either. Finally, after I had given up, a woman in the audience rose abruptly and said something in rapid-fire Spanish. After that, you could have heard a pin drop, and the audience remained silent and attentive for the rest of the session.

What did she say? She had capitalized on her understanding that Puerto Rico is a shame culture, not a guilt culture. My attempts to make the audience feel guilty might have worked in the mainland United States but were ineffective in Puerto Rico. In contrast, the woman pointed out to the audience that if they continued to be noisy, I would leave with a poor impression of the University of Puerto Rico and would undoubtedly report it to others. She said that the audience had no right to convey a bad impression and thereby cast shame on the university. Her appeal was effective in achieving the behavioral change that I had sought unsuccessfully.

The story of the Puerto Rican professors shows the extent to which successful intelligence depends on knowledge of a cultural context. I like to read the *International Herald Tribune*, in part because I find it to be the best daily source of international news, but also because it regularly reports the diplomatic gaffes of our (and others') ambassadors, some of whom do not even speak the principal languages of the countries to which they are representatives. Anyone who has ever had his or her comments in another country translated knows what a grand recipe for disaster it is likely to be. Yet I would be the first to admit that mastery of the mechanics of a foreign language, which draws heavily on analytical intelligence, is not the sole requirement for being an effective diplomat. Tact, the ability to innovate and persuade, an understanding of other points of view, are also necessary —in short, creative and practical intelligence.

Given the importance of successful intelligence in the world, why is it that the students we consider to be bright tend to be bright like Alice? Why are they so often test smart but not necessarily smart in other ways? Children are not born to be smart only in this limited way; rather, we shape them to be. Our system of education, in essence, creates Alices by continually reinforcing or rewarding students for their analytical intelligence. Indeed, the main lesson students learn is that it pays to be smart like Alice. As rewards, they receive good grades, good placements in class, awards, and, later, impressive college admissions.

There is an irony in our scholastic reward system. Children are continually reinforced for being smart like Alice, but in the real world after school, analytical intelligence is no longer enough. It is not that it no longer matters, but it certainly matters less. So people come to be intermittently reinforced rather than continuously reinforced. That is to say, they are rewarded only sometimes for their analytical intelligence. And here is another irony. Psychologists have found that intermittent reinforcement (rewarding behavior some but not all of the time) actually strengthens the behavior.[3] In other words, when IQ-like smarts stop mattering so much, and people are only intermittently reinforced for it, they start relying on it even more strongly, although this response is inappropriate.

The same principle applies at the level of an organization. Several years ago, I was the speaker at a dinner held by a Connecticut technology company that had been very successful but had come on hard times. I spoke about the need for innovation, a choice of topic that I thought was particularly appropriate under the circumstances. The CEO then got up and spoke about how the company was on a tried-and-true path and would continue on it. He gave as evidence for the correctness of the company's ways some of its recent successes. And they were successes—but they were getting to be fewer and further apart, a fact the CEO neglected to mention. There was just enough intermittent reinforcement to keep them on the path they were on, which was too bad, because their fortunes have fallen even more since my speech.

Not all of the executives were happy about the path the company was on, and some of them expressed dissatisfaction even to me, an outsider. One story I heard was an oft-told tale. The executive had been recruited during better times from another company, where he had had a string of successes. If he had known the direction his present company would take, he would never have left his old job. But the decline was gradual, he was, at least in part, responsible, and adverse conditions he once would never have accepted he now was willing to endure, because they came on him so slowly.

The same thing can happen in relationships. We sometimes tolerate dissatisfactions so severe that, had we known they would emerge, we would never have entered into the relationship in the first place. People who stay in unsatisfactory relationships may be smart enough to know the relationship isn't working and maybe even why (analytical intelligence), but they are not smart enough to know what to do about it (practical intelligence). Successfully intelligent people, on the other hand, can make mistakes and get into bad situations in business or in relationships, but they have the judgment and the courage to know when and how to get out.

Consider another example of how intermittent reinforcement can work in intimate relationships.[4] It sometimes comes to pass that one partner realizes that a relationship just isn't working. Suppose that a woman is with a man who keeps beating her, or cheating on her. She eventually decides it's just not worth the pain. So she tells the man that the relationship is over—kaput. We used to call such a message "dumping the guy"; today we call it "restructuring a relationship." But this woman tries to be nice about it. She will still be friends with the man and supportive of him, she says; she just doesn't want to continue an intimate relationship.

What often happens, not surprisingly, is that after receiving this apparently straightforward message, the man tries to get the woman back. And he keeps trying, while the woman finds it totally beyond her grasp why, especially since his behavior has been so outrageous. Sometimes women, and men as well, actually get suckered into taking the offenders back, at which time the old pattern of behavior almost immediately recommences. But why do they keep trying when they are being given the signal that the relationship is over?

They do so because of intermittent reinforcement. By being nice to the man and saying she will maintain the friendship, the woman is inadvertently sending him a mixed message. He is being given some reward. And because intermittent reinforcement strengthens old patterns of behavior, the man tries to maintain the relationship. The nicest thing the woman could do, for him and for herself, is to end the relationship completely and irrevocably.

You can see the effects of intermittent reinforcement on the utilization of analytical abilities. As I have said, those with the very highest IQs are generally not the most successful in life. There is a small but positive correlation between IQ and various kinds of measured success, but at the top, the relationship weakens. And people with extremely high IQs often don't achieve great success because they try to overcapitalize on their analytical intelligence.

The same sort of overcapitalization can happen in relationships. For example, you get into an argument and your partner goes to great pains to dazzle you with his or her impeccable logic and powers of abstract reasoning, pointing out at the same time your own stupidity or emotionality. The technique of logical wizardry is not a successful way of resolving conflicts. People who try to use their analytical abilities where they just aren't appropriate tend to worsen rather than improve a situation. Successful intelligence entails knowing not only when to use your analytical abilities but also when not to use them.

Ruth Duskin Feldman's 1982 book, *Whatever Happened to the Quiz Kids?*, follows the stories of some extremely bright youngsters when they became adults. The radio and later the television show *The Quiz Kids* featured children who had extremely high IQs, in many cases over 160. Traced as adults they were found, for the most part, to have rather ordinary lives, and none of them actually turned out to be a stellar success.

Another indication that schools mold students into Alices comes from Joe Glick's study of the Kpelle tribe in Africa.[5] Glick asked adult members of the tribe to sort terms into categories. For example, they might be asked to group together the names of fruits (apple, orange, grapefruit) or vegetables (celery, lettuce, broccoli) or vehicles (bus, boat, car). Glick found that the Kpelle sorted functionally. For example, they would sort "apple" with "eat" and "car" with "gas," because people eat apples and cars use gas.

In our culture, only young children sort functionally; the Kpelle's functional kind of sorting behavior is considered stupid when it is done by an adult. Older children and adults are expected to sort taxonomically (putting fruits together) or hierarchically (putting the word *fruit* over the names of different fruits and then perhaps putting the word *food* over the whole lot).

Glick tried, without initial success, to get the Kpelle to sort in other ways. When he was about to conclude that they simply didn't have the mental ability to do things any differently, he decided as a last resort to ask them how a stupid person would do the task. At this point, they sorted taxonomically, and with no trouble at all. Why would the Kpelle consider taxonomic sorting stupid? The answer is that the Kpelle do not grow up in our educational system and—even more important—do not take our tests. In everyday life, we tend to think functionally, which is an aspect of practical intelligence. We think of eating apples or using gas in cars. In school, we learn to think taxonomically, which is an aspect of analytical intelligence, but for the most part, this kind of thinking remains limited to artificial settings. A problem arises, therefore, when advanced students or career aspirants have to start thinking in ways that they have not been conditioned in school to think—that is, when they need to start turning out their own ideas rather than parroting or analyzing other people's ideas.

Success in life requires the use of creative and practical skills, but because these skills have not been actively encouraged or selected for, students tend not to develop them. In this respect, then, our schools essentially mislead and misprepare students by developing and rewarding a set of skills that, if important in later life, will be much less so than they were in school. Schools ought to be preparing students to live in a world where what matters is successful intelligence, not just inert, analytical intelligence. Instead, schools largely prepare them in ways that leave them clueless. We end up with doctors who don't know how to relate to patients, psychologists whose understanding of people is limited to textbook cases, and business managers who may know how to analyze a problem but not how to solve it.

I want to emphasize that the kinds of analytical abilities shown by Alice and Ben do matter in later life. It's very hard to get through life without them. For example, when things go wrong at work, you should be able to figure out why. Similarly, in personal relationships, the inability to analyze the source of, say, an argument, or the misanalyzing of it, can be quite a disaster. Couples who repeatedly argue about the same thing often do so because what they are arguing about isn't really the underlying source of friction. Thus, even if they resolve the fight, they don't resolve the problem that caused the fight, and they continue to argue. Clearly, then, analytical abilities are important. But IQ and similar tests measure only a part of analytical abilities, and they make no measure at all of how and when they are most effectively used.

Let's return, for a moment, to the story of the two boys in the forest. The one who survived was not particularly skilled in analytical abilities. But what eventually happened to him? After his close call with the grizzly, naturally enough, he acquired a phobia of forests and decided that the only way to fight it was to learn antiphobic techniques, like deep relaxation, heavy breathing, self-hypnosis, and the like. After mastering these techniques, he returned to the forest to test them out. They worked, and he found himself totally relaxed. But although lightning never strikes twice in the same place, grizzly bears do. The bear, which had not eaten since the last boy, now came charging again. The boy, petrified, quickly analyzed the problem and thought about trying to climb up a tree. But clearly it was too late, and things were looking bad.

Finally, he decided in desperation that the only course of action left was to get down on his knees and pray for his salvation. It was a long shot, but miraculously, just as the grizzly bear was about to attack the boy and eat him alive, it stopped dead in its tracks and got down to pray. Its prayer, however, illustrated the importance of analytical thinking, or the lack thereof. The grizzly bear prayed, "I thank thee, O Lord, for the offering I am about to receive," and that was the end of *that* boy.

Creative Intelligence

A student I will call Barbara (not her real name) exhibited a second way of being intelligent. Her grades were good, although by no means spectacular. And her undergraduate teachers thought she was just terrific, despite the fact that her test scores were very weak. When Barbara applied to our graduate program in psychology, she included a portfolio of her work, and I was tremendously impressed. It occurred to me at the time that her chances of getting a job at Yale as an assistant professor (for which you need a Ph.D.) would actually have been quite a bit higher than her chances of being admitted to graduate school, because getting a job does not require a standardized ability test, whereas getting into graduate school does.

Nevertheless, despite Barbara's mediocre scores, I anticipated that she would be admitted. For one thing, we claim to care about creativity, and Barbara had amply demonstrated creativity in her work.

What better predictor of future creative work could one find than past creative work? (Actually, none.) Certainly, a test like the Graduate Record Examination, which does not measure creativity, will not be as good a predictor of creative work as the creative work itself. In general, the best predictor of any kind of behavior in the future is the same kind of behavior in the past. This principle applies universally. For example, if you are going out with someone who is verbally abusive but promises to stop being verbally abusive after the marriage, the best predictor of what that person will do after the marriage is what he or she has done before it.

At the time of Barbara's application, I was the director of graduate studies for the Psychology Department, so I figured that the other members of the admissions committee would more or less have to listen to me. Besides, I was the expert on the committee with regard to abilities and how to test them. The committee did not, in fact, just blow off Barbara's application. They spent close to a half hour discussing it in great detail, but there was a distressing aspect to this discussion. It became apparent that the test scores were coloring everything else about the application. In other words, having seen the low test scores, committee members were looking to interpret other aspects of Barbara's admissions file as supporting them.

This pattern of behavior is not unusual. Work by Solomon Asch has shown that a person has what he referred to as *central traits,* around which other people organize information about that person. And the pseudoquantitative precision of test scores almost guarantees that they will be interpreted as measuring central traits. So I realized that the committee members were using the central trait of intelligence, as they gleaned it from the test scores, to interpret other information about Barbara. Thus, for example, if a comment in a letter of recommendation could be interpreted either somewhat favorably or somewhat negatively, the members of the committee would interpret it negatively, to make the comment consistent with the test scores.

By the end of the discussion, the members of the committee felt very good about the decision they had made. Barbara was rejected by an almost unanimous vote. I was the only person who voted to admit her. Even though Barbara had included a portfolio of her work, which demonstrated a high degree of competence, the other committee members had made their decisions largely on the basis of her test scores. In other words, they had more confidence in fallible and often weak predictors of creative work than they had in the work itself. We see this odd situation often in education today. The predictor of the performance has become more important than the performance itself! Cases like Barbara's don't occur just at the graduate level.

A study done by Louise Spear-Swerling focuses on Jeannie, another individual with creative abilities.[6] At age six, Jeannie had been a good solid student—above average in most areas but not the kind of exceptional early reader and writer that Ben was. What teachers repeatedly commented on was that Jeannie was "very creative" and "an independent thinker," had "an unusual way of thinking," etc. Some of her artwork was selected to represent her school at a regional art show. But nowhere were Jeannie's abilities recognized on her report cards, because there was no entry, among all the many checkoff boxes, for creativity of performance. Neither Jeannie's school, nor any other I am aware of, has a report card rating students' creativity. It's odd, isn't it? The typical report cards of elementary schools have multiple boxes for the measurement of basic academic competencies and interpersonal behavior but no boxes for creative behavior, which goes totally unrecognized. If anything, teachers tend to penalize it, because creative children can so often be perceived as disruptive.

Jeannie's creative ability was not limited to art. Her favorite subject in school was science, and she frequently initiated her own science projects at home, such as growing bacteria, gathering insect specimens outdoors, and so on. Once, she used a deflated balloon and a diagram of the human digestive tract from a book to make her own "model" of a stomach and intestines. She once saw a children's game on television that interested her; instead of pestering her parents to buy it for her (which she knew would be futile), she constructed her own cardboard version of it. Thus, she was really good at generating interesting ideas and at carrying them out independently.

Some of Jeannie's teachers truly appreciated her creative abilities. But overall, they were less valued than memory abilities. Some people even viewed her negatively, because she tended to have strong preferences for the kinds of problems she wanted to work on and how she wanted to do things. Sadly, parents often find themselves having to encourage their children to suppress their creativity, lest the schools regard them as misfits.

Why was Barbara's future jeopardized, and why is Jeannie's at risk as well? Why do we pay more attention to predictors than to performance? And in general, why do we favor analytical intelligence, as measured on the IQ and similar tests, over creative intelligence? Most of the time, the Barbaras of the world simply get shut out of the system. Barbara was rejected by our graduate program because of her GREs. If she had also applied to other competitive programs, chances are she would have been rejected by them as well, for exactly the same reason. Their admissions committees too might have paid lip service to her portfolio and letters of recommendation—prior to giving her the ax because of low test scores. In fact, many graduate programs prescreen their applicants so that those like Barbara, who have low scores, never even get their applications reviewed by anyone except a secretary, who shunts them aside.

The same unfortunate situation applies across the board. If Barbara had wanted to go to law school, she would have been required to take the Law School Admission Test (LSAT), which is very similar to the GRE. If she had wanted to go to medical school, she would have had to take the Medical College Admission Test (MCAT) and almost certainly wouldn't have done very well on that either. And if she had decided on business school, the Graduate Management Admission Test (GMAT) would almost assuredly have kept her out. All of these tests measure analytical, not creative, intelligence.

After Barbara was rejected by our graduate program, I decided to hire her as a research associate, because I believed that she showed much greater potential than her test scores indicated. And there was another reason. At the time, Barbara was working for one of my main competitors in the field, and I figured it would be better to have her in my camp than in his. And I was not disappointed. Her work as a research associate was highly creative and innovative. Two years later, she was admitted as the top pick into our program. But do you suppose that Barbara's case changed the system? If anything, people like Barbara are often regarded as an odd exception to a sound rule. We still value abstract analytical skills more than creative skills, even though success in today's world requires the kind of creative thinking found in people like Barbara.

The emphasis on analysis is not wrong, just unbalanced. A company like Intel succeeds so fabulously well because of innovation. As one product is being hyped and sold to the market as the greatest invention since sliced bread, its successor is already being developed. So as other companies scramble to try to compete, Intel is already moving way ahead of them, maintaining its position as a market leader. Analytical intelligence is important in knowing the market for any product, but creative intelligence is what produces products in the first place and keeps them coming out.

Practical Intelligence

When Celia (not her real name) applied to our graduate program in psychology, she had grades that were good but not great, test scores that were good but not great, and letters of recommendation that were good but not great. In fact, just about everything in her application seemed to be good but not great. Naturally, we admitted Celia, because every program needs people who are good but not great. Indeed, her work proved to be exactly what we had predicted—good but not great—so we figured we hit it on that one.

But what a surprise Celia gave us when it came to getting a job. Everyone wanted to hire her. And that raised an intriguing question. Why would someone who lacked Alice's analytical ability and Barbara's creative ability do so spectacularly well in the job market? The answer was actually very simple. She had an abundance of practical intelligence, or simple common sense. Celia could go into an environment, figure out what she needed to do to thrive there, and then do it.

For example, Celia knew how to interview effectively, how to interact well with other students, how to get her work done. She was also aware of what kinds of things do and don't work. In other words, she was street smart in an academic setting. She knew something that is true although seldom acknowledged: that in school, as well as in life, one needs a certain amount of practical smartness in order to adapt to the environment.

This talent can be seen in younger children as well. For instance, a television news story reported on a five- or six-year-old child whose mother was epileptic. She had a seizure just as she was about to get into the shower, and was lying unconscious in the tub with scalding water pouring over her. There was no one else in the house but the little boy, who called 911 and gave the dispatcher directions to his house. But the thing that really was impressive was that before calling 911, the boy turned on the cold-water tap full force to keep his mother from being even more badly burned. He had tried to turn off the hot-water tap, but it was too hot to touch.

Sometimes even so-called mentally retarded people have tremendous practical skills. They have to in order to get through life. For example, one study described a mentally retarded man who, unable to tell time, walked around wearing a broken watch. When he needed to know the time, he would ask someone, pointing out that his own watch was broken.[7]

Almost everyone would consider Alice and Ben smart, and many people would regard Barbara and Jeannie as smart (albeit in their own ways), but few people would think of Celia as smart. They might concede that she has common sense, but they would not see that as part of intelligence. They might even say that she was manipulative and reject the idea that being manipulative is an element of intelligence. Not so. The kind of practical intelligence that Celia exhibited is every bit as important as Alice's analytical or Barbara's creative intelligence, for the simple reason that different situations call for different kinds of intelligence. Furthermore, if we value only one kind of intelligence in school, we will seriously underestimate a lot of students, pegging them as much less intelligent than they really are.

This tendency to undervalue certain forms of intelligence became apparent in our own research in California.[8] We compared conceptions of intelligence among parents from different ethnic groups and found that the more parents emphasize social competence skills—such as getting along with peers and helping out the family—in their conception of intelligence, the less bright their children look according to the standards of the schools. In other words, the mismatch between what the parents emphasized in their environment and what the schools required in theirs resulted in kids who might be quite competent in the home and community setting but would be judged as intellectually lacking in the school.

Along a similar line of inquiry, Shirley Heath compared the language behavior of children in three communities:[9] Trackton, a lower-social-class black community; Roadville, a lower-social-class white community; and Gateway, a middle-social-class white community.

Heath found that the children from Trackton performed quite a bit worse than the children from Roadville or Gateway as soon as they started school; she also found, however, that the idea of how smart children are in school was largely dependent on the match between parental and school conceptions of intelligence. The children in Trackton, therefore, might actually have been no less intelligent than the children in Roadville or Gateway.

For example, parents in Trackton were found to emphasize the importance of nonverbal communication. To communicate successfully in Trackton, it was necessary to be very adept at both understanding and transmitting nonverbal cues. In Roadville and Gateway, on the other hand, more emphasis was placed on verbal skills, an emphasis that was a better match to the demands of the school. As a result, children from Roadville and Gateway appeared—but might actually not have been—smarter than children from Trackton. Once again, the middle class (especially the white middle class) benefited from the match between school values and home and community values.

It is quite plausible to argue that white-middle-class culture under-values the importance of nonverbal communication. As an example, many boring teachers or professors can go on being boring year after year precisely because they ignore the nonverbal communication of their audiences. None of their students have the courage to risk a bad grade by telling them they are boring. However brilliant these teach-ers may be, they certainly would not be practically intelligent. If they were to pay attention to nonverbal cues, they would become aware of their failure to command attention and might even do something about it.

Sensitivity to nonverbal communication can be a key to success in an interview setting. Information about how well an interview is going is almost exclusively nonverbal. Interviewers know that they are not supposed to reveal their feelings about the person being interviewed. But at times there might be nothing they would rather say than, "I'm going to do us both a favor. I know that we have another twenty-five minutes left in the interview, but we both know that you are wasting my time and I am wasting yours. So why don't you just bug off?" Though the interviewer certainly can't say this, his feelings are likely to leak out nonverbally, and if the applicant is sensitive to that nonverbal communication, he or she has a chance of changing the way the interview is going.

Another example of the importance of nonverbal skills is found in close interpersonal relationships. When things start to go wrong in such relationships, the initial indications are almost always nonverbal, because the individual who is perturbed does not even realize it consciously. So he or she leaks discomfort nonverbally—in sharp gestures, in leaning away from the other person, in skewed eye con-tact, and in a strained tone of voice. If the partner is sensitive to such cues, he or she may be able to pick up on them and try to find out what the problem is. If not, things are likely to continue to get worse before they can get better.

Nonverbal communication as an aspect of practical intelligence can be useful in business as well. Some Arab businessmen wear dark glasses to hide their eyes during negotiations, because they realize that dilated pupils indicate interest and a poker face can strengthen their bargaining position. Indeed, practical intelligence is what tells us as buyers not to express too much interest before we bid on something, lest the seller realize that we would be willing to pay a higher price than we hope to pay.

To return to the Heath study, it is interesting to compare Roadville versus Gateway. When the children from these two communities started school, they were roughly comparable in their abilities. Within a few years, however, the white-middle-class children from Gateway were doing better than the white-lower-class children from Roadville. What happened? Did the Roadville children have some kind of "inherited cumulative deficit," as some would have us believe? There is a much better explanation. The views about the nature of education and intelligence that were commonly held in Roadville resulted in the appearance that that community's children were less smart in school.

For example, parents in Roadville were more likely to believe that their role as teachers stopped when their children started school. Thus, parents no longer intervened in their children's education. They, like many low-SES (socioeconomic class) parents, had limited educations themselves and may have felt intimidated by the school, or ill equipped to help, especially as their children got older.[10] Gateway parents, on the other hand, continued to intervene, to the advantage of their children.

Moreover, parents from Roadville emphasized memory in their concept of intelligence, whereas parents from Gateway emphasized reasoning. Thus, as the years went by and reasoning became more important, the children from Gateway became progressively more advantaged.

Successful businesses think like Gateway, not Roadville, parents. Many of these businesses place an emphasis on continuing education. They realize that employees are valuable because of the education they may have had when they started work; but they also realize that employees become more valuable for the education they get after they start work. These businesses value lifelong learning, and the emphasis is on developing skills and abilities that will be useful in the business—in other words, aspects of practical intelligence.

Similarly, when we choose professionals—lawyers, doctors, accountants, psychologists, or whatever—we are sometimes impressed by credentials that may matter comparatively little. We may look for expertise as suggested by degrees from prestigious institutions, but what may be more important is the continued expertise that has been developed over the course of a career. In other words, how much a professional knows or where he learned it usually matters less than how he has successfully put that knowledge to use in the practice of his profession—in effect, his practical intelligence.

We cannot consider intelligence in isolation from the broader context of how it is applied. To do so may lead to seriously erroneous conclusions about children's or adults' capacity to learn and ability to perform. But like creative intelligence, practical intelligence is not what our tests measure, nor is it sufficiently emphasized in schools. Educators need to begin to take into consideration not only the analytical intelligence of Alice but also the creative intelligence of Barbara and the practical intelligence of Celia.

Although people usually have a preferred style of thinking, they do not, of course, use only one style exclusively. In everyone, there is some combination of analytical, creative, and practical intelligence. We need to foster *all* these forms of intelligence, not favor just one. Most important, we need to recognize and develop all three forms of intelligence and to foster balance in their use both in school and in the world of work after school. Certain tasks may require the use of greater or lesser degrees of these forms of intelligence, but to be successfully intelligent is to be able to call upon all three at the appropriate time—to analyze a problem, for example, come up with a creative solution, and then turn it into a practical one.

The most successfully intelligent people are not necessarily the ones with the greatest degree of intelligence in any of its three forms. But whether in school or the workplace, they are able to capitalize on their strengths, compensate for their weaknesses, and make the most of their abilities—all of which require analytical, creative, and practical intelligence. It is this view of successful intelligence that we need to adopt in order to obtain the most from our students and ourselves.

Testing the Three Aspects
of Successful Intelligence

Once I had formulated my theory of intelligence, I decided to do a study to check out my views and, further, to test the notion that students can succeed if they are able to capitalize on any or all three aspects of successful intelligence when they are taught and assessed in a way that permits them to do so. Funded by the U.S. Office of Educational Research and Improvement, the study lasted five years. Its goal was simple: to see if students would perform better in the classroom if they were taught in a way that allowed them to make use of the forms of intelligence that came most naturally to them. In other words, if children are taught in a way that fits them, rather than in a one-size-fits-all way, will they learn and perform better? [11]

Here is how the study proceeded. We sent a test based on my three-part theory of successful intelligence to high-school students all around the country and abroad. The test contained analytical, creative, and practical items, in the verbal, quantitative, figural, and essay domains. The idea was to look in a wide variety of ways for students' patterns of abilities. We didn't want to limit ourselves to the analytical kinds of items found on IQ tests, nor did we want to limit ourselves just to, say, the verbal domain or just to multiple-choice items. But testing the three aspects of my theory of successful intelligence in four different domains, we were greatly increasing the chances that if a student had high intellectual abilities of some kind, we would be able to detect them.

What are some examples of the kinds of items that appeared on the test? In the analytical domain, students had to figure out meanings of words from natural contexts, just as they did when they first learned vocabulary. In the creative domain, they had to work with novel number operations that they had never used before and solve verbal analogies with counterfactual premises (e.g., "Suppose it were the case that sparrows played hopscotch. Then what would the solution to the following problem be?"). In the practical domain, they had to use maps to plan routes and schedules to compute times and distances, much as they might do in everyday life. The practical essay required them to describe a life problem they were facing and propose practical solutions to it.

The students taking the test had been identified by their teachers or schools as potential candidates for the program. They were not necessarily identified as conventionally (IQ) gifted. From their test results, we then chose for the program students who met at least one of five criteria. They were either high in analytical abilities, high in creative abilities, high in practical abilities, high (but not necessarily all that high) in all three kinds of abilities, or relatively low in all three kinds of abilities. This gave us five different ability groupings.

It is worth noting that the groups we assembled by these criteria differed from each other not only in their abilities but in some other, fairly obvious ways. For example, the high-analytical group was most notable for its traditional composition in terms of the usual definition of "gifted." It was mostly white, middle to upper middle class, and composed of students who had been identified many times in the past as gifted in their schools. The high-creative and high-practical groups, in contrast, were much more diverse, ethnically, racially, and with respect to socioeconomic class. Many of the students in these groups had never been identified as gifted, and they were generally not the highest achievers in their schools. The high-balanced group (whose members tested well on all three abilities) again looked more like a typical gifted group, presumably because they were high in the more conventional analytical abilities. The low-balanced group was diverse.

The 199 students in the study were brought to Yale to take a college-level course in introductory psychology. All received the same basic introductory psychology text, which is based on my three-part theory of intelligence.[12] And all also received the same lectures in the mornings from one of Yale's best psychology teachers, Mahzarin Banaji.

The critical treatment distinguishing the groups occurred in the afternoons. The five groups received four different types of afternoon instruction, which sometimes matched the natural abilities of the students in each group and sometimes did not. One kind of instruction emphasized analytical thinking: comparing and contrasting, judging, evaluating, analyzing. A second kind emphasized creative thinking: discovering, inventing, imagining, supposing. A third kind emphasized practical thinking: using, utilizing, and applying. And the fourth kind of instruction—the so-called control group—emphasized memory, as do most introductory courses, in psychology or in other areas. These areas of instruction are applicable not just to psychology, of course, but to other fields as well.

In science, analytical thinking is involved in, say, comparing one theory of dreaming to another; creative thinking is involved in formulating a theory or designing an experiment; practical thinking is involved in applying scientific principles to everyday life. In literature, analytical thinking is involved in analyzing plots, themes, or characters; creative thinking in writing a poem or a short story; practical thinking in applying lessons learned from literature to everyday life. In history, analytical thinking is involved in thinking about how two countries or cultures are similar and different; creative thinking in placing oneself in the position of other people from other times and places; practical thinking in applying the lessons of history to the present. In art, analytical thinking is involved in analyzing an artist's style or message; creative thinking in producing art; practical thinking in deciding what will sell, and why, in the art world. Even in sports, all three kinds of thinking are needed: analytical thinking in analyzing an opponent's strategy, creative thinking in coming up with one's own strategy, and practical thinking in psyching out the opponent.

Because we were doing an experiment, we assigned students to sections that emphasized only one type of instruction: analytical thinking, creative thinking, practical thinking, or memory. A good course, however, will be a combination of all of these different types of thinking, for the simple reason that you want to help students learn both in ways that are comfortable to them and in ways that are not. We don't produce successfully intelligent people by coddling them—by always making things easy for them. We produce successfully intelligent people by making some things easy and others hard and by allowing students both to capitalize on their strengths and to compensate for their weaknesses, as well as to make the most of their natural abilities. In my own theory, the "gifted student" is one who is able to do that, which is quite different from the conventional meaning of that term.

This view of gifted people is why we did not rely on conventional tests to select students for our summer program but rather devised our own test. Successful intelligence is not static but dynamic. The traditional psychometric establishment believes that if you take an intelligence test and then retake it at a later date, but within a reasonable period of time, the two scores should be about the same. If the score on the retake goes up or down, maybe there's something wrong with you, or maybe you cheated. I believe that if you work at figuring out your strengths and weaknesses, and at making the most of the strengths and correcting or compensating for the weaknesses, your successful intelligence should show fast improvement. Thus, the true measure of your intelligence is not in a test score; it is in your willingness to develop your own talents.

In our summer course, we evaluated all students for four kinds of course achievement: memory, analytical, creative, and practical. These achievements were measured in a variety of ways: by homework assignments, multiple-choice tests, essay exams, and an independent research project. Students could not succeed just by showing that they had memorized the book. They had to show their degree of proficiency in the three other areas of instruction. I believe that being taught in analytical, creative, and practical ways is important, because it actually enhances learning of material rather than detracting from it. Everyone knows that memorizing a book results in very short-term learning. Most students forget the material as soon as they take the exam, or, unfortunately, sometimes before. By thinking about the material in different ways, students are forced to process it more deeply and thus to learn it better. By thinking to learn, they learn to think.

Our study proved a number of important points relevant to my theory of successful intelligence. First, it is possible to test for creative and practical intelligence, not merely for analytical intelligence. The students who had tested high in creativity, for example, proved to be creative in our program. Second, it is possible to teach in ways that improve all three aspects of successful intelligence. For example, students with high analytical ability who were challenged to be more creative and practical became so. The students in the control group who were relatively low in all three kinds of ability also had a chance to stretch their abilities. And finally, students who were relatively high in all three abilities, while their course work may not always have been brilliant, showed a degree of competence that was well above average. As I studied these results, it became more obvious than ever before that we shortchange our students—and our society—when we measure their intelligence and determine their future on the basis of psychometric tests that may, to a degree, be an indicator of what they already know but not of what they may be able to accomplish.

The most important result was that students who were placed in afternoon sections that matched their natural pattern of abilities performed better than students who were placed in afternoon sections that mismatched. For example, if creative students were given at least some chance to exercise their creative abilities in the course, their performance, on average, was better than if they were not given such a chance. The same was true for analytical and practical students.

In a way, these results were not surprising. It makes sense that students will do better if teaching and testing are tailored to their natural abilities. But that is not the way we teach and test. We value the students with strong memory and analytical abilities, and we practically write off those with strong creative and practical abilities. If we want to capitalize on the gifts of our students, at any level, we need to change our educational practices so that students are taught and assessed in ways that recognize their strengths, not just their weaknesses.

From IQ to Successful Intelligence

It's interesting to look at the careers of some successful people with high IQs, because one soon realizes that their success is not necessarily due to that particular attribute. Again, correlation can be confused with causation. Consider, as an example, Marilyn Vos Savant, who is listed in *The Guinness Book of World Records* as having the highest IQ of any living person on record. She has written a number of puzzle books that challenge people's mental abilities and also has a self-help column in *Parade,* a weekly newspaper supplement of enormous circulation.

How one judges Savant's success depends, of course, on the criteria one uses. From the standpoint of making major contributions to the world, she would probably rank very low among great world thinkers in literature, science, or the arts who may be far less "intelligent" than she is, at least as measured by the IQ scale. Actually, if you read her column, you may well conclude that she is not a world-class psychologist either. But from another point of view, she has been extremely successful—in her career as a writer and media figure. From the standpoint of my own theory of intelligence, Savant is capitalizing on her practical rather than her academic or analytical abilities. And one could argue that she deserves a lot of credit for that. After all, ultimately, that's what successful intelligence is about: finding one's strengths and making the most of them. And she has done that.

Successful intelligence requires one to distinguish between a domain of expertise and a field of expertise.[13] The domain refers to the work itself, the field to the people who do the work. To do outstanding work in a domain is one thing; to be outstanding in the field is another. Domain expertise can be a reflection of some balance of analytical, creative, and practical abilities, but recognition in a field for outstanding work almost always requires a substantial measure of practical intelligence. Artists need to get their work displayed in galleries; authors need to get their work published. We like to think that good work is enough, and sometimes it is. But recognition can also come to those with far less talent in many fields, because they know how to capitalize on what talents they may have to achieve recognition. That too is successful intelligence.

Not only does what is required for success differ in different fields and domains, it also differs over the course of one's career. The characteristics that lead to success in entry-level management jobs, for example, are quite different from those that lead to success at the higher levels of management. At the lower levels, one largely follows; at the higher levels, one largely leads. At the lower levels, one may have little work to delegate; at the upper levels, one may have to delegate almost everything.

Successfully intelligent people are flexible in adapting to the roles they need to fulfill. They recognize that they will have to change the way they work to fit the task and situation at hand, and then they analyze what these changes will have to be and make them.

Andrew Lloyd Webber is a good candidate for the wealthiest as well as the most well known composer alive today. At one level, he has been enormously successful. In the world of "serious music," however—concertos, sonatas, operas, and the like—Webber is not among the elite. Similarly, Leo Buscaglia has had enormous popular success in his work on close personal relationships but is virtually never cited in the work of serious scholars on the subject. Webber and Buscaglia are enormous successes in one respect and not in another. But that is true of everyone who succeeds. What successfully intelligent people have in common is that they decide what their field is and then seek to succeed within it. There is no single criterion for success, and people who are gifted, in a large sense, are those who can find personal success in a field of their own choosing and, sometimes, their own making.

In sum, we need to look beyond IQ to identify intellectually gifted individuals. There are many ways to be gifted, and scores on conventional intelligence tests represent only one of them. Indeed, some of the most gifted adult contributors to society, such as Albert Einstein and Thomas Edison, were not top performers either on tests or in school during their early years. Einstein did not speak until he was three years old, and many other remarkably gifted persons have even shown characteristics associated with mental retardation.

An anecdote illustrates my point. A distinguished historian arrived in a city where he was scheduled to give a talk on memory to the faculty and students of a small college. This was the last in a long string of engagements, and, exhausted, he knew he was incapable of giving a good talk. As he rode in a taxi to his destination, he had an idea. He offered his taxi driver fifty dollars if the man would give the talk for him. The historian didn't know anyone at the college, and he assured the driver that because the talk was completely written out, he didn't have to know anything at all about the topic of the talk; he simply had to deliver it.

Business had been slow, so the taxi driver decided that it was worth going through with the deal for the fifty dollars. He gave the talk, and it went flawlessly. Then the question-and-answer period started, and he found himself unable to answer even the first, trivial question that someone in the audience asked. He knew the answer was in the talk he had given, but he had been so busy concentrating on reading the speech that he couldn't remember a thing he had said. Then he saw the historian who had paid him, sitting way in the back of the auditorium. Thinking quickly, the driver looked the questioner straight in the eye and responded: "Why, that question is so easy even my taxi driver could answer it, and he just happens to be in the audience." The professor may well have been academically brilliant, but the taxi driver showed the analytical, creative, and practical skills that, together, constitute successful intelligence.

CHAPTER FIVE

Key 1: Finding Good Solutions with Analytical Intelligence

Analytical intelligence, the first component of successful intelligence, involves conscious direction of our mental processes to find a thoughtful solution to a problem. Analytical thinking can be used for different purposes. In problem solving, the goal is to move from a problem situation (e.g., not having enough money to buy a car) to a solution, overcoming obstacles along the way. In decision making, the goal is to select from among choices or to evaluate opportunities (e.g., choosing the car that would please you most for the amount of money you have). Let's look at analytical intelligence in both problem solving and decision making, concentrating not on its use in test problems but in everyday life. Analytical intelligence is not equivalent to the academic intelligence measured by IQ tests. Rather, IQ tests measure only a portion of analytical ability—namely, that portion most relevant to performance in school. Here, my focus will be on the broader aspects of analytical ability as it is applied beyond school settings.

Problem Solving

Problem solving requires six basic steps, which constitute a cycle. The cycle develops because the solution to one problem usually becomes the basis for the next problem. For example, you buy a house to solve the problem of needing shelter, but then you are likely to have problems, sooner or later, with repairs and maintenance. Or you form a relationship with someone to deal with a problem of loneliness or lack of intimacy, but then, sooner or later, you are likely to have at least some problems when the person seems never to be around and you're feeling lonely again. Again, problem solving is a cycle, not a straight line.

The six steps in the problem-solving cycle are not always completed in exactly the order described here, although this order is probably the most typical. Moreover, people sometimes return to steps they completed earlier. But in solving a problem, you are likely at some point to pass through all of these steps.

1. Problem recognition.   In order to solve a problem, you first need to recognize that you have a problem. This step is in some sense the most important of all, because if you don't recognize the existence of a problem, you are not going to make any effort to solve it.

Problem recognition is a stumbling block for many people in the use of their intelligence. Alcoholics, for example, commonly fail to admit to having a problem, not only helping to destroy their own lives but also making the lives of many people around them miserable. A common defense mechanism in the case of alcoholism is all-out denial—simply disclaiming that there is a problem in the first place. Another common defense mechanism is projection—arguing that it is the person who is doing the complaining who has a problem, because of an intolerant attitude toward life and the world in general.

Failure to recognize a problem is not limited to alcoholism, of course. For example, some people who have various kinds of sexual problems—affinities for pornography or fetishes—can become rabidly opposed to whatever it is that titillates them. Occasionally, they live a double life, railing in public against the very problem they live out daily. Many psychologists were less than surprised when some televangelists were exposed as clients of prostitutes, the very people they had excoriated in their television addresses. It is also not uncommon for people attracted to pornography to become active in anti-pornography groups and then to "screen" pornography to decide what is safe for others to see. The examples are not always so extreme. There are parents who physically punish their children, sometimes to the point of abuse, in order to teach them not to be aggressive—physically or otherwise—toward other children. All of these cases illustrate a third common defense mechanism used in confronting a problem: reaction formation, in which people convince themselves that their actions or beliefs are exactly the opposite of how they act or believe.

Problem recognition is also important in the corporate world. Intel recognized it had a problem when its Pentium chip turned out to make calculation errors. But the errors were rare and were unlikely to affect normal users. So the company tried to shrug off the problem. When it didn't go away when ignored and initial attempts to solve it —corrections for selected users—faltered, the company eventually offered to correct the problem for all users.

Schools always give kids problems to solve. They are clearly identified as such. They're numbered and have question marks, and they may appear on tests or at the back of book chapters. But real-world problems don't have numbers or question marks, and they occur during the chapters of living, not at the ends. We need to spend much more time helping children (and adult employees) recognize the characteristics of problem situations, and not just assume that our goal is to teach them how to solve obviously recognizable problems.

How do you know when you have a problem? There is no one way. But symptoms indicate that things aren't working as they should; that people, including yourself, are uneasy; that techniques that once produced one set of results are now producing another, less nearly adequate, set of results; that your competitive position is declining; and so on. When people fail to be sensitive to the existence of problems, they often wait to take action until it is too late, or a much more radical solution is needed. Denying the symptoms of serious illness and postponing treatment is an unfortunate example.

Successfully intelligent people don't wait for problems to hit them over the head: They recognize their existence before they get out of hand and begin the process of solving them.

2. Problem definition.   Once a problem is recognized, it still needs to be defined. For example, it is common for people to recognize that they have a problem in their relationships but not be able to define exactly what it is. Or they misdefine it.

Consider a couple who argue because the husband is spending a lot of time out bowling with his friends. Finally, he gives in and promises to cut down drastically on his bowling. Problem solved? Not really. He starts spending his bowling time at bars, and his wife is angry again. So now he becomes increasingly resentful. For him, to stop going to bars will be a second concession. But the problem still has not been solved, because it was never about where he spent his time but rather about how much time he spent away from home and why he did it. Of course, they can solve that problem if the husband stays home. But as often happens in the problem-solving cycle, the problem would be misdefined again, and so the husband would become resentful and take his revenge in other ways. The problem needed to be defined as one of finding a compromise so that the husband would be home enough to satisfy his wife (and perhaps his own desire to spend time with his wife) but away enough to satisfy his need for independence.

The key point here is that we must recognize and correctly define the problems we have, or we can waste a lot of time trying to solve problems we don't have. Typically, the more time we take to figure out exactly what our problem is, the less time it takes to solve it. In fact, studies in my own laboratory of brighter versus less-bright problem solvers showed that in complex reasoning tasks, brighter problem solvers spent relatively more time up front figuring out what to do and less time doing it; less-bright problem solvers spent relatively less time figuring out what to do and relatively more time doing it, because they hadn't really defined the problem.[1]

This difference also characterizes experts versus novices in a number of fields, such as physics.[2] The experts puzzle more over exactly what the problem they face is, while the novices try to solve the problem before they figure out what it is. The same is true in the business world. How many people have changed jobs, seeking a company they will be happier working for, when in fact the problem wasn't the company but the kind of work they were doing? Or how many people have changed the kind of work they do, when in fact the problem was the company for which they worked? Defining a problem correctly can save a lot of grief.

Good definition of a problem paid off for Johnson & Johnson. When someone spiked bottles of Extra-Strength Tylenol with cyanide, the company immediately called together a crisis team, which recommended that all Extra-Strength Tylenol be recalled. Eventually, other Tylenol products were recalled as well. There were those who shook their heads in disbelief, arguing that the recalls would kill the Tylenol brand label. They were wrong. Within a short time, Tylenol had regained the position of market leadership.

Misdefinition of a problem plagues the intelligence-testing business, with regard to both producers of tests and their buyers. The tests they produce and use measure aspects of intelligence that are of some but not great importance to real-life success. But the same tests are produced and used year after year. One cannot help but wonder why. The reason is not complicated.

The first well-known computer, UNIVAC, was created at about the same time as the first edition of the Wechsler Adult Intelligence Scale (WAIS). UNIVAC, which had less power than even the most basic current desktop computers, filled a large room with its hardware. Today UNIVAC would not even be recognizable to the younger generation as a computer, and anyone who used it or a similar device would be met with incredulity. But the latest revised edition of the

Wechsler differs little from the first edition and contains largely the same material, in updated form. Other tests, such as the SAT, have undergone a bit more evolution, but not much.

Why, then, does high technology move at light-speed in comparison to the glacial development of ability tests? Basically, the answer is competition. There are hundreds of major active hardware and software companies; there are only three or arguably four major testing companies, and they are the same ones that were around at the time the Wechsler first came on the market. They are run by largely unimaginative people, who lack even the imagination to know they are unimaginative and who respond to largely unimaginative markets. As long as the markets buy their products and there is no competition, it is really unnecessary to develop more useful and innovative tests. Furthermore, both producers and users have persistently refused to recognize or define the problems with these tests. So, naturally enough, no effort is made to solve them.

The importance of problem definition isn't limited to testing companies. Back in 1974, the Detroit auto industry, confronted by the problem of sagging sales, thought that the royal road to profits was to make larger and larger, more and more expensive cars. When the gas crunch hit, people turned to smaller cars, and the Japanese had them waiting for U.S. consumers to buy. By maximizing size and cost to the consumer, Detroit had clearly misdefined the problem.

Successful intelligence, whether at an individual or a corporate level, requires correctly defining problems just as much as it requires solving them. In fact, problems cannot be solved unless they are correctly defined. But just as schools give children little or no practice in recognizing problems, so do they give little or no practice in defining them once recognized. Try a little exercise. Next time you listen to someone talk about how to solve a problem at work, concentrate on whether that person is really addressing the true problem or, instead, describing a way of solving some other problem. You'll quickly realize that the reason so little often seems to get done is that people spend a lot of time solving the wrong problems.

Successfully intelligent people define problems correctly and

thereby solve those problems that really confront them, rather than extraneous ones. In this way, the same problems don't keep coming back into their lives. They also make the effort to decide which problems are worth solving, in the first place, and which aren't.

3. Formulating a strategy for problem solving.   Once a problem is defined, the individual or the group needs to devise a strategy for solving it. Strategic planning is recognized as important by most businesses, of course. The question is whether they do it, and whether they do it well.

IBM and Apple both devised strategies for maximizing sales of their microcomputer hardware. But the strategies were, to a large extent, diametrically opposed. IBM allowed an open system, which clones could then copy. Apple did not, and aggressively pursued companies that tried to make use of their system (an irony, because their product was quite similar to an earlier product, Xerox's Star System). Obviously, both strategies had advantages and disadvantages. But today IBM has largely come out of an extremely difficult turnaround period, whereas Apple has not. Clones produced competition in the marketing of hardware but also yielded a software explosion for IBM-compatible machines. As people bought more and more of these machines, more and more software was produced to work on them. When IBM started competing on price, the company was able to capture a decent share of an increasing market, whereas Apple found itself isolated with an operating system that could not be found on other machines. Worse, when WINDOWS appeared, people became able to do on IBM-compatible machines some of the graphics that formerly had been far easier on the Apple products.

Successfully intelligent people invest significant resources in strategic planning, and the results show. These people think in terms of long-range rather than bottom-line strategies and are more willing to delay gratification. Indeed, research had found that individuals who were better able to delay gratification as children demonstrate higher scores on tests of cognitive abilities as adolescents.[3] It is difficult to say what causes what. Does delay of gratification lead to higher cognitive abilities, do higher cognitive abilities lead to greater delay of gratification, do both depend on some higher-order factor, or is the relation complex, involving more than one of these options? What is clear is that smarter people, no matter how "smart" is defined, are more willing and able to think for the long term. For example, as children, they are more disposed, on average, to start doing what they will need to do to be admitted to a competitive college. As parents, they are more willing either to start early in saving money for their children's college education or else to start depleting their resources so their children will be eligible for scholarships.

Strategic planning is also important in relationships. For example, suppose you decide you want to attain greater closeness with a partner who seems to be keeping his or her distance. Most people start to employ the same strategy. They bring subtle or not so subtle pressure to bear on the partner to bring him or her closer. They may complain that the partner is too distant or uncaring, or try to make the partner feel guilty for keeping such a distance when they are so giving of themselves. It's a bad strategy, which usually ends up backfiring, driving the partner farther away. A more effective process for achieving the goal is, paradoxically, to create greater distance. As the level of distance becomes greater than that which is comfortable for the partner, then he or she is placed in the position of trying to achieve greater closeness and usually starts to do so in order to reestablish equilibrium.

The importance of strategy formulation to successful intelligence was shown as well as anywhere in the O. J. Simpson trial. The defense decided early on to rely heavily on a jury-selection consultant, who would help decide which potential jurors would be likely to arrive at a not-guilty verdict. The prosecution also hired a jury consultant but decided not to rely on him. This decision proved to be disastrous, especially because the prosecution's consultant viewed the jury that was selected as potentially heavily pro-defense. It is now a matter of history that the defense strategy paid off. One could argue, probably correctly, that the not-guilty verdict was in large measure determined before the trial even started.

Bad strategies can be costly. Recently, a trader in the United States for the Daiwa Bank made some bad decisions and lost about $400,000. Rethinking his strategies, possibly in collusion with high officials of the bank, he kept his bad trades secret and tried to recoup his losses. He never did, and ultimately he was discovered, by which time the bank's losses reached into the billions. As a result, the bank was barred from doing business in the United States.

Bad strategies aren't limited to banks. Recently, Ford had to recall millions of cars for a defect that was recognized years ago. The cost of waiting is in the billions of dollars.

I once consulted for a publishing company whose motto seemed to be: "There's never time to do it right, but there's always time to do it over." The corporate strategy was to act and then think. The result was that projects almost inevitably went off course and had to be reformulated many times and frequently abandoned altogether—a costly way to do business.

Successfully intelligent people carefully formulate strategies for problem solving. In particular, they focus on long-range planning rather than rushing in and then later having to rethink their strategies.

4. Representing information. How one represents information when solving problems has a substantial effect on whether one is able to solve the problems. It also has a substantial effect on what the ultimate solution is. Consider an experiment on dating.[4] College men were told to call a female classmate and have a conversation with her. But because she was a potential date, they were told a little bit about her in advance. Half the men were given predominantly positive information, and half were given predominantly negative information. The men then made the call and, afterward, were asked for their impression of the women. Perhaps it is not surprising that the men who were given the more positive information had a better impres-

sion of the women they called than did the men who were given the more negative information. But the result becomes a bit more surprising when one considers that the information about the women was completely random. The conversations essentially represented self-fulfilling prophecies for the information the men had been given in advance.

The story gets worse. Independent raters who did not know what information the men had been given were asked to assess the attractiveness of the women's personalities on the basis of listening to a tape of their remarks—the men's were erased—during the phone conversation. The women who had been described in advance as more attractive were rated as, in fact, being more attractive. But how could this be, when the information was given out at random? The self-fulfilling prophecy applied not only to the men who had received the information but also to the women they called. In effect, the prophecy was transmitted to them, and they acted as expected. Think about it. When someone treats you as worthless, isn't it likely that, sooner or later, you will start having doubts about your worth?

Prior, and often erroneous, information almost always has this effect. When you meet someone who you are told is brilliant, you are likely to treat the person differently than someone who has been described to you as stupid. And that, unfortunately, is the problem we face in the abilities business. It's no different from the experiment on romance. When people are led to believe that someone will not perform well, the prophecy is often realized.

Investigators have tested this hypothesis.[5] They gave teachers information about children in their classes, specifying those who were likely to bloom that year, information the teachers thought was based on a test of intelligence. Actually, the bloomers of the year were identified at random. The result: Teachers reported that, on average, those identified as potential bloomers did, in fact, bloom during the year. Although the study was not perfect in its design, this kind of result has been confirmed in dozens of studies. In sum, how we represent information about people affects how they will be perceived, how they will be treated, and how they will react, as I myself discovered when my low IQ scores as a child led to my being labeled stupid and to low expectations for me, which I, in turn, fulfilled.

In all forms of interpersonal and other problem solving, representation of information has a great effect on us. For example, consider the simple problem of whether you want to date someone again. In one study, researchers organized a dance and told the students who attended that they were being matched up according to their personal traits.[6] Actually, the couples were paired at random. After the dance, the students were asked how satisfied they were with the date and how likely they were to want to go out with the person again. The investigators used a wide variety of predictors to figure out what factors matter on a first date: personality attributes, family attributes, and the like. They found that only one factor predicted satisfaction and the desire to date the person again: physical attractiveness. But the people who were queried would not have viewed themselves as responding only to physical attractiveness. Rather, the greater physical attractiveness of the date led them to treat the date differently, to encode information about the date differently, and to be more satisfied. Indeed, we now know that physically attractive people do better in life, generally speaking.[7]

Representation of information is important in many life arenas, not just intimate relationships. Many Israelis have viewed Yasir Arafat and the PLO as murderers and liars, whose word could not be trusted in the slightest. Of course, many Palestinians have shared a similar view of Israelis. The correctness of their views is not at issue. But as long as each side continued to represent information about the other in this way, negotiations could lead nowhere. The same is true in business negotiations. If one side or the other is perceived as "the enemy," it will be difficult to reach common ground.

Successfully intelligent people represent information about a problem as accurately as possible, with a focus on how they can use that information effectively.

5. Allocating resources.   In solving a problem, we need to decide what resources we want to allocate to that problem. The decision is

an important one, because we almost always have too much to do in the time available to do it. In our work on intelligence, we frequently look at how people allocate resources, and we always find that better resource allocators are brighter by whatever standard we use.

In one study, for example, we looked at how better and worse readers allocated their time when they were reading.[8] The study was motivated by the belief that typical reading-comprehension tests, such as are found in virtually all the tests used for college and graduate admissions, do not adequately represent the task that either children or adults face when they read. In the tests, you are asked to read a set of passages and to answer similar sets of questions about each of them. Typically, some of the questions will be about main ideas, some about gist, some about details, and some about implications that can be drawn from what you have read. The score is the total number of questions answered correctly.

Why is such a test atypical of actual reading demands? Because most people typically have more to read than they have time to read. Moreover, they read for different purposes. Students read for multiple-choice exams in a way that is different from the way they read for an essay exam. They also read differently depending on whether they are expecting the questions to be general or particular. Adults reading the directions for using an appliance read them quite differently from the way they read the daily newspaper or a weekly newsmagazine. In fact, it would be counterproductive to do things any other way.

In our study, we asked adults to read different materials for different purposes—namely, for gist, for main ideas, for details, and for inference and application. We were particularly interested in how better and worse readers allocated their time. What we found was that better readers showed a differential distribution of time across the different purposes. Good readers spent more time reading for details and analysis, whereas poorer readers actually did not vary their reading time across the different reading purposes. They read everything the same way.

Why are some people so much more productive than others? Why do some people seem to get so much done and others so little in the same amount of time? Allocation of resources is a key to the difference. Smart people allocate time in an effective manner, spending just as long as a task is worth. The not-so-smart allocate time in a more haphazard fashion, with the result that they get less done.

We all develop strategies in order to save ourselves time. For example, as editor of a journal, *Psychological Bulletin,* I read large numbers of manuscripts submitted for publication. If I read them all extremely carefully, I wouldn't have time for anything else, and indeed, some people become nonproductive during their terms as editor because reading is all they do. Instead, I decide rather quickly, on the basis of both my own reading and external reviews, which articles are worth spending time on. The really good ones don't require extremely careful reading, because they are likely to be accepted with minimal changes. The really awful ones won't be accepted, no matter what. So it is those articles in the middle range that warrant my spending the time to read them carefully.

The problem is that sometimes the strategies used to save time are based on rules that do not produce the best possible decisions. For example, consider admissions to gifted programs, college programs, graduate programs, and the like. Many admissions officers save themselves time by eliminating the applications of people with aptitude test scores below a certain point. Why waste time on them when there are so many others to read? The assumption is that people with scores below some cutoff—say, an IQ of 130—couldn't do the work anyway. But can anyone seriously believe that someone with an IQ of, say, 129 could not do the same work as someone with an IQ of 130? Given the error of measurement in the test, the difference is meaningless anyway. Yet programs that use cutoffs function in exactly this way.

Sometimes, not only do the rules become ironclad but institutions seem to forget the reason they were instituted in the first place. Some years ago, a testing company for which I was working over the summer received a complaint from a woman who had taken one of its tests. It was a one-hundred-item, four-choice test, allegedly of higher-order reasoning ability but really more of vocabulary and general information. The school in question required a score of 25 for admission, which in itself was ludicrous, since 25 represents a chance score (100/4) on the test. In other words, someone responding at random would be expected to get a score of 25. The woman making the complaint had received a score of 24. But her other credentials were so outstanding that the school admitted her.

The woman had completed the program and was qualified to graduate with honors. There was just one problem. The school would not give her a diploma because, it said, her aptitude test score was below the minimum required for admission. What had started as a means for deciding to whom the school should allocate its resources—education—had become instead an accomplishment more important than the resources themselves. The school cared more about the predictor of performance than about the performance itself. Fortunately, an accommodation was reached. The woman was allowed to retake the test, got a score of 26, a full point above the cutoff, and was given her diploma. It wasn't the woman who was retarded; it was the school.

The detritus of misallocated resources can be found all over: people who have reached staggering levels of credit-card debt; companies that have made nonproducing acquisitions; governments that build enormous, expensive monuments to their leaders while their people starve. These entities seem never to step back and ask themselves how they are investing their resources. Successful intelligence is not just a cognitive ability—it's in large part a reflective attitude toward life and how one is living it. Successfully intelligent people, like anyone else, will sometimes misallocate resources. The difference is that, every once in a while, they step back and consider the results. If they're not getting the results they want, they reallocate their resources. Less successfully intelligent people just dig themselves deeper and deeper into a sinkhole, usually of their own creation.

Successfully intelligent people think carefully about allocating resources, for both the short term and the long term. They con-

sider the risk-reward ratios and then choose the allocations that they believe will maximize their return.

6. Monitoring and evaluation.   Monitoring simply means keeping track of our progress during the process of problem solving; evaluation is our judgment of the quality of our problem-solving process and the solution we have reached. They are the final, analytical steps in problem solving.

One of the more amazing aspects of our educational system is that so little is evaluated. Programs come and go, but few of them are ever formally evaluated. More typically, educators have subjective impressions, and they are often more likely to focus on the problems of an educational proposal than on its strengths. The result is that we often go through pendulum swings from one extreme to the other.

Present-day testing is a good example of such a pendulum swing. The traditional way of measuring abilities and achievements in the United States has been through multiple-choice examinations. The testing companies produce them and teachers make extensive use of them. In most countries of Europe, such tests are never used; students are evaluated by essay tests. There is no one "right" way to test. And people have long recognized the limitations of multiple-choice testing, even those who use them. They don't allow for creativity, they assume that the test taker defines each problem in the way that the test constructor did, they are stifling, and so on. Moreover, they do not show how an individual can actually go out and use what he or she knows.

Recently, there has been a trend toward what is called *performance testing.* In performance tests, students are asked to do tasks, such as projects and essays, that enable them to show how well they can construct products of various kinds. The nice thing about performance tests is that they have almost none of the limitations of multiple-choice tests. Hence, they are becoming quite popular. But, as is often the case, there is a rub. Performance tests have weaknesses that are virtually complementary to the advantages of multiple-choice tests. It is hard to score them objectively; they tend to be less consistent in the scores they yield from one testing to another; they are, if anything, more culturally bound; and they take a great deal of time to administer.

Performance tests can be just as trivial as multiple-choice tests. Calling it "performance" doesn't make it meaningful. I thought, when I was fifteen and in ninth grade, that I could become very interested in earth science. All I remember from the course is a performance test. The teacher placed rocks around the room, and we had to go from one rock station to another to identify each of the rocks. It was a performance test, but in the most trivial sense of the word. The result was that I never took a course in earth science again. To me, earth science was memorizing rocks, which is to say, boring.

A sensible conclusion would be that we should use both kinds of testing—multiple-choice and performance—and that they complement each other. Even more important, each kind of test has the potential to identify as intelligent the students who are not identified by the other kind of test. But incredibly, the tendency in education is to believe that we need to decide between the two. So we get people in the traditional camp and people in the avant-garde camp, arguing as though the two alternatives were mutually exclusive. No wonder we get so many pendulum swings.

Theorists of intellectual development have suggested that as people grow older, those who truly mature intellectually come to realize that many issues are not black and white and, moreover, that truth often proceeds dialectically.[9] We go from one extreme to the other, but then we find a middle ground that incorporates the best of the two extremes. For example, we might work very hard to achieve some goal and, when we fail, conclude that no goal is worth achieving and simply drop out. Those who are more dialectically intelligent learn to set realistic goals.

In the field of testing, we need to find the same middle ground, to recognize that the solution to our current problems is not to throw out all we have accomplished. Although tests are a long way from being perfect, they are not useless. They provide some information, but that information is far from complete and often not even correct. We need newer, better tests that incorporate the best features of the tests we now have but go beyond them as well.

Failure to monitor and evaluate the way we solve problems can lead to impractical and even wrong solutions. In the field of testing, too many people are so wedded to the solutions they have come up with, the decisions they have made, that they are reluctant to acknowledge that problems continue to exist and better solutions are possible. In business, that attitude can lead to bankruptcy; in marriage, to divorce. It all boils down to what will achieve the desired result—a solution to the problem—and a component of successful intelligence is the ability to focus on results.

Successfully intelligent people do not always make the correct decisions, but they monitor and evaluate their decisions and then correct their errors as they discover them.

Well-Structured and Ill-Structured Problems

Cognitive psychologists distinguish, in general, between two different kinds of problems. Problems with clear paths to solution are sometimes termed *well-structured problems* (e.g., "How do you find the area of a parallelogram?"), whereas those without clear solution paths are termed *ill-structured problems* (e.g., "How do you succeed in a career of your choice?"). Conventional, IQ-based academic intelligence is customarily measured by the ability to solve well-structured problems, whereas real-world successful intelligence is the ability to solve ill-structured problems.

An unfortunate feature of much education today, as well as the assessment of educational progress, is its overwhelming emphasis on well-structured problems. It is easier to teach the facts and only the facts, and then to test on these facts. Facts lend themselves to well-structured problems ("Who discovered X-rays?") with a clear, correct solution. Children learn to become experts at solving such problems.

The strategies that work in solving well-structured problems, however, often do not work particularly well, or at all, for ill-structured problems. There just aren't solutions to major life problems that are as clear as the formula for finding the area of a parallelogram or the identity of the person who discovered X-rays. And confronted with an ill-structured problem, people who are very skilled at solving well-structured problems may be at a complete loss. It is not surprising, since they have never been taught problem-solving strategies, nor have their abilities to solve ill-structured problems ever been tested.

Well-structured problems can often be solved by algorithms, which are formulas that, if followed, guarantee an accurate solution. Algorithms generally involve successive, somewhat mechanical iterations of a particular strategy until the correct solution is reached. Ill-structured problems are not so readily solved. They require entirely different strategies, which fall into the realm of heuristics—informal, intuitive, speculative strategies that sometimes work and other times don't. For example, you might try several ways to resolve a problem in an intimate relationship, none of which is guaranteed to yield a solution. The heuristic approach to problem solving is, by definition, a process that leads a person to find a solution by himself. The difference between the heuristic and the algorithmic approaches can be seen in the way science is taught in our schools and the way it is practiced in a research lab. In a school science lab, students are presented with a problem, then follow a series of prescribed, algorithmic steps to find the solution. In a research lab, scientists do not work on problems that can be readily solved by formulas. Rather, they tackle problems whose solutions are not yet known and must be found by their own work—i.e., heuristically.

Problem solvers apply heuristics in what is referred to as a problem space—the universe of all possible actions that can be taken to find a solution.[10] The search can proceed in a number of different ways, but four heuristics are especially useful in many problem-solving situations.

1. Means-ends analysis. Here, the problem solver approaches the problem by viewing the end—the goal being sought—and then analyzes the means necessary to decrease the distance between the current position in the problem space and the end goal in that space. For example, if you are trying to get from your home in Seattle, Washington, to a friend's house in Poughkeepsie, New York, means-ends analysis might consist of first going from your house to the Seattle airport, flying from Seattle to New York City, and then driving from New York City to your friend's house in Poughkeepsie. You break the problem down into steps.

2. Working forward. In this process, you simply start at the beginning of a problem and then work through it toward the end. Each step in the process takes you closer to your goal of solving the problem, as in writing a book a chapter at a time, starting with the first chapter and proceeding to the end.

3. Working backward. In this process, you start with the solution you want to obtain and then work backward to the problem you are trying to solve. For example, if you know in a mathematical proof what the conclusion is, you can sometimes work back to the premises.

4. Generating and testing. Here, the problem solver simply generates alternative courses of action, not necessarily in a systematic way, and then notices, in turn, whether each brings him closer to a solution. This process works well if there aren't too many possible solution paths. For example, if you have to decide which of several Italian dishes you want to cook for lunch, you might try thinking of some of the alternatives, decide whether each one appeals to you, and then cook the one that most appeals.

Many problems can be solved in more than one way, and often the way we view a problem is shaped by cultural contexts. Suppose that you want to sail from one island to another. If you are a native Westerner, you will probably plan to use charts and navigational equipment. However, natives of some South Pacific islands would probably scoff at such technicalities and even be puzzled by the idea of "going to" another island. They represent information differently, using the concept of the "moving island" to navigate vast expanses of ocean.[11] In their view, each island is adrift, floating along in the ocean, and to get from one floating island to another, they don't "go" anywhere in the usual sense. Rather, they sit in their small boats, watch the changes in the currents and the color of the water, and then "catch" the destination island as it drifts by. In the heuristic approach, there is no one way to solve a problem. The method often depends on what you know or believe to be true. Some methods may seem more obvious than others, but what is considered quite intelligent in one culture may be considered foolish in another.

Mental Sets and Fixation

Many problems are hard to solve because people tend to bring a particular mental set to them—a frame of mind involving an existing predisposition to think of a problem or a situation in a particular way. When problem solvers have a mental set (sometimes called *entrenchment*), they fixate on a strategy that normally works in solving many problems but does not work in solving the problem at hand.

Often, it happens that a manager or an executive who has been enormously successful in one organization is hired away from that organization at a substantial increase in salary and then flops dramatically. Mental set can be the reason. The manager attempts to apply solutions that worked for similar problems in another setting, but in the new setting they don't work.

A particular type of mental set involves "functional fixedness," which is the inability to see that something that is known to have a particular use may also be used for performing other functions. Functional fixedness prevents us from using old tools in novel ways to solve new problems—for example, using a reshaped coat hanger to get into a locked car or picking simple spring door locks with a credit card.

Functional fixedness may be influenced by cultural context in a way that might surprise some Westerners. Writers have hypothesized that there are higher and lower levels of mental development across cultures and that these levels influence the depth or quality of cognitive processes. French anthropologist Claude Lévi-Strauss rejected this hypothesis, instead maintaining that the human mind works in essentially the same way across cultures.[12] The only difference between the thought systems employed by persons in nonindustrialized versus industrialized, specialized societies might be in the strategies they use. Lévi-Strauss noted that scientific thinkers and problem solvers in nonindustrialized societies are generally *bricoleurs* (jacks-of-all-trades). A *bricoleur* has a bag of tools that can be used to fix all sorts of things, whereas the focused expert of an industrialized society might be effective only in a narrow area of expertise. One extension of this line of thinking is that persons who live in less specialized, nonindustrialized societies may not be as subject to functional fixedness as their more specialized, industrialized counterparts.

When we get stuck in solving a problem, whether because of functional fixedness or some other reason, incubation can be a useful technique to break out of it. Incubation involves simply putting a problem aside for a while and then coming back to it later. During incubation, you do not consciously think about the problem. Still, it may be processed subconsciously, resulting in a solution. It is not clear why incubation works, although there have been several suggested explanations. For example, one view is that as time passes, new stimuli, both external and internal, may activate new perspectives on the problem, weakening the effects of mental set.[13] Another view is that when we no longer keep a problem active in our minds, we let go of some of the unimportant details and keep only the more important, meaningful aspects in memory. From these aspects, we are then able to view the problem from a new perspective, with fewer of the limitations of the earlier mental set.[14] In general, incubation seems to work best if we invest enough time initially in the problem to explore it in all its aspects and if we allow sufficient time for incubation to work.[15]

Successfully intelligent people think heuristically to solve problems. They don't formulate or fixate; they incubate. Faced with a problem, they analyze it carefully and then use creative strategies to find a solution.

Decision Making

Economic Models

How do people analyze their options and make decisions? Psychologists once believed in a model that was called *economic man*. According to this model, people use all available information, weigh it rationally and correctly, and reach an optimal decision. But if that were true, we would have no drug addicts, few AIDS cases, and few people going into bankruptcy because they lived beyond their means. Amazingly to us psychologists, economists still, for the most part, use this model of decision making. No small wonder that economics is called the "dismal science."

Utility Models

Economic-man theories were soon replaced in psychology by what is called *utility-maximization theory*, according to which the goal of human action is to seek pleasure and avoid pain. Therefore, in making decisions, people will seek to maximize pleasure (referred to as positive utility) and to minimize pain (negative utility). Utility-maximization theorists suggest that we can predict what people will do by assuming that they will seek the highest possible utility—in other words, whatever decision maximizes pleasure and minimizes pain.

Suppose, for example, you are deciding whether to ask someone out for an evening. It could be someone with whom you've never gone out, or it could be, for that matter, a spouse with whom you've gone out thousands of times. You have the idea to do something unusual—say, go to a belly-dancing show. You are afraid to make the suggestion for fear of being turned down and looking foolish; moreover, you can't be certain you'll have a good time. These factors can be viewed as negative utilities. On the other hand, you have hopes that maybe the evening will turn out to be fun, despite your doubts. Moreover, perhaps the evening will be the beginning of a new, long-term relationship or will help solidify the relationship you already have. These factors provide positive utilities. Whether you make the suggestion will depend on whether the positive utilities outweigh the negative ones in your mind. In effect, you have a kind of decisional balance sheet, and you weigh, perhaps subconsciously, the pluses and minuses on the balance sheet.

Although it is certainly appealing to come up with mathematical models for decision making, in practice it is very difficult to assign objective utilities to decisions, and models based on such assignments are likely to produce inaccurate representations of reality. As a result, cognitive psychologists interested in decision making introduced subjective-utility theory, which acknowledges that utilities for a given action may be different from one person to another, depending on the person's system of values. But even this system proved insufficiently complex to do justice to people's decisions.

Game Theory

Game theory suggests that many decisions, especially those involving more than one person, have gamelike aspects. Sometimes, the game-like properties of a decision are simple. For example, in a game of chess or checkers, one person wins and the other loses. Such a game is called a *zero-sum game,* because a positive outcome for the winner is balanced by a negative outcome for the loser—positive plus negative equals zero. Some games are more complex than chess or checkers, however.

One such game is the *prisoners' dilemma.*[16] Suppose that two men have been arrested and are charged with pulling off a bank heist. Each man is found to have an unregistered firearm at the time of arrest. The police do not have conclusive evidence that the two men actually robbed the bank, and they need a confession from at least one of them so that the district attorney can win the case. The district attorney hatches a Machiavellian plan in order to wring out a confession from at least one prisoner.

She separates the two prisoners, preventing them from communicating with each other. She then tells each of them that what happens to him will depend not only on what he does but also on what the other prisoner does. If neither prisoner confesses, the district attorney will be unable to prove the bank-robbery charge, but she will prosecute both of them on the charge of illegal possession of a firearm, and each prisoner will be jailed for a term of one year. The district attorney informs the prisoners that if they both confess, she will recommend an intermediate-length term for each of them: ten years. In addition, however, she offers each prisoner immunity from prosecution if he is the only one to confess. In this case, the prisoner who confesses will go scot-free, whereas the prisoner who does not confess will be slapped with the maximum possible sentence: twenty years.

This situation presents a complicated dilemma for the prisoners. The greatest individual payoff is for the prisoner who pulls a double-cross on his partner, gains immunity, and goes scot-free. However, if both prisoners double-cross each other, both will go to jail for a decade. The greatest individual loss is for the prisoner who does not double-cross his partner and thereby has to spend the maximum term in prison. The best deal for both prisoners together is for each to remain silent—a potentially costly strategy if one partner is less altruistic than the other.

Subjective-utility theory does not do a good job of explaining how to make decisions in the prisoners' dilemma and similar situations, because the decision maker cannot identify the subjective utilities without knowing the decision of the other party. But there is no way of knowing the other party's decision before making one's own decision.

Game theory suggests various strategies a person can use in a gamelike situation such as the prisoners' dilemma. According to the minimax loss rule, you make a choice that minimizes your maximum loss. Using this rule, the prisoner in the prisoners' dilemma will confess because he wants to minimize the possibility of going to jail for twenty years, the maximum loss. In investing, you would choose investments like money market funds with high-grade, very short-term securities in order to minimize your possible losses.

Another strategy is the maximin gain rule, according to which you maximize your minimum gain—for example, you might stay with a dull job at a modest salary (a rather minimal gain) rather than take a chance on starting a new business. Staying with your old job maximizes your minimum gain, whereas opening a new business might maximize your potential maximum gain but not your potential minimum gain.

Using the maximax gain rule, the strategy is to maximize the maximum gain. For example, an investor using this strategy is likely to maximize potential gain, at the possible risk of maximizing the possible loss of all her money. She is also a good candidate for buying lottery tickets. The maximum gain is huge, but the chances of winning it are remote.

Game theory has been of considerable interest to psychologists, because it seems to represent the situation in many negotiations, especially international ones. One never knows for sure what other parties will do or what their motivations really are. In business negotiations as well, it is often hard to decipher just what the intentions of other parties are. The prisoners' dilemma is a one-shot deal. But in many negotiating situations, the parties come back to the bargaining table again and again, each time with a somewhat greater knowledge of the decision they have to make to gain their objectives.

Computer simulations have been done in order to determine what strategy maximizes gains in the prisoners' dilemma. Some of them are extremely complicated, but interestingly, the one that maximizes outcomes turns out to be a very simple one—namely, tit for tat. If the negotiations with the district attorney are conducted on an ongoing basis, in the first round you give the other party the benefit of the doubt, acting in his or your best interest. After that round, you always do exactly what he does. If he should act in a trustworthy fashion, you do too. If he doesn't, you don't. If he should act to maximize joint gain, you do too; if he doesn't, you don't. And so on. Of course, you risk the possibility of going to jail for ten years if you both confess, but if you both do not, your prison time will be just a year —in this case, the maximum joint outcome. This same strategy is often used in business situations. As long as both parties act for their mutual benefit—the maximum joint gain—the negotiations will probably proceed to a successful conclusion; if they do not, negotiations will come to an end. Perhaps it is no coincidence that this very simple negotiating strategy is so popular around the world and in so many cultures across time and space.

It is always tempting to try to get the upper hand in negotiations, capitalizing on your strengths and exploiting your counterpart's weaknesses. But successfully intelligent people are rarely exploitative, and an analysis of the prisoners' dilemma shows why. Unless they are in positions of absolute or almost absolute power, they know that what goes around comes around. If they exploit their colleagues, clients or customers, competitors or employees, all will tend to give back in kind.

Successfully intelligent people also don't fall into the trap of thinking life is always a zero-sum game—with a winner and a loser. By thinking about their own interests and those of others, they are often able to negotiate toward a solution that is maximally effective for everyone, rather than effective only for some at the expense of others.

Satisficing

The economic model and all of the various game theory rules are based on the notion that decision makers are both rational and objective in making their decisions. They decide what criteria to use to maximize or minimize and then make the optimal decision for doing so. Even in the 1950s, however, some psychologists were beginning to recognize that we humans do not always make ideal decisions, that we usually include subjective considerations in our decisions, and that we are not always entirely rational.

The most well-known challenge to the conventional economic model is the view that we humans are not irrational but rather exhibit bounded rationality—we are rational within limits.[17] In this view, one of the most typical decision-making strategies is satisficing. In this process, we do not consider all possible options and then carefully compute which of them will maximize our gains and minimize our losses. Rather, we consider options one by one and then select the first option that we find satisfactory—just good enough. Thus, we will consider the minimum possible number of options to arrive at a decision that we believe will satisfy our minimum requirements. For example, you may use satisficing when considering what car to buy. You don't look at every model on the market or go to every showroom in the state that sells cars. Rather, you might choose the first model that meets your criteria for acceptability, or the first dealership that provides you with satisfactory terms. Some people also use this strategy in romantic decision making, marrying the first person who comes along who meets minimum criteria of acceptability. Of course, if someone else then comes along who exceeds the minimum criteria, there can be a problem.

The trend that led from fully rational models of decision making to models of bounded rationality involved the increasing recognition that people are not perfect decision makers. We make decisions in less than ideal circumstances, given inadequate or incomplete information and using limited objectivity and rationality. Often, we are even willing to settle for the first acceptable option that becomes available, fully aware that other options may be better but not wanting to allocate the time or resources to consider them.

Representativeness Heuristics
and Base-rate Biases

Sometimes, in our rush to make decisions, we fall prey to invalid heuristics and biases. If asked about the probability that flips of a coin will yield the sequence H T H H T H, people will judge it as higher than the sequence H H H H T H. Why do people believe one sequence to be more likely than others? Apparently, it is because they use the heuristic of representativeness, in which we judge the probability of an uncertain event according to *(a)* how obviously it is similar to or representative of the population from which it is derived and *(b)* the degree to which it reflects the salient features of the process by which it is generated (such as randomness).[18] If you expect a sequence to be random, you tend to view one that "looks random" as more likely to occur. Indeed, people often comment that the ordering of numbers in a table of random numbers "doesn't look random," because they underestimate the number of runs of the same number that will appear wholly by chance.

Representativeness helps explain why low test scores can be such a killer when it comes to gaining admissions or even respect. Test scores are assumed to "represent" a person's abilities. Good scores seem to require intelligence, and the more representative the test is of our notions of what intelligence is (e.g., an IQ test is more representative than is a test of finger-tapping speed), the more we are likely to place confidence in the test. We may be 100 percent dead wrong. But once we start using the heuristic of representativeness, we are often scarcely even aware we are doing so. Similarly, we may expect an attractive person to have a certain personality, viewing his or her physical attractiveness as representing generalized attractiveness. Small wonder that attractive people are at an advantage.

In order fully to understand the representativeness heuristic, it helps to understand the concept of base rate—the prevalence of an event or a characteristic within its population of events or characteristics. People often ignore base-rate information, even though it is important to effective judgment and decision making. In many occupations, the use of base-rate information and the representativeness heuristic is essential for adequate job performance. For example, if a doctor were told that a ten-year-old girl was suffering from chest pains, he would be much less likely to worry about an incipient heart attack than if told that a fifty-year-old man had the identical symptom. Why? Because the base rate of heart attacks is much higher in fifty-year-old men than in ten-year-old girls.

Some undergraduates at good universities are abysmal students. They are there because of athletic prowess, or because their parents are alumni or are viewed as potential megadonors. Yet when we hear that someone attends a good university, we may be impressed. Why? Base rates. For the most part, students at good universities have good academic credentials. Similarly, when we hear that something is made by a company whose products we generally like, we will probably buy it. Why? Base rates again. The company has had a good batting average in the past. Base-rate biases thus help us make decisions. But if we let them dominate our decisions, we may prevent ourselves from ever changing our minds about anything. We also may make base-rate decisions on the basis of wholly inadequate information, as when a woman decides never to marry a man from New York again because her first husband, from New York, was a loser.

Sometimes, the base rates of events are quite surprising. For example, how often, do you believe, planes have accidents? In fact, fewer than 1 in 250,000 plane flights have even the most minor of accidents, and fewer than 1 in 1.6 million scheduled flights end in fatalities.[19] The odds were 1 in 2.2 million of being killed in an airplane crash in 1988.[20] With odds like that, companies that sell flight insurance in airports make a bundle.

Although the chances of dying during any given car trip (however brief) are low, more than 1 in 125 Americans will die in a car-related accident.[21] Drivers who are eighteen-year-old, intoxicated, non-seatbelted males are 1,000 times more likely to die in a car crash than are forty-year-old, sober, seat-belted men or women drivers.[22] When insurance companies charge vastly different rates for different groups, they do so on the basis of averages, or base rates.

Availability

Given these statistics, why is it that many more people are afraid of flying in airplanes than of riding in cars? One reason is the availability heuristic, according to which people make judgments on the basis of how easily they are able to call to mind what they perceive to be relevant instances of a phenomenon. Newspapers give much more play to plane crashes than to car crashes, and it is usually easier to call to mind grim instances of plane crashes than of car crashes. Hence, people tend to fear riding in planes more than they fear riding in cars.

The availability heuristic can also be shown by giving people five seconds to estimate the product of either of two sets of eight numbers: $8 \times 7 \times 6 \times 5 \times 4 \times 3 \times 2 \times 1$ or $1 \times 2 \times 3 \times 4 \times 5 \times 6 \times 7 \times 8$. When researchers tried this out, the median (middle) estimate for the first sequence was 2,250. For the second sequence, the median estimate was 512. By the way, the actual product is 40,320. The two products are the same, as they must be because the numbers are exactly the same (applying the commutative law of multiplication). Nonetheless, people provide a higher estimate for the first sequence because their computation of the first few digits multiplied by each other makes a higher estimate more plausible—hence, available—for the first string of numbers than for the second.

Sometimes, availability and representativeness work together to lead to a less than optimal conclusion. For example, consider the following true story.[23] A high-school senior has thoroughly checked out two colleges, College A and College B. He has looked in guidebooks and spoken to people who are well acquainted with each college. On the basis of all the available information, College A looks better. Yet when he visits both campuses, he likes his host at College B more than his host at College A, and the class he attends at College B is more interesting than the one he attends at College A. Moreover, on the day he visits College B, the weather is excellent, whereas on the day he visits College A, it is terrible. He finds it hard not to prefer College B. Actual visits seem more representative in their information about the colleges than does secondhand information, and the information from the visits is also more readily available. Yet College A is probably the better choice, because it is almost certainly a mistake to judge two colleges on the basis of a single host, a single class, and the weather on the day of the visit.

It is important to realize that heuristics such as representativeness and availability do not always lead to wrong judgments. Indeed, we use them because they are so often right. For example, in buying a computer, you may decide to buy from a company whose name is readily available in memory, based on the view that you are taking a bigger risk in buying from a company that is relatively unknown. The known company does not necessarily make a better computer, but because a computer is a large purchase, you may not want to take the risk of buying from an unknown manufacturer. Sometimes that is the right decision, sometimes not. My son insisted on buying a computer from an unknown manufacturer because it had much better features at the same price that the better-known company charged for fewer features. The computer soon had a glitch, which was very tough luck for him, because the company had already gone out of business.

Other Judgmental Phenomena

There are other oddities in people's judgments. One is overconfidence —an individual's overvaluation of her or his own personal skills, knowledge, or judgment. In one study, people were asked to respond to two hundred two-alternative statements, such as: "Absinthe is *(a)* a liqueur, *(b)* a precious stone." (Absinthe is a licorice-flavored liqueur.) When they were then asked how sure they were that their answers were correct, they were strangely overconfident. For example, when they were 100 percent confident of their answers, they were right only 80 percent of the time.[24] Other investigators asked people questions such as: "I feel 98 percent certain that the number of nuclear plants operating in the world in 1980 was more than _____ but less than _____ ." Nearly one-third of the time, the correct answer to questions such as these (exactly 189 at that time) was outside the range that people gave. It is not clear why we tend to be so overconfident in our judgments. One simple explanation is that we prefer not to think about being wrong.[25] Another is the belief that we have not been wrong in the past, so we have demonstrated our invulnerability to making bad judgments.

Overconfidence in test scores is one of the more frustrating phenomena I have to deal with in my own work. I have addressed many audiences, but none has seemed quite so self-confident as the group of admissions people I spoke to at a College Board meeting. They really believed in their test. At best, the test had only modest to moderate correlations with college grades in the first year or two, and lower correlations with other measures of success, either in college or thereafter. I suspected that few people in that audience, perhaps none of them, knew the statistical data. And there was no apparent evidence that they cared.

Another common error in judgment is caused by the gambler's fallacy, a belief that just by the nature of things, a person's luck is bound eventually to change. Thus, the gambler who loses five successive bets may believe that a win is more likely the sixth time. In truth, of course, the gambler is no more likely to win on the sixth bet than on the first—or on the thousand and first. Another frequent error of judgment is caused by the fallacy of composition, which we commit when we believe that what is true of the parts of a whole must necessarily be true of the whole as well. Yet often, when a whole comprises many parts, the quality of the integration of those parts strongly influences the quality of the whole. For example, all-star baseball teams, ballet companies composed of prima donnas, and blue-ribbon panels may end up being ineffective because the members, despite their stellar individual abilities and credentials, find themselves unable to work together.

One of the reasons that psychologists have been so slow to make any serious changes regarding the testing of intelligence is that when major committees are appointed to study existing practices, they are carefully chosen to include experts representing diverse points of view. In my experience, the experts agree on relatively little and, as a result, cannot arrive at any consensus regarding what should be done. Thus, little changes.

Much of the work that has been done on judgment and decision making has focused on the errors people make. But people do act rationally in many instances. Nonetheless, rationality can be limited by any number of factors involved in the way we solve problems and make decisions.

Successfully intelligent people recognize the limits of rationality and are also aware of the traps into which they can fall in their thinking. Their solutions and decisions may be either intuitive or reasoned, or a combination of both, but they are seldom guilty of those thought processes that can lead to errors in judgment.

Despite limitations, analytical intelligence is certainly important in good problem solving and decision making, the hallmarks of successful intelligence. But it alone, as measured by conventional tests, is no guarantee of academic success, nor, as applied in nonacademic settings such as the business world, is it a guarantee of good judgment. Analytical intelligence is the first, but not the only, key to successful intelligence.

CHAPTER SIX

Key 2: Finding Good Problems with Creative Intelligence

"Alice is intelligent, but she doesn't have a drop of creative talent in her."

"John is wonderfully creative, but he does terribly on standardized intelligence tests."

How many times have we heard remarks like these? And how many times have we concluded that abilities, like hieroglyphics, are etched in stone, as inexplicable but also as unchangeable as those peculiar markings?

Since we have long had such a difficult time defining intelligence, let alone measuring it, it is not surprising that creativity is equally hard to pin down. What does it mean to be creative? Can creativity be measured? Perhaps the two concepts are not mutually exclusive and there is such a thing as creative intelligence. If so, how is it defined and measured? More important, how can it be developed? To answer these questions, we first need to understand something about what creativity is.

The Investment Theory of Creativity

Creatively smart people are like good investors. They buy low and sell high.[1] But whereas investors typically do so in the world of financial instruments, creative people deal in the world of ideas. Specifically, they generate ideas that are like undervalued stocks, which are generally rejected by the public at large. When their ideas are proposed, others frequently view them as counternormative, counterproductive, and even foolish. The result is that they are often summarily rejected, and the person who proposes them is viewed with suspicion and perhaps disdain and derision.

Creative ideas are, by definition, both novel and valuable. Why, then, are they rejected? Because the creative innovator defies the crowd, standing up to vested interests in a way that makes people who have those interests uncomfortable. Members of the majority do not maliciously or even purposely reject creative notions. Rather, they simply do not realize—and often do not want to realize—that creative ideas represent a valid and often superior alternative to the way they think. To them, creative people tend to be somewhat oppositional in nature, a tendency they find annoying or even downright offensive.

Successfully intelligent people buy low and sell high. They defy the crowd and, eventually, come to lead it.

There is good evidence that creative ideas tend to be rejected.[2] For example, reviews of major works of literature and art are often initially negative. Consider the following quote, from *The New Yorker*: "heavy-handed, and ultimately unintelligible . . . topples into dreadful pits of bombast." That's from a review of *Tar Baby*, by Toni Morrison, today widely acclaimed as a great American novel. Now try this one: "Highly autobiographical and . . . since it represents the views of a girl enduring a bout of mental illness, dishonest." That's from the *Atlantic Monthly*, in a review of *The Bell Jar*, by Sylvia Plath, another classic. The reviewers definitely missed the creativity of these great works of literature.

Some of the greatest scientific papers are rejected not by one but by several journals before they are eventually published and later hailed as classics. For example, John Garcia, a distinguished biopsychologist, was summarily denounced and called almost every imaginable name when he first proposed that classical conditioning, a learning procedure, could be produced in a single trial of learning.[3]

In 1769, Sir Richard Arkwright patented the spinning jenny, a machine to make thread from cotton. This invention was received with hostility from hand spinners and weavers, who burned Arkwright's mills and boycotted his thread. Around the same time, Edmund Cartwright invented a mechanical loom, and his textile mills met a similar fate. In the nineteenth century, Ignaz Semmelweis, a Hungarian obstetrician, suggested that hospital medical staff might be infecting patients by not washing their hands properly before operations. The not-yet-accepted germ model of disease made good sense and fitted the evidence: When Semmelweis introduced a chlorine disinfectant, the rate of puerperal fever in the wards dropped substantially. However, he was ridiculed by his medical colleagues and eventually went crazy.

By the time I left graduate school, I had developed a new theory of intelligence that I hoped would break what I saw as gridlock in a field that seemed unable to get beyond IQ-based conceptions of the construct of intelligence. One of my first invitations to speak was from the Educational Testing Service, a company that produces many standardized tests, such as the SAT, the GRE, the LSAT. Naively, I expected that people would be delighted to hear my new point of view on intelligence. Instead, their reaction was: How can this twenty-five-year-old twerp presume to tell us what intelligence is? We've been studying it for as long as he has been alive, and he's telling us? In short, the reaction was not what anyone would call warm and friendly. However, the point isn't whether the theory was right or wrong. It is that when people have a vested interest in a given set of ideas, and especially when they have millions of dollars invested in those ideas, they may not be eager to hear other ideas.

In the investment view of creativity, then, the creative person buys low—comes up with an idea that is likely to be rejected and derided.

That person then attempts to convince other people of the value of the idea and thus increase the perceived value of the investment. If he has finally convinced others of its value, the creative person sells high—leaves the idea to others and moves on to the next unpopular idea.

In order to foster creativity, we need to encourage people to buy low and sell high—to defy the crowd. Creativity, then, is as much a matter of an attitude toward life as it is one of ability. Young children naturally display this kind of creativity. It is only in older children and adults that it is so hard to find, not because the potential is missing but because creativity has been suppressed by systems of raising and teaching children that encourage intellectual conformity. Children start to suppress their natural creativity when, both figuratively and literally, they are instructed to draw within the lines and are rewarded when they do so.

The Role of Creative, Analytical, and Practical Intelligence in Creativity

I define creativity not only as the ability to come up with new ideas. I believe it is a process that requires the balance and application of the three essential aspects of intelligence—creative, analytical, and practical, the same aspects that when used in combination and balance make for successful intelligence.[4]

The first and most important aspect of creativity is *creative intelligence,* which is the ability to go beyond the given to generate novel and interesting ideas. Often, someone who is creative is a particularly good synthetic thinker, seeing connections (syntheses) other people don't see. Creative intelligence is an important part of creativity in general, but it is not the whole thing.

The second aspect of creativity is *analytical intelligence,* the ability to analyze and evaluate ideas, solve problems, and make decisions. All people—even the most creative among us—have better and worse ideas. But creative people, in particular, must also have the ability to analyze their own ideas and evaluate their merit. Otherwise, they are as likely to push forward in pursuit of weaker ideas as to pursue better ones. Moreover, they have to use their analytical ability to work out the implications of new ideas and perhaps to test them.

The third aspect of creativity, *practical intelligence,* is the ability to translate theory into practice and abstract ideas into practical accomplishments. An implication of the investment theory of creativity is that good ideas do not just sell themselves. We have to go out and convince other people of their worth. Anyone who has ever worked in a school will understand this principle. In a school, as in any organization, there exists an entrenched set of ideas about how things should be done. If someone proposes a new way of doing things, it is incumbent upon that person to sell the idea and to convince other people of its worth. Practical ability is also needed to recognize which of one's ideas will have pragmatic application, however it may initially be received.

Thus, creativity provides a bridge between analytical intelligence, considered in the previous chapter, and practical intelligence, considered in the next. The central span of the bridge is creative intelligence, but to be creative requires a balance among all three aspects of intelligence. The person who is high only in creative intelligence may come up with innovative ideas but will not recognize which are good ones and will not know how to sell them, in any case. The person who is high only in analytical intelligence may be an excellent critic of other people's ideas but is not likely to generate creative ideas of his or her own. The person who is high only in practical intelligence may be an excellent salesperson but will be as likely to sell ideas (or products) of little or no value as to sell genuinely creative ones. In promoting creativity, therefore, we need to provide a balance of these three skills.

This idea of balance is particularly important in my concept of successful intelligence. Our society is preoccupied with amounts. More is better. More money is better, more food is better, more intelligence is better. Many cultures, however, especially Eastern ones, put greater emphasis on balance than on amounts. Successful intelligence is at least as much a matter of balance as amount, both in the development of the necessary skills and in knowing when to use them.

This balance applies equally to the use of creative skills. No one is more supportive of the importance of creativity than I am. Yet creativity needs to be balanced against practicality. Some ideas are creative, but they are not practical. Moreover, there is a time and place for creativity. My son has a creative turn of mind and will often champ at the bit when confronted with boring school assignments. Yet these assignments must be done, unless there is some compelling reason not to do them. I tell my son to choose his battles carefully. If he believes an important principle is involved, he should by all means fight for it. But a lot of creative people lose their support because they fight every little battle and other people tire of them. Successfully intelligent people fight their battles well, but first they carefully pick the battles to fight.

We also need to promote the attitude that all three kinds of intelligence are important—that is, to remember ourselves and to teach our students that to be truly creative, it is necessary to find a balance among the creative, analytical, and practical aspects of intelligence. This *creative attitude* is at least as important as any creative-thinking skills.[5]

Testing the Investment Theory

In testing the investment theory, my colleagues and I have used a product-centered approach, as have many other researchers—including those who study creative greats.[6] In our research, we have tested creativity in the domains of writing, drawing, advertising, and science.[7] We do not claim that these domains are representative of all possible domains, and obviously they are not exhaustive. But taken together, the four give at least a sampling of the many different kinds of creativity. The tasks we use in our tests have a parallel form across the four domains and include topic selection as an integral part of the creative process. In each domain, subjects are asked to be as imaginative as they can be. And ideally, they should be given as much time as possible to produce their work.

In the domain of writing, people are asked to pick two titles from a list and write a brief story for each. We choose titles that they are unlikely to have thought about before, such as: "Beyond the Edge," "A Fifth Chance," "Saved," "Under the Table," "Between the Lines," "Not Enough Time," "The Keyhole," "The Octopus's Sneakers," "2983," or "It's Moving Backwards." These are titles that can lead to a wide diversity of stories.

In the domain of art, people are given materials and asked to produce drawings for two of the several suggested topics. Again, we choose topics that they are not likely to have drawn or even thought about before as themes for artistic compositions: "A Dream," "A Quark," "Hope," "Rage," "Pleasure," "Earth from an Insect's Point of View," "Contrast," "Tension," "Motion," and "Beginning of Time."

In the domain of advertising, people are asked to come up with TV commercials for two products. We try to select products that are as boring as possible and for which the subjects are not likely to have seen commercial. Topics include "Double-Pane Windows," "Brussels Sprouts," "Internal Revenue Service" (a positive image), "Broom," "Iron," "Cuff Links," "Bow Ties," "Doorknobs," and "Sugar Substitute."

Finally, in the domain of science, people are asked to solve two problems that are rather different in kind from those they are likely to have encountered. Examples are: "How could we find out if extraterrestrial aliens are living among us?" "How might we determine if someone has been on the moon in the past month?" and "How could we solve the problem of decoys in a Star Wars defense system?" Maybe the extraterrestrial problem wasn't as unusual as we thought. We later found an article in a tabloid newspaper providing tips for identifying extraterrestrials (for example, they wear oddly mismatched clothes and have bizarre senses of humor). Another tabloid identified twelve U.S. senators as space aliens.

In one of our studies, forty-eight individuals—twenty-four males and twenty-four females, ranging in age from eighteen to sixty-five, with an average age of thirty-three—completed two products in each of the four domains. People were recruited through an ad in a local newspaper and were paid to participate. The only requirement for participation, other than a minimum age of eighteen, was that the candidate be a high-school graduate. A second group, of fifteen adults, rated for creativity the products of the members of the first group, using a 1 (low) to 7 (high) numerical scale. Each judge used his or her own view of creativity when rating the products. The judges' ratings were averaged to form a creativity score for each product.

The first question that needs to be raised, of course, is whether judges can even reliably rate creativity. Some of the makers and users of conventional standardized tests argue that, at least with their tests, there is agreement as to the right answer, whereas with products that require creative or other skills, there will be no consensus about what is good and what is bad. We found, on the contrary, an interrater reliability (consistency across judges) among our raters of .92, on a 0 to 1 scale where 0 would indicate no consistency at all and 1 would indicate perfect consistency. This interrater agreement is high by any standard and indicates that people do show considerable (although not perfect) agreement about what they judge as either creative or uncreative. In several other studies, judges (peer or expert) have been used, and similar good interjudge reliability has been found.[8]

In our study, the story and art products were in general judged to be significantly more creative than the advertising and scientific products. This difference probably resulted from people having more experience in writing stories and drawing pictures than they do in formulating TV advertisements and answers to scientific questions.

Now consider the question of whether there is a "general creative ability." In other words, are the people who were creative in one task necessarily creative in the others? The question can be dealt with in several ways. One way is to divide people down the middle in each domain on the basis of whether their products were judged as being above or below average. The question then becomes one of what percentage of people were above (or below) the average in various domains. In the limiting case, if creativity were just a single ability, we would expect 50 percent of people to be above average in no domains, and 50 percent to be above average in all domains. On the other hand, if there were absolutely no general-ability factor of creativity, we would expect roughly 6 percent to be above average in no domains, 23.5 percent to be above average in one domain, 41 percent to be above average in two domains, 23.5 percent to be above average in three domains, and 6 percent to be above average in all four domains.

We found that 19 percent of the subjects were above average in no domains (that is, all their products were judged as below average), 31 percent were above average in one domain, 17 percent above average in two domains, 15 percent above average in three domains, and 18 percent above average in all four domains. Obviously, these results are intermediate between the two extremes. They suggest that creativity is neither completely domain-general nor completely domain-specific, but if asked to which extreme it is closer, one would have to vote for domain specificity rather than domain generality. In other words, people tend to be creative in certain domains but not in others. Most people are above average in creativity in at least some domains but below average in others.

Another way of checking cross-domain generality is to look at statistical correlations of creativity ratings across domains. These scores, on a -1 to $+1$ scale, indicate the degree of consistency people show in creativity across domains. A correlation of 1 would indicate perfect consistency across domains, with the same people always creative or uncreative. A correlation of 0 would indicate absolutely no consistency whatever across domains. In this case, creativity in one domain would not at all predict creativity in any other domain. A correlation of -1 would be strange, indicating that high creativity in one domain implies low creativity in another. The median correlation across domains was in fact .37. This number reinforces our above analysis. Creativity is neither completely domain-general nor domain-specific but tends more toward domain specificity than toward domain generality.

These results have important implications both for the way we think about creativity and for the way we act on the basis of these thoughts. In some schools, we have classes in which we place the children who are identified as superior to others; children who are not "gifted" remain in regular classes. Our results suggest that with respect to creativity, there is no one group that can be properly identified as "gifted." Some people are gifted in one or several domains, others in other domains. One could, in fact, be very highly gifted creatively in one domain and not at all so gifted in another. It would not make sense, then, to have an overall "creatively gifted" group that is separated from all other children. Rather, we could possibly identify creatively gifted children, but the children (or adults, for that matter) so identified would vary across domains.

This result also contains an important message about successful intelligence. To some extent, it too is domain-specific. People who are successfully intelligent in one domain (e.g., business) are not necessarily successfully intelligent in another (e.g., intimate relationships). The notion of someone's being "gifted" or not is a relic of an antiquated, test-based way of thinking. People can be gifted, but with respect only to some set of performances. It is for this reason that it is so important to identify one's areas of strength and weakness. Quite simply, no one is good at everything. The successfully intelligent person finds, sometimes develops, and always makes the most of what he or she is good at.

Similarly, if a business wished to select creative people for employment, its policy makers would have to ask themselves, "Creative with respect to what?" For example, the people who would be creative in the marketing department would not necessarily be creative in the finance department, and vice versa. Creativity is not just a single thing—it varies across domains. But even if we were to identify people as creative in various domains, we would have to remember something else. Creativity within a domain can be developed. So although we can measure creativity, we are measuring it in a time and place.

We can see the effect of product within domain simply by correlating the ratings of creativity that subjects received for each of the two products they created in each of the four domains. If creativity were completely consistent within a domain, we would expect the correlation of rated creativity across products (for example, drawing 1 and drawing 2 for each participant) to approach 1. But if creativity were completely random within a domain, we would expect the correlation of rated creativity across products to be close to 0. In our data, the average correlation between rated creativity for two products within a given domain was .58. Clearly, people are more consistent within domain than they are between domains (where, you may remember, the average correlation was .37). But they are by no means perfectly consistent even within the domain. Thus, we have to be very careful about generalizing across products.

I should point out that our correlations were probably lower than they might have been if it were not for what is called *measurement error*. That means that no measurement of any psychological attribute is perfect, and to the extent that our judges were less than perfect evaluators (which certainly they were), correlations would have been reduced because of errors in their judgments.

I cannot emphasize enough the importance of the issue of error in judgment. Like others, we have found that various judges are fairly consistent in what they believe to be creative and uncreative.[9] There is quite good agreement among them. Each judge has a unique opinion, and the average judgment for each product reflects a central view of creativity. Sometimes, however, one whole set of judges may fail to see the value in a certain work, or all may see value where it hardly exists, as compared with another set of judges. There is no absolute standard for what constitutes creativity. What one society or culture or group considers creative another group may not.

Here is an example of a hazard in the measurement of creativity. In one of our studies, forty-four participants were asked to produce creative products in the domains of story writing and art.[10] In this particular study, we predicted that people who were generally more willing to take risks would be judged as producing more creative products than people who were not generally willing to take risks. As it turned out, the results were supportive of our thesis in the domain of art but not in the domain of writing.

Out of curiosity, we decided to inspect the written products of our subjects who were risk takers but were not judged as creative in their writing. What we found was totally unexpected. We thought that the products of the risk takers *were* creative, although they had not been so evaluated by our judges. But the products had represented risks —for example, some of them were critical of such institutions as government or religion—and our judges had not reacted favorably to their content.

The general point is that creativity ratings depend on those who make them. One can have a group of judges agree that a product is not creative, and by their standards, it may not be. But another group may find the same product to be very creative. Creativity is not something that exists in the abstract—it is a sociocultural judgment of the novelty, appropriateness, quality, and importance of a product. Thus, when we look at assessments of creativity—or anything else, for that matter—we should consider who is doing the judging.

Fans of conventional standardized tests may take these remarks as a stake through the heart of creativity measurement. They might argue that with their measurements, at least we don't have to worry about subjectivity. But in fact, the same limitations apply in *all* measurements. The very same behaviors that in one society or context are considered smart are in other contexts or societies considered stupid. The point, however, is that the same limitations that apply to the measurement of creativity apply to all measurements. There really is no such thing as a wholly "objective" measurement of intelligence, creativity, or anything else. Measurement is always related to the norms and expectations of a particular group in a particular time and at a particular place.

We often forget this fact when we are evaluated. People's evaluations differ. Thus, we need to consider not only the evaluation but also its validity. Several years ago, a well-known journal in psychology published an article arguing, in essence, that pretty much everything you need to know about a worker can be measured by his or her so-called general intelligence. My colleague Richard Wagner and I were incensed. Hadn't anyone reviewed the article before it was published? We wrote what we believed was a careful reply and sent it to the journal. It then became obvious why the article had been published. The editor was extremely sympathetic to its point of view. Our reply was sent to two assassins, whose reviews could hardly have been more critical. We were flatly rejected with a letter from the editor just short of questioning our sanity for submitting the reply in the first place.

Years later the editorship changed hands, and we submitted a very slightly revised version of the original article. The reviews were glowing, and the article was published with almost no revisions, vivid proof that how work is evaluated depends on who evaluates it. Similarly, measures of creativity must be seen in the context of the interaction between the product and those who are evaluating it.

Developing Creative Intelligence

I have never met parents, teachers, or employees who believe themselves to be suppressing creativity. On the contrary, the overwhelming majority of people want to encourage creativity in others and in themselves but often are not sure of how to go about doing so. An IQ myth is that abilities cannot be developed. The truth is that they can be.[11] And the best proof of that can be found by examining twelve characteristics of successfully intelligent creative people and exploring how these characteristics can be developed.

1. Successfully intelligent people actively seek out, and later become, role models.   When all is said and done, the single most powerful way of developing creative intelligence in your employees, your students, or your children is to serve as a creative role model yourself. People develop creative intelligence not when you tell them to but when you show them how.

Ask yourself who the teachers are that you most remember from your days in school and who most affected what you became. They are probably not the teachers who crammed the most content into their lectures but rather those whose ways of thinking and acting served as role models. The teachers we remember tend to be those who balanced teaching of content with teaching us how to think with and about that content.

Occasionally, I will give a workshop on developing creativity, and a teacher, parent, or manager will ask exactly what to do and how to do it. Bad start. You cannot follow a cookbook recipe for developing creativity—first, because there is none, and second, because such a stock prescription, if it existed, would hamper creativity. To encourage creativity, you yourself have to be creative.

Successfully intelligent people, as a rule, have had good role models. It's in part for this reason that it is so difficult to take older children from poor environments, put them in a new environment, and expect sudden changes. The problem is that they have not had good role models. If we want to develop successful intelligence, the earlier we start, the better. It's never too late, but neither is it ever too early.

2. Successfully intelligent people question assumptions and encourage others to do so. We all tend to have assumptions about the way things are or should be. Usually, such assumptions are widely shared. But creatively intelligent people question many assumptions that others accept, eventually leading others to question those assumptions as well. For example, when Copernicus suggested that the earth revolves around the sun, the suggestion was viewed as preposterous because for centuries it had been assumed that the sun revolved around the Earth.

Sometimes, unfortunately, it is not until many years later, and perhaps even after the death of the creatively intelligent person, that others realize the limitations or errors of their assumptions. Yet without the impetus of those who question assumptions, little or no progress would ever be made in any human endeavor.

Teachers and parents should encourage children to question assumptions. That way, they will also encourage them to think creatively and express their own ideas about the way things are or should be. Many assumptions are, of course, valid. Even so, it is important for children, or adults, for that matter, to understand why we think or act the way we do. It is probably safe to assume that all creative thinking begins with one question: "Why?"

3. Successfully intelligent people allow themselves and others to make mistakes.   Buying low and selling high carries with it a danger. Most unpopular stocks are unpopular for a reason. People think they aren't very good investments. Put another way, people often think a certain way because it's safe and they don't want to make mistakes. But every once in a while, a great thinker comes along—a Freud, a Piaget, a Chomsky, or even an Einstein—and shows us a new way to think. That is not to say that great thinkers never make mistakes. On the contrary, making mistakes is inevitable when you're exploring new territory. But they learn from their mistakes—or enable us to learn from them.

Schools tend to be unforgiving of mistakes. When children hand in workbooks, their errors are often marked with a large and pronounced *X*. When they answer a question incorrectly in class, some teachers pounce on them, and their classmates snicker. When children go outside the lines in a coloring book, or use the wrong color, they are corrected. In hundreds of ways in the course of their schooling, children learn that it's not all right to make mistakes. As a result, they become afraid to err and thus to risk the kind of independent, if sometimes flawed, thinking that can lead to the development of creative intelligence.

Too often we have a coloring-book mentality about the way we think. If our ideal child is the one who stays within the lines and uses the "right" colors, who is our ideal adult—the one who stays within the lines at work? Usually so. We can't reward a coloring-book mentality in our children and then hope for creativity when the children become adults.

Sometimes what may seem like a mistake on the part of a child isn't one. The response just doesn't fit conventional wisdom. Some years back, a colleague of mine, Wendy Williams, observed a class in which the teacher asked the children who discovered America, and a child blurted out, "The Indians." Everyone laughed, and the teacher hastened to correct the mistake, naming the great explorer Christopher Columbus. Today, perhaps, a teacher would not be so quick to correct such a "mistake." More to the point, however, is the realization that insisting on "right" answers and the "right" way of doing things encourages conformity, not creativity.

4. Successfully intelligent people take sensible risks and encourage others to do the same.   When you buy low and sell high, you always take a risk. But creative people are willing to take that risk. They have to be, in order to produce the work that others will ultimately admire and respect. And in taking risks, creative people will sometimes fail and fall flat on their faces. We have to let them do so.

It is important to emphasize the word *sensible* in relation to risk taking, because I am not, of course, talking about the kinds of risks that endanger life and limb. Rather, I am talking about the risk that is always involved when we explore new ideas and new ways of doing things. It is the risk of being "different."

Schools, for the most part, discourage risk taking. Children learn early how the system works. To succeed, you have to get high grades, and to get high grades, you've got to stay on the straight and narrow. You need those grades to get into better sections, to be admitted to advanced courses, to get into college, and, later, to get advanced training or the best job. Risk taking, it might seem, is for suckers, because even a few low grades can put you out of the running for the greatest advancement.

When my daughter, Sara, was in third grade, the children were studying the planets, and the teacher assigned a lesson in which they were to simulate being astronauts, dressing up in astronaut fashion and pretending to fly to Mars. Sara suggested that she dress up as a Martian and meet the astronauts when they arrived. The teacher immediately told her that she couldn't do that, because space probes had indicated there were no Martians. Sara took a risk by suggesting an interesting and creative idea, and she was shot down.

Perhaps it is no wonder that it is so much easier to observe creative intelligence in young children than in older children and adults. It is not that the older individuals lack creative intelligence but rather that they have suppressed it. Only by allowing and even encouraging intellectual risk taking can we help our students, and even ourselves, unleash creative potential. Further, teachers should reward risk takers. If students take a sensible risk on an assignment or a project, they should be given credit for their creativity, even though there are ways in which their project might be improved.

In one of our studies, my colleagues and I examined risk-reward options using multiple measures of risk taking and creative performance in drawing and writing.[12] Forty-four adults completed creativity tasks, risk-taking measures, and other tests. The creativity measures for drawing and writing involved expanding a title into an actual product (as described earlier). We measured risk taking in three ways: contests, hypothetical scenarios, and a self-report questionnaire.

Two contests provided behavioral measures of risk taking. People were given the opportunity to enter their drawing in one contest and their short story in another. Each contest established two "pools" of work from which the best entries would be selected. One pool was described as high risk and high payoff. In this pool, there would be one winner of twenty-five dollars. The other pool involved lower risk and lower payoff, with five winners of ten dollars each. The instructions allowed participants to enter one pool for the drawing contest and a different pool for the writing contest. Based on our judges' ratings, prizes were awarded at the conclusion of the study.

The hypothetical scenarios measured risk-taking propensity in a very different way. Three choice-dilemma questionnaires assessed risk taking in the drawing, writing, and general-life domains.[13] Each questionnaire contained twelve hypothetical situations in which people were asked to imagine themselves, and each scenario presented a choice between two courses of action: (a) a high-risk, potentially high-payoff alternative and *(b)* a low-risk, low-payoff alternative. People selected the minimum odds for success that they would require before pursuing the high-risk option. A sample scenario from the art-domain questionnaire follows:

> You are a potter, making a large vase to be displayed at a craft show. You hope to receive recognition in the pottery guild's magazine, which will be doing a feature story on the show. You have two ideas for the vase. Idea A would use a potter's wheel to form a vase with smooth contours that are pleasing to look at. You know several other potters at the show use the same method, but you feel confident that you will receive some recognition for technical skill. Idea B would use a hand coil method in which you roll clay into strips and piece the strips together. This method yields an unusual primitive vase. The magazine editors may feature your coil vase because of its uniqueness, or they may not even mention it because it could be seen as too far out of the mainstream. Listed below are several probabilities or odds that the coil vase (idea B) will turn out successfully. Please check the lowest probability that you would consider acceptable to make it worthwhile to pursue the coil vase.

The possible odds for success were: 1 in 10, 3 in 10, 5 in 10, 7 in 10, or 9 in 10. A subject could also refuse the risky alternative "no matter what the possibilities" and would then receive a score of 10 out of 10 for that scenario.

Risk taking was further assessed with a biographical questionnaire. People used a 7-point scale to describe their tendencies toward risk in drawing and writing for the overall task, topic selection, topic development, and materials and style used. They were also asked if they would describe themselves as a high- or low-risk taker in the drawing and writing domains. A separate group of fifteen participants judged the creativity of the drawing and writing work. They showed good interrater reliability (.81 for drawing and .75 for writing on a scale of 0 = low and 1 = high).

In agreement with previous research, our findings showed that people were relatively risk avoidant. For example, in the drawing contest, thirty-two of the participants chose the low-risk, low-payoff option, in contrast to twelve who chose the high-risk, high-payoff alternative. In the writing contest, twenty-nine participants selected the low-risk and fifteen the high-risk alternative. In both cases, the bias toward lower risk was significant.

The main question of interest in our study, however, was whether higher levels of risk taking were associated with higher levels of creative performance. For the drawing contest, people choosing the high-risk, high-payoff option showed an average creativity score of 4.21 (on a 7-point scale), whereas people choosing the low-risk, low-payoff option showed an average score of 3.90. When creativity ratings were obtained from three additional judges with artistic training, the basic results were accentuated. The high-risk group received an average creativity score of 4.36, whereas the low-risk group's average score was 2.86. Thus, more creative people leaned toward taking more risks.

The scenario-based measures of risk taking also supported a connection between risk taking and creativity. Risk taking on the artwork scenarios correlated significantly with creativity in drawing ($r = .39$). An analysis of the artwork, writing, and general-life scenario scores with regard to creative performance on the drawing task tested the extent to which the relationship between creativity in drawing and risk is domain-specific. In other words, does creative artwork depend on whether someone takes risks generally or just when engaged in artwork? We found support for domain-specificity. Creativity in drawing is related to risk taking in the artwork domain but not especially related to risk taking in writing or general-life situations. This finding is consistent with other research on risk taking in various domains. For example, the extent to which a person takes risks with money is not very predictive of the risks taken in physical situations (sports, sex) or in social situations.[14]

In contrast to the scenarios and the behavioral contest measures of risk, self-report items showed little relationship to creative performance. Only one item that assessed "overall" risk taking in drawing related to creative performance ($r = .34$). In summary, we found some support for the hypothesized link between risk taking and creative performance in the drawing domain. Successfully intelligent people are willing to take sensible risks.

5. Successfully intelligent people seek out for themselves and others tasks that allow for creativity. If the only assessment students receive in a course is a multiple-choice test, they will learn quickly enough what is valued, no matter what teachers say they value. If our schools want to encourage creativity and the display of creative intelligence, they need to include in their assignments and tests at least some opportunities for creative thought.

I teach an introductory course in psychology for college freshmen and have also designed an advanced-placement high-school psychology course. But their underlying principle can be used in any course at any level, and that is to ask in class and on examinations questions that not only require factual recall and analytical thinking but allow creative (and practical) thinking as well.

For example, I may ask students to recognize the basic tenets of existing theories of depression, but I will also ask them to synthesize existing theories and show how they might be integrated with each other and with ideas of the students to produce a new theory. I do not expect publishable new theories. My goal is to get the students to think creatively, because by practicing creative thinking they will develop their creative thinking skills.

The same principle can be applied in any course. In English, students can be asked to write short stories, poems, or even alternative endings to existing stories. In history, they can be asked to imagine that they are some figure in the past, and then to say what decisions they would have made in his or her place and why they would have made them. Or they can be asked to speculate on aspects of the future history of the world. In science, students can be asked to propose intuitive theories of phenomena, to design simple experiments, or to do independent research projects (library or empirical). In mathematics, they can invent their own word problems or systems of enumeration or measurement. In foreign-language classes, they can be asked to create skits taking place in the foreign country, simulating not just the language but the cultural customs. Really, the only limitations in terms of assignments are the limitations in the imagination of the teacher.

6. Successfully intelligent people actively define and redefine problems, and help others to do so.   A high-level executive in one of the "Big Three" automobile firms in the United States was faced with a dilemma. On the one hand, he loved his job and the money he made doing it. After all, high-level executives in Detroit are paid well, whether or not their cars are selling. On the other hand, he absolutely detested his boss. He had put up with this would-be ogre for a number of years and just couldn't stand it anymore. After carefully considering his options, the executive decided to visit a headhunter —a specialist in finding high-level executives new jobs. He went to the interview not knowing exactly what to expect, but fortunately, the headhunter indicated that there would be no problem in placing him somewhere else.

The executive told his wife about how the interview had gone and that he was confident he would find another job. After he described his day, his wife, a teacher, described hers. At the time, she happened to be working with my book *Intelligence Applied*, a program for teaching thinking skills to high-school and college students. She described the technique she had gone over that day—*redefining a problem*. The basic idea is that you take a problem you are facing and then turn it on its head. In other words, you look at the problem in a totally new way, one that is different not only from how you have seen it in the past but also from how other people would be likely to see it. As she described her lesson, the executive felt an idea sprouting in his head. He saw how he could use the technique his wife was teaching in her class to his personal advantage.

The next day, he returned to the headhunter, gave him his boss's name, and asked him to look for another job—for his boss. The headhunter agreed, and before long he found something. When the boss received a phone call offering him another job, it happened that he was tiring of his current job, and in short order he accepted the new position. The icing on the cake was that when the boss's old job became vacant, our high-level executive applied for it and ended up with the higher-level job.

This true story—told to me by the wife of the executive—illustrates the importance of redefining problems. The executive had originally defined his problem as one of finding himself a new job. He solved it by turning the problem on its head—that is, by finding his boss rather than himself a new job.

A couple of years ago, I faced an annoying problem. Every morning, I would wake up and discover garbage strewn all along my driveway. Opened, overturned garbage cans provided what seemed to be the obvious clue. A raccoon had knocked the can over and was eating the garbage. The problem was how to trap and remove the raccoon.

The solution seemed obvious. I went to the local hardware store and bought a trap designed not to hurt the raccoon. You put bait (such as the contents of a can of sardines) in the center of the trap, open the side doors, and place the trap near the garbage cans. As soon as the raccoon enters to eat the bait, the doors slam shut and the animal is trapped. You then drive out to some country road and release the raccoon.

I followed the prescribed steps and assumed I had solved my raccoon problem. However, my garbage cans continued to be overturned every night. The doors of the trap had closed and the bait had been eaten, but there was no raccoon inside. Apparently, the animal was able to enter the trap and eat the bait without stepping on the spring mechanism that closed the doors. I was dealing with a very smart raccoon.

I decided to redefine the problem and find a professional animal trapper to do the job. I called one, and he came to the house with a bunch of traps that looked curiously like the one I had used. He placed the traps, with bait inside them, in the area occupied by the garbage cans, and indeed they trapped animals—several squirrels and my neighbor's cat. It was two hundred ten dollars later, and I had yet to see a trapped raccoon.

Further information about the problem became evident one morning around three, when I was awakened by a loud, clanging noise that emanated from the area of the garbage cans. I got up and saw an enormous dog reaching his paws inside the trap. The doors had closed, but not completely. Thus, the dog was able to pull out the bait, and the doors shut only after it had departed. Basically, I had not solved my raccoon problem because there was never any raccoon. Redefining the problem once more, I went to the hardware store and bought garbage cans with handles that locked the lids. Indeed, the dog was unable to open the lids, and the problem was solved. But several months later, the new garbage cans were attacked by the real thing—hungry, clever raccoons, which, unlike the dog, had no trouble opening the lids and eating the garbage.

Not one to be beaten out in a test of wits by raccoons, I bought a few bungee cords and crisscrossed them over the top of each can. After several days, however, the raccoons had figured out how to get through the cords. Eventually, I solved the problem by redefining it one last time. I built an enclosure with locking doors that completely surrounded the garbage cans—this the raccoons could not enter. And from that day to this, even though it took much trial and error to solve the problem, only the trash collectors and I can get to those cans.

My raccoon problem may seem mundane, especially in the context of creative thinking. But successful intelligence can find application even in mundane contexts. It's not only about once-in-a-generation ideas such as few of us ever have, like Einstein's theory of relativity. It's also about solving problems, making decisions, and improving situations in our daily lives. Creatively successful intelligence is in the everyday turn of mind, not just in occasional flashes of genius.

One way you can encourage creative intelligence is by allowing people to choose their own ways of solving problems and, sometimes, to choose again when they learn that their selection was mistaken. For example, I often require several brief papers in my courses, and I allow students to choose their own topics for at least one of these papers, subject to my approval only to make sure that the topic is in some way relevant to what I am teaching and that the paper has at least a chance of being completed successfully. Obviously, students should not *always* choose. There are particular topics that teachers believe they need to explore. But if they are *never* given the opportunity to choose, they will never learn how to do so.

Choice should be taken seriously. In the project fair at a school, each child got to choose the state of the United States about which he or she would do a project. Not much of a real choice. The more latitude you give students, the more they will learn how to choose wisely the problems and projects they want to pursue, an essential element of creativity.

7. Successfully intelligent people seek rewards for, and themselves reward, creativity.   I explicitly reward creative efforts among my students. For example, when I assign papers, I tell them that I will look for the usual things—namely, a demonstration of their knowledge, their display of analytical skills, and, of course, good writing. But above and beyond that, I will look for and reward creativity. The question is not whether I agree or disagree with what they will say, but whether they come up with new ideas that represent a synthesis between ideas they have heard or read about and their own ways of thinking.

Some teachers complain that they cannot evaluate creative responses with the same objectivity they apply to multiple-choice or short-answer tests. At one level, of course, they are correct. There is some sacrifice of objectivity. But our research, as well as that of others, shows that evaluators are remarkably consistent in their assessments of creativity.[15] Moreover, our main goal in assessment really ought to be instruction—students learn through assessment, just as they do through any kind of instruction. Better that students do creative work that is evaluated with somewhat less objectivity than that they never be allowed to do creative work, just so that teachers can maintain the semblance of objectivity in evaluation.

8. Successfully intelligent people allow themselves and others the time to think creatively.   We are a society in a hurry. We love fast food, we rush from one place to another, and we value quickness. Indeed, to say that someone is quick is one way to say the person is smart, which squarely shows where we place our values.[16] Moreover, our standardized tests tend to have large numbers of (usually multiple-choice) problems squeezed into very brief time frames. Who would have time to think creatively, even if they were allowed to?

Contrary to popular myths, most creative insights do not happen in a flash.[17] People require time to understand a problem, mull it over in their minds, and come up with a creative solution. If teachers stuff questions into exams, or give students so many homework assignments that they scarcely have time to complete any of them, they will not have the time they need to think creatively. If employers never give employees time to think, the resulting work will not be, on average, creative.

Unfortunately, very heavy demands are placed upon teachers in the United States, and they are given substantially less free time than, say, in Japan.[18] The result is that the teachers, like the students, have scarcely any time to think, much less to think creatively. If we want students, or people in the workplace, to develop creative thinking skills, they have to be given time to do so.

9. Successfully intelligent people tolerate ambiguity and encourage tolerance of ambiguity in others.   Americans, as a general rule, have a low tolerance for ambiguity. Historically, we have always liked things to be delineated in black and white. We like to think that one way of doing things is "right" and another "wrong," or that a certain idea is "good" or "bad." The problem is that in the realm of creative work, there is usually a period of time when there are a lot of grays.

And even when things are worked out, a creative idea, like any other, may have its pluses and minuses.

The development of a creative idea almost always takes time, and during that time we tend to be uncomfortable and impatient. You want the solution now, when you have only half of it. Without time or the ability to tolerate ambiguity, you may jump to a nonoptimal solution prematurely. Linus Pauling lost credit for the discovery of the structure of DNA because he was not able to tolerate ambiguity quite long enough. He had a structure, but it was not quite the right one. He published the structure—a helical one—and his notion provided some of the missing pieces Francis Crick and James Watson needed to complete their work on the right structure.

Creative writers learn to live with ambiguity, especially when they are not quite certain how their work is going to turn out. In regard to his novels *Night Rider* and *At Heaven's Gate,* Robert Penn Warren said, "What I want to emphasize is the fact that I was fumbling rather than working according to plan and convictions already arrived at." [19]

Even the study of the physical sciences has its ambiguities. In the eighteenth century, Antoine Lavoisier, a founder of organic chemistry and biochemistry, had very imprecise measuring tools. As a result, he worked with "messy," ambiguous data and had to decide which observations were meaningful and which were not. Lavoisier "lived with incoherence" for long periods. [20] For example, in his work on oxidation and combustion, he grappled for two years with contradictory characterizations of air as either a single changeable substance or as a composite of several basic substances.

Because ambiguity is uncomfortable and anxiety-provoking, people strive to resolve it. Moreover, the pressure for resolving it is often not completely internal. Your employer or your partner in a relationship may put as much or more pressure on you than you yourself do. The employer may need to get the new product out. The spouse may be uncomfortable not knowing how you really feel about your relationship. The publisher may want the novel tomorrow and not next year. From all sides, therefore, you may be experiencing pressure to get the damn thing—whatever it may be—over with.

But to make the most of our creative potential, we need to be able to tolerate the discomfort of an ambiguous situation long enough so that what we produce is the best or closest to the best we are capable of. Any number of products have come on the market—cars, books, pens, or whatever—that weren't quite right. If the company had waited just a bit longer, it might have made a better product. Sometimes, in business situations, a competitor steps in and does get it right. And what could have been a stunning success becomes a modest one, or even a failure.

When a student has almost the right topic for a paper, or almost the right solution to a difficult math problem, it is tempting to just say go with it and accept the near miss. When a manager makes almost the right decision, he will probably stick with it. When a person looking for a new house sees almost the right house, or the person looking for a partner finds almost the right partner, it's tempting to call it quits and end the search. Creative intelligence includes a tolerance for ambiguity and a willingness to take all the time necessary to come up with good solutions and make good decisions.

10. Successfully intelligent people understand the obstacles creative people must face and overcome. Creative people *always* encounter obstacles. It's the nature of the enterprise. When medical scientists first proposed that the reason antacid drugs were not particularly effective against ulcers was that ulcers were caused by bacteria rather than stomach acids, the pharmaceutical companies were not standing in the wings, waiting to be told that their multimillion-dollar investment in antacids was in vain.

Creative thinking almost inevitably encounters resistance. The question is not whether it will encounter resistance but whether the creative thinker will have the fortitude to persevere in the face of it. I used to wonder why so many young and promising creative thinkers disappear into the woodwork. Now I better understand. Sooner or later, they give up. They decide that being creative isn't worth the effort, especially when they find that creativity is punished rather than rewarded. Yet the truly creative thinkers who stay the course and are willing to pay the short-term price will, in the long term, reap the richest rewards.

11. Successfully intelligent people are willing to grow.   Once a person has a major creative idea, the tendency may be to stop there and spend the rest of a career following up on that idea. It is frightening to contemplate that the next idea may not be as good as the last one, or that the success to which one has become accustomed may disappear with the next idea. Or we simply become complacent and stop being creative.

Complacency can also come about because of our own expertise. We can become so comfortable with it that we assume we know all there is to know and stop growing. We come up with no new ideas and are reluctant to consider new ideas from others. Meanwhile, the world has passed us by.

Several years ago, I visited a famous psychologist in another country. He wanted to show me the zoo in his city, so we went there and headed for the cages of the primates. As it turned out, just as we reached the cages, the primates were engaging in what could euphemistically be called "strange and unnatural sexual behaviors." Being New Jersey born and bred, I of course turned away. But the man I was with didn't have my refined breeding. He stared intensely at them and, a few minutes later, began analyzing their behavior in terms of his theory of intelligence.

There are very few things I think I know for sure, but one of them is that whatever it is that motivates sexual behavior, it has nothing to do with that man's theory of intelligence. And I started to wonder how such an intelligent man could seriously believe that it did. Then I realized that he, like so many other experts, had succumbed to tunnel vision. You come up with an idea that works, and soon you're trying to apply it to everything, whether it is appropriate or not.

We can all fall into that trap. For example, my theory of intelligence has three parts. A couple of years after I proposed it, I proposed another theory, a theory of love, that also had three parts. Then came a three-part theory of creativity. Soon people were asking me why all my theories had three parts. I told them that there were three good reasons. I intended the remark as a joke, but I could see that I too had become entrenched.

We often encounter examples of the costs of knowing too much in everyday life, but is the phenomenon demonstrable under the more carefully controlled conditions of a laboratory? Peter Frensch and I tried to show in such controlled conditions that being an expert can actually hurt you under certain circumstances.[21] Our experiments involved having expert and novice players compete against a computer in a game of bridge. Since computers can be programmed to play quite well, it is no mean challenge, even for experts. In one of the experiments, both experts and novices played bridge against a computer, while the computer kept score. It will come as no surprise that the experts played better than the novices. But the point of the experiment was not merely whether experts play better than novices (of course they do) but rather the effects of knowledge on how people play.

In addition to a standard-play condition, there were two other conditions of play. One was a "surface-structural" change condition, in which people played bridge against the computer but the form of the game was slightly altered. What was altered was either the rank ordering of the suits (which is, normally, from lowest to highest, clubs, diamonds, hearts, spades) or the names of the suits, which were changed to made-up words, such as "gleebs," "fricks," and so on. We called these changes "surface-structural" because they altered only the most superficial aspects of the game, and the new conditions of play could be mapped in a one-to-one fashion to the old conditions. Nothing fundamental about the game was really different. When the players were subjected to this surface-structural alteration, their play suffered momentarily but quickly recovered. All they had to do was learn the new order or names of the suits. And again, experts played better than novices.

In a "deep-structural" change condition, a more fundamental change was made. The game of bridge starts with a bidding phase and then converts into a playing phase that occurs in a number of successive rounds. The player who puts out the high card in a given round takes the trick and is normally the one who leads off play in the next. Our deep-structural change made it so that the player who puts out the low card takes the trick and leads off the next round. To total novices, the change would make little difference. It wouldn't disrupt their complex strategies of play because they didn't have any. But experts who had developed such strategies would be more likely to be disrupted, because they could no longer use them.

The results came out exactly as predicted. Experts were more hurt by the deep-structural changes than novices. Although the experts eventually recovered, it was hard for them because they were used to their normal strategies of play. Thus, their expertise got in the way of their adapting to the new rules.

As we age, we face the issue of growing not only older but, potentially, more set in our ways—more entrenched. For example, there are trends in my own field, psychology, that I don't like. I see the field as leaping from one bandwagon to the next. But is it the field, or my own inability to keep up? I can never really know for sure, but I have to be aware of both possibilities.

I tell my students that we have an equal exchange. My advantage over them is knowledge. To be creative, you have to be knowledgeable about a field. You can't move a field beyond where it is if you don't know where it is. But the advantage my students have is flexibility. Precisely because they know less, they are not as likely to be set in their ways. If they listen to me, but I listen also to them, we both profit from the exchange. In the same way, senior managers can learn by listening to junior managers who don't yet have a vested interest in the systems that are currently in place.

Occasionally, I may not like a student's or a junior colleague's idea. I'll tell the person as much. But I'll also encourage the person to try the idea out on me again, perhaps in a few weeks. I may see value in the idea a few weeks later that I didn't see the first time. And even if I don't, I won't conclude that the idea is no good. I'll encourage the person to get feedback from others. Someone else may see in the idea something I didn't see. We don't throw away creative ideas in my work group, because I won't let us.

When I was a graduate student, a world-famous psychologist came to deliver a talk, and he prefaced it by saying that he had funded his latest research himself. No one wanted to fund him. Why? Because the work was in an area different from the one in which he traditionally worked. The funding agencies were willing to let him work in his usual area but not willing to trust him in a new one; they had placed him in a box and did not want him to step outside it. Deciding to step outside it anyway, he later became famous for work in the new area and then easily obtained the funding he needed.

We are all susceptible to becoming victims of our own expertise, entrenched in ways of thinking that may have worked for us in the past but will not necessarily do so in the future. Being creative means that we are willing to step outside the boxes that we as well as others have built for ourselves, before we become trapped inside.

12. Successfully intelligent people recognize the importance of person-environment fit.   The last strategy is one that is as important to teachers and parents as it is to students. It stems from the fact that creativity is not really an objectifiable phenomenon. What is judged as creative is an interaction between a person or persons and the environment in which they work.[22] The very same product that is rewarded as creative in one time or place may be scorned as pedestrian in another.

Some years ago, I had a very talented graduate student who received two job offers, one from a highly prestigious institution, the other from a good but less prestigious one. The highly prestigious institution, however, did not seem particularly to value the kind of creative work the student did, whereas the less prestigious institution did seem to be such a place.

I gave the student what was probably the worst advice I ever gave anyone. I recommended that he take the prestigious job, because if he didn't, he would always wonder whether he could have made it in that place. Unfortunately, the student took the advice and did all right, but probably not as well as he would have done at the other place. There is a lesson to be learned. Find the environment that rewards what you have to offer, and then make the most of your creativity and of yourself in that environment.

A good example of environmental misfit can be found in the movie *Dead Poets Society*. A teacher who is clearly very creative is judged incompetent by the school in which he works, and he has to leave. This story is repeated many times daily, in many settings. Because there is no absolute standard for what constitutes creative work, the same lesson, school-reform idea, or student product that is valued in one setting may be devalued in another. People to whom that happens should look for a setting in which their creative talents will be encouraged and their unique contributions as creative thinkers rewarded rather than punished.

We all should be encouraged to develop our creativity in the areas where we have a contribution to make. We need an environment that lets us capitalize on our strengths. Research shows that people do their most creative work when they love what they do.[23] Too often, young people follow one career path or another not because it is what they love but because it's what other people, usually their parents, want. They may do good work in such a career path, but they probably won't do great work and almost certainly won't do creative work.

It is very unfortunate that we do not do more to encourage and develop creative intelligence. Even the most unimaginative and convention-bound parents or teachers want their children or students to succeed. If anything, our society worships success—but usually after the fact, without giving much thought to *how* it was achieved. There can be, of course, many contributing factors, but creative intelligence is always part of the mix.

Key 3: Making Solutions Work with Practical Intelligence

All of us know people who succeed in school but fail in their careers, or vice versa. They are a constant reminder that there must be more to success than school smarts.

Making It in the Real World

Consider the person who succeeds in school but doesn't make it in the world. We had one such student at Yale—an example of what, to many people, appeared to be the best Yale had to offer. Penn was brilliant in his schoolwork and, moreover, had ideas of his own. What more could you want than someone who is both analytically and creatively brilliant? As it turned out, quite a bit.

Penn had a couple of quirks that proved to be definite drawbacks on the job market. For one thing, he was unbelievably arrogant. Maybe too many people had told him he was brilliant. Maybe he had just been born a jerk. Whatever the cause, his arrogance hardly endeared him to people with whom he had to work. But his second quirk was worse—an almost total lack of practical intelligence. If there were a part of the brain that specialized in practical intelligence

—there almost certainly isn't—one might have concluded that someone had gone into Penn's brain with a vacuum cleaner and sucked it out completely.

Penn was offered job interviews from all the most prestigious organizations in his field. He seemed to be everyone's first pick. You could feel the envy among his fellow students—a green mist seemed suddenly to permeate a room when this fellow walked in. The problem was, Penn was so rock-bottom in practical intelligence that he couldn't hide his arrogance during his job interviews. He cleaned up on getting interviews, but he was just about taken to the cleaners when it came to job offers. He got only one offer, from a second-rate organization, and he lasted less than two years there.

Ironically, Penn had a classmate who lacked his academic brilliance but was a master of one aspect of practical intelligence, which is sometimes referred to as social intelligence.[1] Everyone liked Matt, because he was not only adept interpersonally but also a genuinely nice person. He wasn't a first-round choice, but he got interviews in the second round when recruiters hadn't yet filled their quotas that year. Matt ended up with seven job offers out of eight job interviews and has since been quite successful in his career. He hasn't been a mover or shaker, to be sure, but he has been solid, productive, and well liked.

Maybe, ultimately, Penn would have had more to contribute to an organization than Matt. But no one wanted to hire him, and given his experience at Yale, my guess is that no one would have much enjoyed working with him either. As someone who studies intelligence, I find it sad when I see students rewarded bountifully by their schools for their analytical intelligence, which won't be quite enough to achieve success in life—a fact Penn never quite understood. On the other hand, some less brilliant academic lights may have a lot more on the ball when it comes to practical intelligence, or common sense. Consider the following true story told to me by my colleague Richard K. Wagner, a former student of mine and now a professor of psychology at Florida State University in Tallahassee.

One of the advantages of an office job is that you can stay out of the summer heat, especially if you work in a hot, humid city like Tallahassee. As if it is not enough that the summer heat makes any outdoor work unbearable, the city of Tallahassee prides itself on the services it provides its citizens, and it requires of its sanitation crews physical labor far beyond the ordinary lifting and tossing of standard-size garbage cans placed at curbside. In Tallahassee, each household uses a huge, city-issued trash container, which is kept in the backyard. Trash collectors have to locate every container from every backyard, haul it to the curb, heave it into the truck, and then drag it back to the yard.

Many of the garbage collectors are young high-school dropouts who, because of their lack of education, might not be expected to do well on intelligence tests. And on the surface, the job appears to be physically but not intellectually challenging. Each stop simply requires two trips to the backyard, one to retrieve the full can, another to replace it when it's empty. Or so Wagner thought.

After observing this collection routine one summer, Wagner noticed that an older man had joined the crew and that the routine had changed. Except for the first and last houses, the new routine consisted of wheeling one house's empty can into the next house's backyard and leaving it to replace the full can, which was, in turn, wheeled to the truck to be emptied. After all, the containers were identical, issued by the city rather than purchased by each household. What had required two trips back and forth to each house now required only one. The new man's insight cut the work nearly in half.

Successful practical intelligence enables a person to come up with this kind of strategy for solving real-life problems, a strategy that had eluded well-educated observers such as Wagner, other garbage collectors, and the managers who trained the collectors. But how well is this kind of intelligence reflected in an IQ score? An anecdote told me by Seymour Sarason, a psychologist at Yale, provides little grounds for optimism.

When Sarason reported to his first job—administering intelligence tests at a school for the mentally retarded—he could not begin testing because the students had cleverly eluded elaborate security precautions and escaped. When they were rounded up, Sarason proceeded to administer the Porteus Maze Test, a paper-and-pencil intelligence test that involves finding the ways out of labyrinths. To his surprise, he discovered that the very same students who had been able to outwit the staff and escape from the facility were unable to find their way out of even the first, easiest maze on the test.

Sometimes those who are not considered brilliant or even bright by society get the last laugh. Consider a story told to me by my wife, who is originally from León, Mexico. A young Mexican went to work for a shoe factory in León, the capital of shoe manufacturing in Mexico. He was an effective worker, but when his boss discovered that he was illiterate, he was promptly fired. The young man went on to start his own shoe business and, ultimately, bought the business of the man who had fired him. Years later, when he had become one of the wealthiest men in Mexico, he was interviewed by a magazine reporter, who asked him whether he had learned to read. He replied that he had not. The reporter asked him to consider whether he wouldn't have been even more successful, and wealthier, if only he had learned to read. "On the contrary," the megaindustrialist replied. "If I had learned to read, I would still be on the assembly line in the shoe factory where I had my first job."

How Well Does IQ Predict Real-World Success?

The degree to which intelligence tests predict out-of-school criteria, such as job performance, has been an area of long-standing controversy in psychology. Opinions range from the view that there is little or no justification for tests of cognitive ability for job selection[2] to the view that cognitive-ability tests are valid predictors of job performance in a wide variety of job settings,[3] or even in all job settings.[4]

Even the most charitable view of the relationship between intelligence-test scores and real-world performance leads to the conclusion that much of what makes people more or less successful in real-world performance is not whatever it is that intelligence tests measure. The validity of these tests, as mentioned earlier, is evaluated on a scale from 0 to 1, where 0 means that it is completely invalid as a predictor of success and 1 means that it is completely valid as a predictor (that is, it predicts with 100 percent accuracy who will succeed and who won't).

The average validity coefficient between cognitive-ability tests and measures of job performance is about .2.[5] To find out how well these measures account for individual differences, you need to square the validity coefficient. Thus, at this level of validity, only 4 percent of the variation among people in their job performance is accounted for by cognitive-ability test scores. Scarcely something to write home about.

The average validity coefficient between cognitive-ability tests and measures of performance in job training programs is about double (.4) that found for job performance itself, which suggests that the level of prediction varies as a function of how comparable the criterion measure is to schooling. Put people into a course that prepares them for a job, rather than into the job itself, and the ability test will indeed be a better predictor than it is of the job performance.

What all this means is that, on average, having a higher IQ will lead to better performance on the job. But the effect isn't large. Of course, a lot depends on just what job we're talking about. A competent doctor or physicist will probably need a higher IQ to succeed on the job than will a competent assembly-line worker. But it is easy to lose sight of the extent to which IQ isn't really enough for success, even in what would seem to be the most intellectually demanding jobs.

Many of us have been to doctors who probably have high IQs, and may have gotten good grades in medical school, but are truly lousy doctors. They seem to have learned their interpersonal skills in a boxing ring, and their physical-examination skills in a butcher shop. If we have a choice of physicians, chances are good that the next time around we'll look for someone else. Why put up with the abuse? Such a doctor may find that all the degrees from the fanciest medical schools are not enough to save a foundering practice. Practical intellectual skills may count for little in getting into medical school, but they count for a lot in building up a successful practice.

A physicist, ensconced in the ivory-tower world of academia, would seem even more immune from the need for the social skills that characterize the practically intelligent. But in experimental physics, at least, we find only the illusion of immunity. Today, because of the complexity and expense, most significant research in physics is done in large teams. Research reports may have ten, twenty, or even more collaborators. Physicists who cannot work as part of a team may find themselves iced out of the most important projects. Indeed, in my own academic group at Yale, one of the main things I look for in making hiring decisions is the ability of the individual to work as part of a team. Those who don't have these practical skills, regardless of their academic skills, aren't hired; if they somehow slip through the net, they don't stay very long.

Some psychologists nevertheless argue that IQ not only matters for job success but matters a lot. They have suggested that the validity coefficient of IQ tests and related measures for predicting job performance is really about .5, not .2.[6] That's a pretty big difference. How did they get a figure so much higher than that reported by the commission appointed by the prestigious National Academy of Science?

They used a variety of what euphemistically might be called *statistical corrections* in order to jack up these validity coefficients. For example, they argue that tests are not perfectly reliable instruments—if you give people the same test twice, their scores won't be exactly the same. So, they say, when you look at the validity of the test, you should correct for the imperfect reliability of the test and present a validity number that would be true if the test were perfectly reliable —that is, if people always got the same scores when they took the test more than once. I would be glad to make these psychologists a deal. If they can show me a test that is as perfectly reliable as a precision thermometer, I'll accept their statistics. We all like to think about perfect worlds, and someday maybe we'll live in such a world. In the meantime, our statistics should pertain to the world we live in.

By the way, psychologists interested in raising the predictive validity of IQ tests for job performance also correct for the fact that when people are hired by organizations that use these tests, only high scorers are hired. In other words, their validation samples do not include those who were not hired. This practice makes tests look awfully good, and here's why: Suppose you include in your sample both low-grade idiots, who can't hold a pencil and hence get 0 on all the tests they are given, and super-geniuses, who ace practically any test they take. Chances are the super-geniuses will do better in lots of jobs than the idiots, especially if the jobs require them to hold a pencil. But why even bother to do this kind of statistical sleight of hand? You can save yourself a lot of money just by asking people to hold a pencil and not hiring those who can't.

The inflated estimates actually might be viewed as correct—but, again, only in a theoretically perfect world where tests always measure things reliably and where everyone who might take a test in a population, or a perfectly representative sample, is tested. The problem is that when we live in the real world, the estimates just don't apply.

I have gone into some detail on the statistical manipulations of the IQ-test crowd for several reasons. First, to understand what the fuss is all about, you have to understand just a bit about statistics. Otherwise, you quickly get lost in the numbers and tend to accept how they are interpreted at face value. And second, you can't make statistics show everything, but you can make them show an awful lot, figuring that those who read them won't know any better. In my opinion, many, although certainly not all, of the users of IQ statistics are suckering their readers, who therefore should remember that familiar warning "Buyer beware!"

John Hunter and Frank Schmidt will "correct" statistics in order to make them look more impressive.[7] They, at least, write for professional audiences who know how to interpret what they do. If you are going to talk, as did Mark Twain, about lies, damn lies, and statistics, then you've got to talk about Herrnstein and Murray and *The Bell*

Curve.[8] Herrnstein and Murray, like Hunter and Schmidt, would have their readers believe that IQ tests predict practically everything, including real-world as well as academic success. But they play with statistics, and with their readers.

Every student of elementary statistics soon learns that correlation does not imply causation. In other words, the fact that one variable is related to another variable does not mean that the first variable causes the second variable. The second variable may cause the first, or both may be related to some third variable, which causes both of them. For example, suppose we compare Norwegians to Nigerians. There is a strong correlation between being black and being Nigerian. But being black does not make you Nigerian, nor does being Nigerian make you black. A Norwegian who moves to Nigeria may take up Nigerian citizenship but is unlikely to turn black. Rather, the correlation is based on a third, higher-order variable—namely, where people of different skin colors have tended to settle. Again, correlation does not imply causation.

Now consider a typical Herrnstein-Murray example. They state that 10 percent of very bright individuals, 14 percent of bright individuals, 15 percent of normal individuals, 19 percent of "dull" individuals (their term), and 22 percent of "very dull" individuals spent a month or more out of the labor force in 1989.[9] Here, as elsewhere, they are intent on convincing you that being dumb leads to bad news —in this case, being out of a job. But does low IQ *cause* unemployment? In fact, we now know that when people are not challenged intellectually through work, their intelligence suffers.[10] So one might argue that being out of work can hurt IQ. But more plausibly, low scores on IQ tests and being out of work could both be due to higher-order causes, such as our society's failure to provide educational and job opportunities for many individuals, or lack of parental models that lead to the development of both school-related and job-related skills.

Although Herrnstein and Murray know that you cannot infer causality from correlation, they often speak as though you can. All of the data in their book are correlational. All of them! They do show that there is a statistical association between IQ and various aspects of their interpretation of life success. Their graphs are impressive. But after more than eight hundred pages of mind-dulling text and graphs, you will probably never get to Appendix 4. And even if you do, chances are you won't understand it unless you have a background in advanced statistics. What does this appendix say, when you strip away the complex equations and terminology?

It admits that the majority of statistical relations about which Herrnstein and Murray have made so much in their book are weak. The typical proportion of variation across people accounted for in their analyses is less than 10 percent. That's right, less than 10 percent. Their whole edifice is based on statistical relations that are so weak they would be laughable had the book not become a best-seller and its message so widely cited. Their arguments are built on a foundation of papier-mâché shaded to look like concrete.

So we're back to where we began. Even if you accept Herrnstein and Murray's statistics, IQ accounts for less than 10 percent of the variation among people in a variety of real-world outcomes. If we are talking about job performance, I believe the 4 percent figure is the best we have. But no matter whose figures you accept, the percentage is small. Even if you accepted what is in my opinion the inflated figure of Hunter and Schmidt—25 percent—you are still seeing 75 percent of the variation unexplained. Clearly, we need other constructs beyond IQ to explain why people differ in various kinds of real-world success.

I believe that academics and others love statistics because they cover up how poorly things are going at the level of individual cases. When statistical measures account for 10 or even 25 percent of the variation in a group, the level of individual prediction is quite poor. People are getting mispredicted all over the place. If you care only about the group data, perhaps you think you're not doing so badly. But when you consider the large numbers of people who are put into the wrong piles—the rejects who should have been accepted or hired and the accepted or hired who should have been rejected—the results look quite different.

Real-World Success
and Practical Intelligence

Remember the important distinction between academic intelligence, on the one hand, and practical intelligence, on the other.[11] Any way you look at it, real-world tasks—the kinds that matter in most people's lives—don't look very much like academic tasks:

1. Academic tasks are given to you on a silver platter, although sometimes the silver is plenty tarnished. The teacher tells you what to do. The textbook gives you a concrete problem to solve. The test asks you a question. You become the answer part of a question-answer machine. In the real world, there is no one to serve as the question part. Often, it's not even clear what the question or problem is. For example, what, exactly, is wrong with your relationship and in need of improvement? In an academic context, you would be told what's wrong and asked to fix it. In a real-world context, you have to figure out not only how to fix it but what "it" is in the first place.

2. Academic problems are often of little or even no intrinsic interest. When all is said and done, you don't really care what the answer is—or what the question is, for that matter. You're just answering questions in the hope of getting an A in a course you may not even want to take, or you thought you wanted to take and now realize you didn't. In real life, the questions and answers often matter, and in major ways. The decisions you make in a relationship or on a job can make or break your marriage or your career. A lot more is often at stake than an A on a test.

3. Academic problems are disembedded from people's ordinary experience. How many times have you had to solve a verbal-analogy problem like EVANESCENT : FLEETING :: EPHEMERAL : (a) permanent, (b) long-lasting, (c) temporary, (d) instant, in your everyday life? How many times have you sat down for forty minutes and filled in some answers that are supposed to determine whether you've got what it takes? In everyday life, people are judged for the quality of their work on the job, on their contributions to the give-and-take of interpersonal relationships, or on their contributions to organiza-

tions, or whatever. They are not judged—at least, not properly—by their answers to fairly artificial problems created for quick solution in a forty-minute time period.

4. Academic problems often have just one "correct" answer. On an intelligence test, you are expected to produce the right answers, and either you produce enough of these right answers or you are judged as lacking in intelligence. In everyday life, there usually are no clearly right or wrong answers, although there may be better and worse ones. Even when some answers are better than others, what makes an answer better depends on the values that are brought to bear on the situation. One business may go for a deal that another will pass up, because the two businesses differ in their values. Tests don't allow for value differences, even though such differences may, in fact, affect the way a person approaches a test.

I could go on, but the point is that real-world and testlike problems are quite different. Moreover, they show different courses over a life span. Men and women past the age of sixty-five were interviewed about their perceptions of changes in their ability to think, reason, and solve problems as they aged.[12] Although performance on traditional cognitive-ability measures typically peaks at the end of formal schooling, 76 percent of the participants in the study believed that their ability to think, reason, and solve problems had actually increased over the years, with 20 percent reporting no change and only 4 percent reporting that their abilities had declined with age. When confronted with this decline in psychometric test performance upon completion of formal schooling, the participants said that they were talking about solving different kinds of problems than those found on cognitive-ability tests—problems they referred to as "everyday" or "financial" problems.

In fact, there is good evidence that people's abilities to solve everyday problems do increase with age, at the same time that certain abilities that are particularly relevant to IQ-type tests decrease. Particularly relevant here is the theory of fluid and crystallized intelligence.[13] Analyses of thousands of data sets collected in studies of intelligence have confirmed the usefulness of this distinction.[14] *Fluid intelligence* is required to deal with novelty in the immediate testing situation (e.g., figuring out the next letter in a letter series problem, such as c, d, f, i, . . .). *Crystallized intelligence* reflects acculturated knowledge (e.g., the meaning of a low-frequency vocabulary word). A number of studies have shown that fluid abilities are vulnerable to age-related declines but crystallized abilities are maintained and generally increased throughout the life span.[15]

Practical problems are characterized by, among other things, an apparent absence of the exact information necessary for solution and also by their relevance to everyday experience. Thus, crystallized intelligence in the form of acculturated knowledge is particularly relevant to practical problems. Without such knowledge, you just can't solve the problems life throws at you. In contrast, fluid intelligence, as is required to solve letter series or figural-analogy problems, is more relevant to the solution of academic problems and IQ-like tests. It is also important in everyday life for situations that require flexibility of thinking. Thus, it follows that the judgments people make about changes in intelligence with age are correct. Their intelligence does increase, but it is their practical intelligence that does so, not their academic intelligence, which, in fact, probably does decline. As you get older, your ability to perform effectively on the job may well increase, but at the same time your ability to be an effective college freshman decreases.

Some Empirical Studies
of Practical Intelligence

The idea that practical and academic abilities follow different courses in adult development finds support in a variety of studies. For example, in one study, eighty-four adults between the ages of twenty and seventy-nine were given two types of reasoning problems:[16] a traditional cognitive measure, the Twenty Questions Task,[17] where you have to figure things out by posing artificial questions of a kind you are not likely to pose outside a game situation ("Is it living? Is it human?"); and a problem-solving task involving real-life situations such as: "If you were traveling by car and got stranded on an interstate highway during a blizzard, what would you do?" or: "Now, let's assume that you lived in an apartment that didn't have any windows on the same side as the front door. Let's say that at 2:00 A.M. you heard a loud knock on the door and someone yelled, 'Open up. It's the police.' What would you do?" The most interesting result of this study for the purposes of understanding practical intelligence was a difference in the shape of the age curve for performance on the two types of problems. Performance on the traditional, academic, gamelike measure decreased linearly after age twenty. Performance on the practical-problem-solving task increased to a peak in the forty- and fifty-year-old groups, and only then declined.

Similar results were obtained in a study of 126 adults between the ages of twenty and seventy-eight.[18] The study examined the relationships between fluid intelligence, crystallized intelligence, and everyday-problem solving. Participants were given traditional measures of fluid intelligence (such as letter series) and crystallized intelligence (such as vocabulary), as well as an everyday-problem-solving inventory that sampled the domains of consumer problems (e.g., a landlord who won't make repairs), information seeking (additional data are needed to fill out a complicated form), problems with friends (getting a friend to visit you more often), and work problems (you were passed over for a promotion).

The measure of crystallized intelligence was given to determine whether the development of everyday-problem solving was more similar to the development of crystallized than to fluid intelligence. Performance on the measure of fluid intelligence increased from age twenty to thirty, remained stable from age thirty to fifty, and then declined. Performance on the everyday-problem-solving task and on the measures of crystallized intelligence increased through age seventy. Although participants in this study showed peak performance later in life than did participants in the previously cited study, the pattern of traditional cognitive task performance peaking sooner than practical task performance was consistent across the studies. In addition to the developmental pattern of task performance, this study compared performances on the fluid-ability and everyday-problem-solving tasks and reported a modest correlation. The correlation of the crystallized task with everyday-problem solving was no higher. In other words, there is more to practical intelligence than there is even to crystallized abilities of the kind measured by tests of vocabulary and general information.

In sum, there is reason to believe that whereas the ability to solve strictly academic problems declines from early to late adulthood, the ability to solve problems of a practical nature is maintained or even increases through late adulthood. The available evidence suggests that older individuals compensate for their declining fluid intelligence by restricting their domains of activity to those they know well and by applying specialized knowledge.[19] For example, we know that age-related decrements at the "molecular" level (e.g., speed in the elementary components of typing skill) produce no observable effects at the "molar" level (i.e., the speed and accuracy with which work is completed), because older adults learn to compensate—e.g., making up for slower finger movements by looking further ahead while they type.[20]

The difference between academic and practical intelligence shows itself in many ways, but most importantly in the activities of daily life. Consider some of the studies showing that IQ tells you little of what you want to know about what makes for success, regardless of life pursuit. One such study looked at the strategies used by milk processing plant workers to fill orders.[21] Workers who assemble orders for cases of various quantities (e.g., gallons, quarts, or pints) and products (e.g., whole milk, 2 percent milk, or buttermilk) are called *assemblers*. The study found that rather than employing typical mathematical algorithms learned in the classroom, experienced assemblers used complex strategies for combining partially filled cases in a manner that minimized the number of moves required to complete an order. Although the assemblers were the least educated workers in the plant, they were able to calculate in their heads quantities expressed in different base number systems, and they routinely outperformed the more highly educated white-collar workers who substituted when assemblers were absent. The order-filling performance of the assemblers was unrelated to measures of school performance, including intelligence-test scores, arithmetic-test scores, and grades.

A further study examined expert racetrack handicappers—in particular, the strategies they used to predict post-time odds at the track.[22] Expert handicappers used a highly complex algorithm for predicting odds, which involved interactions among seven kinds of information. One obvious piece of useful information was the horse's speed on a previous outing. By applying the complex algorithm, handicappers adjusted times posted for each quarter mile on a previous outing by factors such as whether the horse was attempting to pass other horses, and if so, the speed of other horses passed and where the attempted passes took place. These adjustments are important because they affect how much of the race is run away from the rail. When posted times for these factors are adjusted, a better measure of a horse's speed is obtained. Use of the complex interaction in prediction would seem to require considerable cognitive ability (at least as it is traditionally measured). However, the study reported that the degree to which handicappers used the interaction was unrelated to their IQs. Moreover, the mean IQ of the group of handicappers was only average.

Another series of studies of everyday mathematics involved shoppers in California grocery stores who sought to buy at the cheapest cost when the same products were available in different-size containers.[23] (These studies were performed before cost-per-unit quantity information was routinely posted.) For example, oatmeal may come in two sizes, 10 ounces for 98 cents or 24 ounces for $2.29. One might adopt the strategy of always buying the largest size, assuming that it is the most economical. However, the researchers (and savvy shoppers) learned that the largest size did not represent the least cost-per-unit quantity for about a third of the items purchased. The findings of these studies were that effective shoppers used mental shortcuts to get an easily obtained answer accurate (although not completely accurate) enough to determine which size to buy. For the oatmeal example, the strategy used by effective shoppers was to recognize that 10 ounces for 98 cents is about 10 cents per ounce, and at that price, 24 ounces would be about $2.40, as opposed to the actual price of $2.29.

Another common strategy involved mentally changing a size and price to make it more comparable with the other size available. For example, one might mentally double the smaller size, thereby comparing 20 ounces at $1.96 versus 24 ounces at $2.29. The difference of 4 ounces for about 35 cents, or about 9 cents per ounce, seems to favor the 24-ounce size, given that the smaller size of 10 ounces for 98 cents is about 10 cents per ounce. These mathematical shortcuts yield approximations that are as useful as the actual values of 9.80 and 9.33 cents per ounce for the smaller and larger sizes, respectively, but much more easily computed in the absence of a calculator.

Another result of interest was that when the shoppers were given the MIT mental arithmetic test, no relation was found between test performance and accuracy in picking the best values.[24] The same principle that applies to adults appears to apply to children. A study found that Brazilian street children could apply sophisticated mathematical strategies in their street vending but were unable to do the same in a classroom setting.[25]

One more example of a study of everyday mathematics was provided by individuals asked to play the role of city managers for the computer-simulated city of Lohhausen.[26] A variety of problems was presented to these subjects, such as how best to raise revenue to build roads. The simulation involved more than one thousand variables. Performance was quantified in terms of a hierarchy of strategies, ranging from the simplest (trial and error) to the most complex (hypothesis testing with multiple feedback loops). No relation was found between IQ and complexity of strategies used. A second problem was created to confirm these results. Called the Sahara problem, it required participants to determine the number of camels that could be kept alive by a small oasis. Once again, no relation was found between IQ and complexity of strategies employed.

The Nature of Tacit Knowledge

The distinction between academic and practical kinds of intelligence is paralleled by a similar distinction between two types of knowledge.[27] An academically intelligent individual is someone who is characterized by facile acquisition and use of *formal academic knowledge,* the kind of knowledge sampled by IQ tests and other tests of their ilk. Conversely, the hallmark of the practically intelligent individual is facile acquisition and use of *tacit knowledge.* Tacit knowledge refers to action-oriented knowledge, which is typically acquired without direct help from others and which allows individuals to achieve goals they personally value.[28] The acquisition and use of such knowledge appears to be uniquely important to competent performance in real-world endeavors.

What, exactly, is tacit knowledge? It has three characteristic features. First, tacit knowledge is about knowing how—about doing. It is procedural in nature. Second, it is relevant to the attainment of goals people value, not the kind of academic drivel without practical value that teachers sometimes try to stuff in students' heads. And third, it is typically acquired with little help from others.

Knowledge with these three characteristics is called *tacit* because it often needs to be inferred from actions or statements. But it can be, and sometimes is, brought out into the open, although usually with difficulty and often with resistance. For example, there may be a big difference between what gets you a promotion according to a rule-book and what gets you a promotion in reality. A company may not be eager for the true criteria—the tacit ones—to emerge. But they can, and sometimes do, come to light.

Promotions are, in fact, a particularly good example of the importance of tacit knowledge to practical intelligence. The people who get promoted within an organization are usually the ones who have figured out how the system they are in really works, regardless of what anyone may say about how it is supposed to work. Many lawyers quickly figure out that billable hours are the key to success in a law firm, but they may also need to figure out that not all billable hours are equal—that some cases may be far better as career builders than others. In many fields, what matters even more than the work you do is the reputation you build for that work, and reputation is not always tantamount to the quality of the work. People are often promoted more on the grounds of the reputation they have built than for the quality of their work, which may not be, in fact, as good as that of people who are left behind. The winners figured out what would lead to their advancement, and it was more than just the quality of their work.

Usually, tacit knowledge is expressed in the form of a sequence of if-then conditionals, which can be rather complex. For example:

If (you need to deliver bad news to your boss)

and

If (it is Monday morning)

and

If (the boss's golf game was rained out the day before)

and

If (the staff seems to be "walking on eggs")

Then (wait until later to deliver the news).

You can see from this example that tacit knowledge is always wedded to particular uses in particular situations. People who are asked about their knowledge in practical situations will often begin by articulating general rules in roughly declarative form (e.g., "A good leader needs to know what people are like"). When such generalizations are probed, however, they often reveal themselves to be summaries of much more specific, and more useful, tacit knowledge.

Indeed, tacit knowledge is practically useful—it is knowledge that is instrumental to attaining goals, such as how to lead or how to get promoted. For example, knowledge about how to make subordinates feel valued is practically useful for managers or leaders who want to attain that goal but is not practically useful for those who are unconcerned about it. Thus, tacit knowledge is distinguished from knowledge, even "how-to" knowledge, that is irrelevant to goals people care about personally.

An important feature of tacit knowledge is that it is usually acquired without direct help from others, and sometimes even despite barriers to its acquisition. That may make it sound somehow underhanded. But there is a reason for such barriers. Consider, for example, how to get a promotion. In a typical company, not everyone can get that promotion. There is knowledge about what matters to the higher-ups that distinguishes those who are more likely to get the promotion from those who are not. But suppose everyone had that knowledge. Then it would not distinguish among people and would be useless in determining who got the promotion. Very quickly, another piece of inside information that some people know and some do not would become the factor that distinguishes those who forge ahead from those who are left behind.

The stock market provides another example. Information about a stock is useful only if others either don't have it or don't know how to use it. If everyone has the information and knows how to use it, then it is immediately incorporated into the price of the stock, and some other information becomes the key to future trends in the price of that stock.

The implication of all this is that practically intelligent people do not simply try to acquire as much knowledge as they can about the system in which they are working. They know that they need to acquire information about the system that is not readily accessible to everyone.

Consider two further examples. These days, it is very hard to get funding for projects that any individual or organization might want to undertake. In my own profession, people have traditionally applied for grants from the National Science Foundation or the National Institutes of Health, to name two. But now it is almost not worth the bother to submit applications to them. Why? Because everyone knows about them. The people who are successful in getting funding—the practically intelligent ones—are going after the pockets of money others don't even know are there. For a similar reason, when my children decided they wanted to apply for internships, they bought a book about them. They learned a lot of useful information but were somewhat discouraged to read that for each of the internships listed in the book there are usually close to fifty rejected applications for every one that is accepted. My advice to them: Look for internships that aren't in the book and apply for them. The chances of being accepted will be much better.

Testing Tacit Knowledge

The tacit-knowledge aspect of practical intelligence can be effectively measured.[29] The measurement instruments my colleagues and I used consist of a set of work-related situations, each with between five and twenty response items. Each situation poses a problem for participants to solve by rating the various response items. For example, in a hypothetical situation presented to a business manager, a subordinate whom the manager does not know well has come to him for advice on how to succeed in business. The manager is asked to rate each of several factors (usually on a 1 = low to a 9 = high scale), according to the importance of each for success in the given situation.

What do we find when we test people's tacit knowledge? One of the first questions we asked is whether tacit knowledge predicts performance of managers. We were particularly interested in managers because they are people who are judged on their practical, not their academic, intelligence. No one cares about their IQ or SAT scores or their college grades. Their superiors do care, however, about their ability to perform effectively for their companies.

Does performance on measures of tacit knowledge actually predict performance in management? We found that it does. For example, in two of our studies, we found correlations (on a 0 = low to 1 = high scale) of .2 to .4 between tacit-knowledge scores and criteria such as salary, years of management experience, and whether the manager worked for a company at the top of the Fortune 500.[30] In another study, tacit knowledge was significantly correlated with managerial compensation (.39) and level within the company (.36). Tacit knowledge was also correlated, although more weakly, with job satisfaction (.23).[31] These correlations were as good as or better than the .2

correlations typically found when IQ tests are used to predict managerial performance.[32]

When more precise criteria were used to assess managerial performance, the tests of tacit knowledge looked even better. In a study of bank managers, for example, we found correlations of .48 between tacit knowledge and average percentage of merit-based salary increase and of .56 between tacit knowledge and "generating new business for the bank."

Further support for the tacit-knowledge approach came out of a study done at a leading management training center, the Center for Creative Leadership in Greensboro, North Carolina.[33] In this study, we were able to examine correlations among a variety of measures, including an intelligence test, a well-known personality test, several tests of cognitive styles, a test of preference for innovation, a test of job satisfaction, and a test of orientation in interpersonal relations. We found the test of tacit knowledge to be the single best predictor of performance on two managerial simulations, called Earth II and Energy International. The correlation was .61. In contrast, IQ correlated only .38 with performance.

One might wonder whether that aspect of practical intelligence measured by tests of tacit knowledge is itself related to IQ. The answer, as far as we can tell, is no. We typically get correlations at the level of .1, which are not even statistically significant. In other words, contrary to the claims of Herrnstein and Murray, IQ is not the only, and probably not even the best, measure of practical performance in organizations or elsewhere. In fact, we used a statistical procedure to look at the correlation of tacit knowledge with managerial performance, taking into account every other measure the Center for Creative Leadership used. The result: Tacit knowledge was still a significant predictor of performance, even after everything else was taken into account.

The lesson of these studies is that tacit knowledge often matters as much as or more than academic intelligence for job success. And it seems not to matter what the job is. Even in ivory-tower academic jobs, tacit knowledge is key to success. Knowing the ropes is more important than most of what you learn in school. Indeed, some of those who best know the ropes may have done poorly in school.

Are you born with tacit knowledge? Of course not. Then where does it come from? Experience. In a study of fifty-four business managers, fifty-one business-school students, and twenty-two undergraduates, we found, as you would predict, that tacit knowledge for management increases, on the average, with business experience. No surprise there. But IQ does not increase. So tacit knowledge is like other aspects of practical intelligence in that it increases over the course of the life span, in contrast to academic intelligence, which decreases. It is important to keep one additional finding in mind, however. People with more business experience did not score uniformly higher than those with less such experience. In fact, some people with many years of business experience performed quite poorly. The point here is that what matters most is not how much experience you have had but rather how much you have profited from it—in other words, how well you apply what you have learned.

In a later study, which focused on the development of tacit knowledge over the managerial career, we used extensive interviews and observations to construct measures of tacit knowledge for different levels of management.[34] We administered this measure to all executives in four high-technology manufacturing companies. We also obtained nominations from managers' superiors for "outstanding" and "underperforming" managers at the lower, middle, and upper levels. This approach enabled us to delineate the specific contents of tacit knowledge for each level of management (lower, middle, upper) by examining what experts at each level knew that their poorly performing colleagues did not.

Our results showed that there was indeed specialized tacit knowledge for each of the three management levels and that this knowledge is differentially related to success. We derived these results by comparing outstanding and underperforming managers within each management level on inventories specific for the various levels of management. For example, within the domain of knowledge about oneself, knowing how to seek out, create, and enjoy challenges is substantially more important to upper-level executives than to middle- or lower-level executives. Knowledge about maintaining appropriate levels of control becomes progressively more significant at higher levels of management. Knowledge about self-motivation, self-direction, self-awareness, and personal organization is roughly comparable in importance at the lower and middle levels, and becomes somewhat more important at the upper level. Finally, knowledge about completing tasks and working effectively within the business environment is substantially more important at high levels. In general, the lower the level of management, the more important it is to know how to get day-to-day, operational tasks accomplished, whereas the higher the level of management, the more important it is to know how to set a vision for the company to follow.

Some psychologists, as mentioned earlier, hold to the importance of a general ability or g-factor—roughly IQ—which they believe explains almost everything involving intelligence that you can relate to job performance.[35] They have criticized our work for ignoring this general ability. In fact, we have not ignored it. Our studies at the Center for Creative Leadership showed that our measures of tacit knowledge were more accurate in predicting managerial skill than IQ-type tests. But it turns out that managerial ability itself shows some "g-like" qualities.

We analyzed scores from our tacit-knowledge tests and found that, in fact, people who tend to be good at acquiring and using some aspects of tacit knowledge also tend to be good about others. In other words, there was something like a general factor. Moreover, when people were tested for their tacit knowledge in two domains—business management and a field that is as different as one could find, academic psychology—the correlation between scores in the two domains was .58. Thus, people who are good at acquiring and using tacit knowledge do appear to have a generalizable skill. In everyday parlance, they are high in common sense. But common sense is *not* academic intelligence. In study after study, we have found only trivial correlations between tacit knowledge and IQ.[36]

We put our belief that tacit knowledge is not IQ to a rather severe test when a student of a "true believer" in IQ, Malcolm Ree, correlated scores on a tacit-knowledge test with scores on the Armed Services Vocational Aptitude Battery, which is essentially a very sophisticated and relatively broad-ranging IQ test.[37] In a sample of 631 Air Force recruits, of whom 29 percent were women and 19 percent members of minority groups, the median correlation between tacit-knowledge scores and ASVAB scores, on the 0 to 1 scale, was a mere .07. Statistical analysis revealed that when scores were grouped according to the underlying constructs they measured, all the ASVAB tests tended to cluster together, but separately from tests of tacit knowledge. Quite simply, practical and academic intelligence are not the same, never have been, and, in the foreseeable future, never will be.

Interestingly, both IQ and tacit knowledge are related to education. We have found correlations with both years of higher education (.37) and self-reported school performance (.26). We have even found correlations with quality of college (.34). The fact that IQ also correlates with these measures tells us that tacit knowledge is predicted by educational variables—but those aspects of education that are not correlated with IQ. In short, it is what you gain in college other than straight academic smarts that matters for tacit knowledge. Thus, from our point of view, what students learn in courses is truly only a minor part of the college or any other educational experience.

One other result stands out from the tacit-knowledge and ASVAB comparisons. Scores on the ASVAB were significantly related to both sex and race, in that women and minority-group members performed more poorly than men and majority-group members. However, tacit-knowledge scores were unrelated to either sex (correlation of .02) or race (correlation of .03). In other words, tacit knowledge, unlike IQ, is not sex or race loaded.

Beyond Business

Although our focus has been on business management, tacit knowledge is related to success in other domains as well. For example, in two studies of academic psychology professors, we found correlations in the .4 to .5 range between their tacit knowledge and various criteria, such as number of citations to their work reported in the *Social Science Citation Index* (a measure of impact upon the field) and the rated scholarly quality of their departmental faculties.[38]

More recently, we have studied the role of tacit knowledge in the domain of sales.[39] In a sample of life insurance salespersons, we found correlations in the .3 to .4 range between measures of tacit knowledge for sales and criterion measures such as sales volume and sales awards. In this work, we were also able to express the tacit knowledge of salespeople in terms of sets of *rules of thumb*—rough guides to action in sales situations. Not only does knowing the rules of thumb for sales help to assess sales tacit knowledge, it also potentially could help to devise a training program for more effective sales work.

Are measures of tacit knowledge predictors of performance that apply to adults but not to adolescents or children? Not at all. In a study of tacit knowledge in the college environment, done in collaboration with Wendy Williams, we found that such knowledge predicted academic success as well as conventional psychometric tests such as the SAT, and predicted personal adjustment substantially better than the SAT.[40] The kinds of tacit knowledge needed for success on the test bear a lot more similarity to what you needed to know to succeed in college than the more abstract and far-removed scores you may have attained on tests like the SAT or the ACT.

We have also studied the role of tacit knowledge for children quite a bit younger than college students, because tacit knowledge is important at all ages. Consider an example of how. Some years back, my son, Seth, showed me a paper he planned to hand in to his teacher. He was in fifth grade and had not yet mastered the fine points of tacit knowledge in terms of teacher expectations. In fact, many students of all ages are academically able but just never quite understand what teachers and schools expect. When I saw Seth's paper, I said, "You're not really going to hand this in, are you? It's full of typographical errors—errors in spelling, punctuation, and capitalization. Besides, it's pretty messy." Seth assured me—he had no doubts—that his teacher didn't care about trivia like spelling and capitalization. She didn't care if the paper was messy. All she cared about were the ideas. I told Seth that I wasn't so sure he was correct —that virtually all teachers care about spelling, grammar, punctuation, and appearance. Seth continued to insist his teacher was the exception. He handed the paper in. He was wrong.

It is our belief that students, as much as anyone else, need to learn about tacit knowledge as it applies in school. My colleagues and I, together with a team at Harvard headed by Howard Gardner, instituted a six-year program of research called Practical Intelligence for Schools (PIFS). It involved intensive observations and interviews of students and teachers in order to determine the tacit knowledge necessary for success in school. Curricula designed to teach the essential tacit knowledge were then developed and evaluated in a variety of Connecticut and Massachusetts school districts. The curricula have since been sent to hundreds of schools and are now being widely used.

The results of the curricula evaluations have been uniformly positive. For example, students in the PIFS program showed significantly greater increases in reading, writing, homework, and test-taking ability over the school year, compared with students in the same schools who were not in the program. Furthermore, teachers, students, and administrators reported fewer behavioral problems in classes using the program.[41] In other words, children can not only be assessed for tacit knowledge, they can also be taught it and can benefit by it.[42]

Beyond Adaptation

Tacit knowledge is the aspect of successful intelligence that helps people adapt to their environments—learning how the system works and making it work for them. All the academic knowledge in the world doesn't serve that purpose, although tacit knowledge can be taught. For example, I give a seminar on professional psychology, which teaches students how to apply for jobs, how to write résumés, how to do job interviews, how to give talks, what to do if they are fired, and so on. Even though this seminar deals with the world that the students will have to deal with, many of the other professors in the department don't particularly like the idea of such a course, perhaps because it is practical rather than theoretical.

Learning adaptive skills is essential to the development of successful intelligence, but there is more to it than that. Suppose, for example, you go to work for a computer company because you are eager to write software for educational or business purposes. But you're plunked down in the industrial-espionage division, where your job is to steal ideas from competitors. Or suppose you go to live in a community that you thought was everything you wanted, and it *is* everything you wanted—for your worst enemy. Or suppose you are in an intimate relationship with someone who is repeatedly unfaithful. Successfully intelligent people don't adapt to such circumstances. They get out.

Successful intelligence requires striking a balance between knowing when to adapt and when to select another environment. Successfully intelligent people also recognize a third option in dealing with the environment—shaping. They know that virtually no environment is going to be absolutely perfect. You don't leave your marriage when you have your first big fight. You don't leave your kids because they behave badly. And you don't leave your job because sometimes your boss really ticks you off. Rather, you find ways to shape the environment to make it better conform to your needs. If you look at the most successfully intelligent people, they're shapers. They don't follow the trends set by other people; they set the trends. They don't live with problems; they solve them. And they do so, at least in part, by adapting to, selecting, and shaping their environments.

In summary, then, people with practical intelligence actively seek out the tacit knowledge that is implicit and often hidden in an environment. They recognize that this tacit knowledge may differ from one environment to another. They further recognize that the tacit knowledge needed for success changes with advancement in a career and may also change as a function of a different environment (a company merger, for example). They discard tacit knowledge that is no longer useful and embrace what is. They use tacit knowledge to select, adapt to, and help them shape environments. They realize that what is important is not how much experience they or others have had but how much they or others have profited from the experience. They make the most of the opportunities they have. Clearly, practical intelligence is key to success in any field. And those who can combine it with analytical and creative intelligence will be the most successful.

PART IV

The Countdown Continues:
Activating Successful Intelligence

CHAPTER EIGHT

Self-activation Versus
Self-sabotage

Up to now, I have concentrated on the hard, cognitive side of successful intelligence—how we think as it is related to how well we perform —and successful performance is the only true test of successful intelligence, however else it may be measured or defined. Success, however, is a relative term; like beauty, it may be in the eye of the beholder. Even so, I have found that successfully intelligent people have many things in common, whatever the degree or nature of their success. Let's look at several of these characteristics and attributes. Their absence in our own line of work and personal lives can lead to self-sabotage and failure. Their presence, conversely, can serve as self-activators and can lead, ultimately, to success.

1. Successfully intelligent people motivate themselves.   It scarcely matters what talents people have if they are not motivated to use them. In many if not most environments, motivation counts at least as much as intellectual skills in the attainment of success. Individuals within any given environment—for example, a classroom or an entry-level job—tend to represent a relatively narrow range of ability but a much broader range of motivation. Motivation thus accounts for individual differences in success. For some people, motivation

will come from external sources—the approval of peers, the desire for recognition or monetary rewards, and the like. For others, it will be internal, deriving from their own satisfaction with a job well done. Most people will be both internally and externally motivated in different proportions. Whatever the source of motivation, it is critical to the expression of intelligence and to success. You have to *want* to succeed. And it is important to remember that the environment may or may not provide much motivation, so that you may have to find ways to motivate yourself.

On the whole, it is probably preferable for motivation to be internally—rather than externally—generated, for the reason that external sources tend to be transient. As a result, people who are primarily externally motivated are likely to lose their motivation when those external rewards diminish or disappear. Internally motivated individuals are able to maintain their motivation over the rises and falls of external rewards. For instance, children who are motivated to learn primarily by stars, stickers, or other tangible rewards often lose their motivation when the rewards are unavailable, whereas children who have an intrinsic interest in a topic have a natural motivation for learning that is more easily sustained.[1] Creative intelligence in particular seems to rely heavily on internal motivation. Creative people almost always love what they are doing.

Parents tend to make several mistakes with regard to motivating their children, with the result that they achieve less rather than more than they hope for. First, especially today, they tend to push too hard. Some parents are literally obsessed with their children's success. They may push them to ever higher performance in school, never satisfied unless their children are at or at least near the top of their class. They may even end up doing some or most of their homework for them. Anyone who has ever gone to a science fair for children has seen the results: professional-looking science projects that are a credit to the parents but say nothing about the children's capabilities, because the children had little or nothing to do with them.

It's not just parents; it's schools as well. I have been asked to write letters of recommendation for children applying to private kindergartens. They not only have to fill out applications (or have their parents do it for them), they also have to take an IQ test—usually, a preschool version of the Wechsler—in order to be admitted. No wonder so many kids freak out by the time they reach adolescence.

Both the children and the parents pay a price. When finally the children have to be on their own, they haven't the foggiest idea how to motivate themselves. As a college teacher, I see again and again students whose parents pushed them into a competitive school who, when they are away from home, do not know how to work on their own. No matter how strong they are intellectually, they are often motivationally impotent without parental pressure.

That is not to say that parental pressure should never be applied; rather, it should be appropriate in degree. And parental approval can be an especially effective motivator when it encourages children to undertake and complete tasks of their own volition.

The second mistake with regard to motivation is seeking for their children what parents want for themselves—by inducing them either to follow in the parents' footsteps or to live up to some ideal image. I have met any number of students in my own institution who are studying for careers because their parents have insisted on it. They have no real love of or, often, even genuine interest in what they are studying. They may become competent in the fields into which they have been pushed, but they won't be intellectual leaders in them, simply because leaders are self-motivated and always love what they are doing.[2]

My own parents wanted me to be a lawyer. When I decided to go to graduate school in psychology, my mother was not thrilled. When I got my Ph.D., she pointed out that the president of Rutgers University at the time had both a law degree and a doctoral degree in psychology, and look how successful he was. When I got tenure, she commented to the effect that I had shown myself that I could make it as a psychologist; it wasn't too late to go to law school. At this point, she was probably at least half joking. But when parents have dreams and ambitions for their children that their children do not share and wish to achieve, it is rarely a joke. There is often a residual disappointment on both sides.

Of course, it is sometimes easier to point out this parental error to others than to correct it oneself. When my son wanted to learn to play the piano, I was delighted. But he didn't practice, and eventually, to my great annoyance, he quit. So when, a few months later, he wanted to take trumpet lessons, I told him to forget it. I had already seen what had happened with the piano, and I wasn't going to buy him a trumpet and pay for lessons, only to see him quit again.

Later, when I thought about my reaction, I realized it was much too strong for the situation. Then I realized why I was so negative about Seth's playing the trumpet. I was a pianist, and I very much liked the idea of my son's becoming a pianist. When he quit, I felt as if I were giving up a part of myself. And when he wanted to play the trumpet, I was still annoyed. But in addition, I just couldn't imagine a Sternberg kid playing the trumpet. It didn't fit my image of my own child at all. Then I remembered my mother's image of me as a lawyer, and I knew that Seth was never going to realize his intellectual and other potentials if I tried to turn him into me. I had to help him become himself. He learned to play the trumpet. And today, hard to believe though it may be for me, my daughter plays the oboe.

When Seth was sixteen, he decided he wanted to become a pilot. I was convinced that despite my own total lack of interest in flying, it was the right thing for Seth. He is incredibly spatial and proved so even when he was young. Once, I brought home a piece of exercise equipment and asked him to help me put it together. He was done assembling it before I had even finished reading the instructions. Seth took flying lessons and got his pilot's license when he was seventeen. His teacher told me that Seth had soloed after less time than any other student, of any age, he had taught. Will Seth ultimately become a pilot? I don't know. What matters is that he was self-motivated to achieve a goal that was important to him. That's how people develop successful intelligence.

Teachers and employers of successfully intelligent people would do well to learn this lesson in their work with others. In my own department, I let students and junior colleagues follow their own interests, within reason, even though they may not correspond with my own. I let them find their own way not only to maximize their intellectual potential but to maximize mine. By letting students lead me, I have entered areas that I never would have explored had I insisted on their doing exactly what I, not they, wanted.

The third mistake is to rely exclusively on one kind of motivator, whether internal or external. Of course, it is important for people to do what they love. But they also need to be rewarded for their accomplishments. Successfully intelligent people combine internal and external motivation. In particular, they find ways of getting external rewards for the work they are internally motivated to accomplish. They, like myself, often marvel that they are paid for doing what they would love to do even if they weren't paid.

2. Successfully intelligent people learn to control their impulses. There are times in life when impulsive behavior is unavoidable and may even be necessary, but it tends to hinder rather than enhance intellectual work. Teachers sometimes encounter children who are capable of doing excellent work but whose capabilities are largely unrealized because of their tendency to act impulsively and without reflection. In one of his earliest books, L. L. Thurstone, an intelligence theorist at the University of Chicago, claimed that a key feature of intelligent persons is their ability to control impulsive responses.[3] Many years later, a comparative psychologist, D. Stenhouse, independently came to the same conclusion.[4] Habitual impulsiveness gets in the way of optimal performance by preventing people from bringing their full intellectual resources to bear on a problem. While endless reflection is also clearly undesirable, people should not let themselves get carried away by the first solution that occurs to them in attempting to solve a problem. Better solutions may arise after further thought.

Successfully intelligent people, whatever their line of work, may act swiftly in solving problems and making decisions, but usually only in familiar situations. They are acting from experience, not on impulse. Otherwise, they take the time necessary to think through a problem or decision.

3. Successfully intelligent people know when to persevere. Some people, even very intelligent ones, give up too easily. If things do not immediately go their way, or if their initial attempts at doing something are unsuccessful, they simply quit. They thereby lose the opportunity to complete, possibly in a highly suitable way, the tasks they undertake. It is as if the least frustration is enough to keep them from persevering.

A common characteristic among successfully intelligent people is perseverance. Success may have come only after a long string of frustrations and failures. Dean Koontz is an enormously successful writer of horror and other fiction, whose books shoot quickly up the best-seller lists. His success has enabled him to reprint, sometimes under new titles, some of his early works, which sold relatively few copies when they were first published. Upon being reissued, they are instant hits. Koontz is only one of many authors who have found that in order to achieve success, they first have to experience repeated lack of it.

At the other extreme are people who continue working on a problem long after it should have become clear that they are not going to be able to solve it, at least at that time. Alternatively, they may basically have solved the problem, but they then go on to solve it again and again. One can see in certain careers the existence of this tendency toward perseveration—continuing to try when there is no realistic hope of success. For example, a person may make an important discovery or come up with a useful invention, and thirty years later, he is still working out minor implications of the discovery or peddling the same, now outmoded, invention. At some point, colleagues expect, or at least hope, that he will move on to another problem, or try a different approach to the same problem. Instead, he continues to do the same thing, over and over again.

Not all perseverators keep going because of an initial success. Some keep going despite their lack of it. Several years back, I heard a scientist give a talk about her work on a particular biological problem. Oddly enough, she spoke about the seven years she had spent on attempts to demonstrate a particular phenomenon, all of which had failed. I expected to hear her say that she was going either to move on to a new problem or to try a new approach to the problem she was currently addressing. But amazing as it seemed, she said she planned to keep forging ahead with the approach that she had amply shown was really quite useless.

Sometimes, the environment conspires to encourage perseveration. People get pigeonholed for doing a certain thing, and then others expect them to keep doing more of it. For example, I started off studying intelligence. But during the mid-eighties, I decided I was interested in branching out and studying a new area, love. I had some ideas, and I thought that they could profitably be applied to understanding the psychology of love. My colleagues were not exactly thrilled about the expansion of my work into this new domain, however. Typical reactions were that perhaps I had run out of ideas about intelligence, or was getting soft in the head, or wanted to be another Dr. Ruth. The work was actually quite successful, and one of my articles became the first theory of love ever to be published in *Psychological Review*, the premier theoretical journal in psychology. But I reached that point because I persevered despite the lack of support.

Perseveration is not limited to career decisions. It occurs in other areas of life as well—for example, a person continues to pursue a potential romantic partner despite repeated rejections. Successfully intelligent people persevere, but when it becomes clear they are making no headway, they know it's time to quit.

4. Successfully intelligent people know how to make the most of their abilities. Many people become aware, at some time during their lives, that they are not particularly well suited to their jobs. It is as if the work they are doing requires one set of abilities, when their real strength lies in a different set of abilities. This phenomenon, of course, can occur during their schooling as well as in later life. They

may find themselves in law school and realize that their cognitive abilities would have suited them for an academic career. Or they may find themselves in medical school and come to the conclusion that their real abilities lie in business.

Such discoveries usually lead to the choice of another academic or career path. It is not unusual to find that successfully intelligent people have explored a number of options before they finally take up the pursuits for which they have the greatest ability and in which they will thus be able to excel.

Schools, unfortunately, often encourage students to capitalize on the wrong abilities. They teach career-preparation courses in which the abilities needed for success in the classroom are different from those fundamental for success in that career. For example, a law student might write brilliant legal essays but not have the ability to argue cases in a courtroom. Schools also often discourage students from pursuing careers in which they might be quite successful. Students who do not excel academically will probably not be admitted to graduate schools, when, in fact, they may have the ability to become great teachers. Conversely, those who do excel and go on to earn graduate degrees may not be able to teach at all. Successfully intelligent people know their strengths and capitalize on them.

5. Successfully intelligent people translate thought into action. Some people are very adept at coming up with solutions to the problems in their lives as well as the lives of others, but they seem unable to translate their thoughts into action. In the words of the psychologist E. R. Guthrie, they become "buried in thought."[5] No matter how good their ideas, they rarely seem to be able to do anything about them. Successfully intelligent people, on the other hand, not only have good ideas but also have the ability to act on those ideas. The same holds true of the decision-making process. People who make good decisions but who are unwilling or unable to act upon them will never benefit from them, whatever their level of intelligence. Successfully intelligent people put their decisions into action.

Having a high IQ can become a disincentive to action. People with high IQs and analytical abilities often can see more and more layers to a problem, and as a result, they become paralyzed because they can't see their way through to a solution. When action is needed, they may be unable to take it. Psychologists have studied relationships between IQ and leadership.[6] They have found that during times of relative calm, when there is no great premium on quick action, people with higher IQs are more effective as leaders than are those with lower IQs. But in times of stress, the relationship actually reverses itself. High IQ becomes an impediment to action, and the higher-IQ individual becomes a less effective leader than the lower-IQ one. Thus, the ability to think through alternative courses of action is important, but it is equally important to know when to wait and when to act.

6. Successfully intelligent people have a product orientation. Some people seem more concerned about the process by which things are done than about the resulting product. Yet it is primarily on the basis of what we produce that our accomplishments are judged, whether in school or in later life. I have had students who do first-rate research but do a clearly second- or third-rate job writing it up. They were very skillful in the process of research but less skillful in turning that process into a final product. Successfully intelligent people are concerned with process, but their ultimate focus is on product; they want results. Process without product is like a beautifully designed car without an engine. It may take intelligence to build, but it will never get you where you want to go.

The nub of the problem, I believe, is that our society encourages a consumer rather than a producer mentality. In school, for example, students spend much of their time reading and listening and taking notes. At all levels, they are merely consuming what their teachers and their textbooks tell them, while the only products they learn to produce are usually in the form of tests that measure comprehension rather than intelligence.

Are essay tests an exception; surely they measure intelligence? Perhaps so, but an essay test I took in college is not atypical. I was under the impression that essays were an opportunity to express one's creativity. But the professor really couldn't have cared less. The essays were scored on a scale from 0 to 10, and the final scores referred to the number of points the students had made that the professor wanted them to make. If we demand that students merely "consume" information and feed it back on tests, once again we are depriving them of the kind of learning experience that will be of greatest benefit in the real world, and that is how to use their intelligence. We should be just as concerned with the products our schools turn out as with the process of education.

7. Successfully intelligent people complete tasks and follow through.   The one certain prediction about "noncompleters" is that whatever they begin they will not finish. Nothing in their lives ever seems to draw quite to a close. Perhaps they are afraid to finish things because they will not know what to do with themselves next. Or they may so overwhelm themselves with the details of a project that they are unable to progress.

These people remind me of Zeno's paradox: A body in motion wishing to reach a given point must first traverse half the distance, then half of the remaining distance, then again half of the remaining, and so on ad infinitum. And if the body always goes half the remaining distance, it will never arrive at the destination. Successfully intelligent people get where they want to go, and if their goal is to solve a problem or make a decision, once they have reached it, they follow through.

I recently ventured into an intercontinental collaboration examining health-related antecedents of school failure in children living in a third-world country. The project studied, in particular, effects of parasitic infections on cognition and school performance. All of the collaborators were as pleasant as could be. But one collaborator, perhaps the most pleasant of all, almost completely sabotaged the project. Anytime he was given a task to do, he managed to find some reason not to get it done. I was reminded of the old "dog ate my homework" excuse. Ideally, we would simply have bypassed him altogether, but for political reasons we were unable to. The result was that one person almost, but not quite, caused a multiyear, multiperson, multimillion-dollar effort to go down the drain, all because he just would not follow through.

8. Successfully intelligent people are initiators. Many people seem unwilling or unable to initiate projects; they wait to be told what to do or they spend time mulling over ideas without ever making up their minds about which projects to pursue. Often, their inability to initiate comes from a fear of commitment. Consider, for example, the problem of a student trying to decide on a dissertation topic. Some students fail to complete graduate school because they can never commit themselves to a topic. A dissertation requires a substantial investment of time and energy, and they are simply unwilling to make this commitment.

Students who succeed in high school, and sometimes business people who succeed in one company, may not be particularly successful when they move on to college or to another company. They are often so used to success coming to them that they just sit back and wait for it to come to them. But in the new environment, they have to prove themselves again. And the more competitive the environment, the more they have to make things happen rather than wait for them to happen. They have to initiate and commit themselves completely to the tasks at hand.

Many people fail to initiate relationships for fear of becoming too committed. As a result, their relationships are superficial and short-lived. In terms of my triangular theory of love, they lack commitment, one of the three ingredients (the other two being intimacy and passion) needed for a complete loving relationship.[7] Even friendship requires commitment. It is a characteristic of successfully intelligent people that pertains in every aspect of their lives.

9. Successfully intelligent people are not afraid to risk failure. Fear of failure seems to start early in life and is very common especially in

individuals at the extremes of the continuum in achievement. Perhaps low achievers fear failure because they have experienced too much of it; some high achievers may not have learned to accept occasional failures as a normal part of learning. Fear of failure has been linked to low levels of motivation to achieve.[8] In contrast, those with high need to achieve tend to undertake tasks that have moderate levels of risk, tasks in which they have a good chance but no certainty of succeeding. If we always encourage our children and students to get the highest grade, we may discourage them from seeking challenges that are optimal for their level of possible accomplishment.

I have seen many able students who occasionally seem unwilling to undertake projects for fear of failing at them. As a result, they do not realize their full intellectual potential. Later on, as lawyers or doctors or scientists or business executives, they may, unless certain of success, shy away from projects that could really make a difference to their careers. Making mistakes is not tantamount to failure. We all make mistakes, and it is usually a good indication that we have not thought a problem through or have made a hasty decision. We have more work to do to get it right the next time. Successfully intelligent people make mistakes, but not the same mistake twice. They correct their mistakes and learn from them. And if they do, in fact, experience failure, they learn from that too.

10. Successfully intelligent people don't procrastinate. Procrastination seems to be a universal fact of life. We all, at some time or another, put off until later the things we know should be done now. Procrastination becomes a serious problem only when it is a uniform strategy in our way of doing things. Procrastinators look for little things to do in order to put off doing the big things. They somehow manage to get their daily work done but seem to take forever before tackling the important projects that could make a real difference in their course work or their career.

Procrastinators are always pressed for time, simply because they put things off until the last possible minute. Many students start studying for a test the night before or postpone a written assignment until a day or two before it's due. The claim that they work better under pressure is usually a rationalization. The fact is that their grades and assignments would be much better if they took the time necessary to do good work. In the business world, habitual procrastinators don't get their work done at all and may soon find themselves out of a job.

My colleague Richard Wagner and I studied procrastination in the business world.[9] We found that less senior executives had a variety of strategies for fighting procrastination. More senior and more successful executives did not have them, for the simple reason that they had no need for such strategies. Perhaps that is part of what made them both senior and successful. It goes without saying that successfully intelligent people are well aware of the penalties for procrastination. They schedule their time so that the important things get done—and done well.

11. Successfully intelligent people accept fair blame. Some people feel they can do no wrong and look for others to blame for even the slightest mishap. Some people blame themselves for everything, even if they are in no way responsible. Misattribution of blame can be seriously debilitating in both academic and business settings. One of my colleagues had a graduate student working with him who was very able and competent in research. The faculty thought the world of her, and yet she always blamed herself for anything that went wrong. It reached the point where she felt that she could do nothing right, and eventually she left our program. Another graduate student was exactly the opposite. He blamed others for things that went wrong in his work, and although it was clear to practically everyone around him that he was just not working very hard, he always blamed someone else for his inability to get things done. He too soon left the program. When something had gone wrong, successfully intelligent people accept responsibility if it is their fault. They don't make excuses for themselves or try to put the blame on someone else. And they expect others to do the same. A candid admission that you are in the wrong is the first step in getting it right the next time.

12. Successfully intelligent people reject self-pity. When things do not go just right, it is difficult not to feel sorry for ourselves. But constant self-pity is highly maladaptive. One of the students in our graduate program had certain clear disadvantages in terms of preparation and obviously felt sorry for himself. At first, others felt sorry for him too and encouraged him to pull himself up by his bootstraps and make a go of things. But the self-pity never seemed to end, and as he became sorrier and sorrier for himself, others became less and less sorry and finally impatient with him. Still, he spent more time feeling sorry for himself than making the effort required to try to compensate for his disadvantages. Self-pity for whatever reason is a barrier to doing good work. And it is no excuse for doing bad work. Successfully intelligent people have no time for self-pity. If they feel that they have been somehow wronged or put at a disadvantage, they immediately try to remedy the situation.

13. Successfully intelligent people are independent. In most of the tasks people face, they are expected to acquire a certain degree of independence. Even in the early elementary grades, children usually are expected gradually to assume some independence—remembering to bring papers home, working on their own in the classroom, completing homework on time, and so on. The inability to be independent in age-appropriate ways can seriously compromise children's chances of school success.

To some extent in school and college, and especially in graduate work and in their careers, people are expected to work independently and think for themselves. Many students seem not to learn this and rely on others to tell them what to do and, in some cases, even show them how to do it. Without such aid, they are at a total loss. The result is that they often have to seek less responsible jobs, or they never do as well as they should in the jobs they have. Successfully intelligent people rely primarily on themselves. If they want to get something done, they know the best way to do so is either by doing it themselves or by taking responsibility for someone else's getting it done. They don't expect others to take on the responsibilities that are theirs.

14. Successfully intelligent people seek to surmount personal difficulties. Inevitably, people will have personal difficulties in the course of their lives. We all can expect some real joys, but also some real sorrows. The important thing is to try to keep both the joys and the sorrows in perspective. Some people let personal difficulties interfere grossly with their work. Major life crises will almost always have some effect, whether you like it or not. But the best thing is to accept that this will happen and take it in stride. Don't wallow in your personal difficulties and let them drag you down. Indeed, in times of personal hardship, your work, as well as other people, may provide some of the help and solace you need. Successfully intelligent people know that it is a mistake to try to avoid the personal difficulties that they must often face, but to the greatest extent possible, they keep their professional and personal lives separate.

15. Successfully intelligent people focus and concentrate to achieve their goals. There are any number of people who, despite their intelligence, never seem to be able to concentrate on anything for very long. They are easily distractible, tend to have short attention spans, and thus don't get much done. To some extent, distractibility is a variable over which we do not have total control. For people who do have good concentration, it is not something they have to worry about particularly. But people who have difficulty concentrating should do their best to arrange their working environment in order to minimize distractions. In effect, they have to create an environment in which they can achieve their goals. If they do not, they will have difficulty in reaching those goals. Successfully intelligent people are aware of the circumstances under which they are able to function at their best. They create those circumstances and then use them to their maximum advantage.

16. Successfully intelligent people spread themselves neither too thin nor too thick.   People who spread themselves too thin often find they get nothing done, not because they don't work hard enough but because they make only small degrees of progress on large numbers of projects. They should recognize this tendency and try to counteract it. If they undertake multiple projects, it is important they allocate their time so that there is a reasonable probability of finishing them.

People who are unable to undertake more than one or at most two things at a given time are not necessarily at a disadvantage, as long as they do not fall behind. But undertaking too little at one time can result in missed opportunities and reduced levels of accomplishment. Successfully intelligent people avoid undertaking either more or less than they know they can handle at a single time. And they allot their time to maximize their performance.

17. Successfully intelligent people have the ability to delay gratification.   People who are unable to delay gratification seek rewards for achieving short-term goals but miss the larger rewards they could receive from accomplishing more important, long-term goals. Scientists and scholars often fail to undertake the really big projects that could make the critical difference in their careers. They write short articles instead of books because of their inability to delay the gratification that would come from the completion of longer but more substantial projects. Success is never achieved overnight; it requires one to delay gratification, sometimes for long periods of time. Successfully intelligent people do not deny themselves life's many small rewards and pleasures. But their time and intellectual energies are chiefly devoted to those achievements—and personal relationships— that will bring them the greatest pleasure in the long run.

18. Successfully intelligent people have the ability to see the forest and the trees.   I have worked with several students who, though intellectually very capable, are relatively unsuccessful in their careers because of their inability to see the forest for the trees. They obsess over small details and are unwilling or unable to see or deal with the

larger picture in the projects they undertake. They become so absorbed with the microstructure that they ignore or pay only minimal attention to the macrostructure. Similarly, some teachers become so bogged down in the everyday demands of planning individual lessons, correcting papers, and so on that they lose sight of the broader goals they want to accomplish.

There are times and places where minutiae can become important. In designing computers or spacecraft or cars, even the most minor slips can become major when the product malfunctions. But in many aspects of life, it is necessary to concentrate on the big picture, or at least never to lose sight of it. It is very easy for students, scholars, scientists, and businesspeople to become bogged down in the day-to-day details of life. If they do, they should take time to ask themselves two important questions: Why am I doing this? and What do I hope to achieve? Successfully intelligent people distinguish between the consequential and the inconsequential. They are aware of what they are doing and whether or not it will lead them where they want to go.

19. Successfully intelligent people have a reasonable level of self-confidence and a belief in their ability to accomplish their goals. Everyone needs a hefty measure of self-confidence to get through life. There can be so many blows to our self-esteem and so many setbacks that without self-confidence, we may never achieve our goals. Lack of self-confidence can gnaw away at our ability to get things done well because self-doubts become self-fulfilling prophecies. Self-confidence is often essential for success. After all, if people do not have confidence in themselves, how can they expect others to have confidence in them.

At the same time, it is important not to have too much or misplaced self-confidence. As many students fail through too much self-confidence as through too little. Individuals with too much self-confidence do not know when to admit they are wrong or in need of self-improvement. As a result, they rarely improve as rapidly as they could; sometimes they don't improve at all.

Too little or too much self-confidence can be especially damaging in job interviews. An applicant with limited self-confidence fails to inspire the confidence of those who might hire her. Excessive self-confidence can also put people off and lead to the suspicion that the applicant is not as wonderful as she thinks. Either way, the applicant doesn't get the job.

The same is true in the business world. Executives and managers with low self-confidence have trouble commanding respect and cooperation from their coworkers and employees. On the other hand, those who are *too* confident can cause resentment and block the free exchange of ideas. It is important, here as elsewhere, to strike just the right balance between too little or too much of a good thing.

20. Successfully intelligent people balance analytical, creative, and practical thinking. There are times in life when we need to be analytical; times when we need to be creative; and still other times when we need to be practical. It is important to know when to apply these thinking skills. Some students seem frequently to make the wrong judgments on this matter. They complain that their teachers fail to recognize their creativity on objective, multiple-choice tests, or that they are not given credit for how well organized their uninspired papers are. Although these students may have both analytical and creative abilities, they often put them to inappropriate use. For example, standardized multiple-choice mental-ability tests do not usually provide an opportunity to demonstrate creativity, unless they are explicitly designed to measure creativity. Research projects, on the other hand, are excellent opportunities to show creativity. The point is that it is important not only to have analytical, creative, and practical abilities but to know when to use them.

Successfully intelligent people learn what kind of thinking is expected of them in different situations and then bring to those situations the appropriate intellectual skills. Further, in problem-solving and decision-making situations, they use a continuum of all three thinking skills; they analyze the situation and come up with solutions or decisions that are both creative and have practical application.

• • •

I have described twenty characteristics of successfully intelligent people as they are reflected in both their personal attributes and their performance. They are not characteristics measured by conventional intelligence tests. We must never lose sight of the fact that what really matters most in the world is not inert intelligence but successful intelligence: that balanced combination of analytical, creative, and practical thinking skills. Successful intelligence is not an accident; it can be nurtured and developed in our schools by providing students, even at a very early age, with curricula that will challenge their creative and practical intelligence, not only their analytical skills. It is my contention that successful intelligence *should* be taught, because it is the kind of intelligence that will be the most valuable and rewarding in the real world after school—both in our work and in our personal lives. Our ultimate goal in understanding and increasing our intelligence should be the full realization in our lives of the intellectual potential we all have.

A C K N O W L E D G M E N T S

I am grateful to many individuals and organizations for their support of my work. This book was written while I was supported by major grants from the U.S. Office of Educational Research and Improvement (OERI) and the U.S. Army Research Institute (ARI). Of course, their support of my work does not imply that the position taken in this book in any way reflect official positions of these organizations or of the U.S. government.

Over the years, the members of my research group at Yale have made important contributions to my thinking, and any work I have done has drawn on the collaborative efforts of us all. I am especially grateful to my main collaborator in my work on creative intelligence, Todd Lubart; to my main collaborators in my work on practical intelligence, Richard Wagner and Wendy Williams; and to my main collaborator in work on learning disabilities, Louise Spear-Swerling, for their formative roles in the work described here. Fred Hills and Burton Beals, my editors at Simon & Schuster, provided many valuable suggestions for improving the manuscript, and Jeff Herman, my agent, helped me place the manuscript with Simon & Schuster in the first place. I cannot fail to thank as well my wife, Alejandra Campos, and my children, Seth and Sara Sternberg, whose many lessons can be found sprinkled throughout these pages.

Chapter One
Beyond IQ to Successful Intelligence

1. R. Herrnstein and C. Murray, *The Bell Curve* (New York: Free Press, 1994).

2. S. E. Morison, *The Oxford History of the American People*, vol. 2 (New York: Penguin Books, 1972).

3. S. J. Ceci, *On Intelligence . . . More or Less: A Bio-ecological Treatise on Intellectual Development* (Englewood Cliffs, N.J.: Prentice-Hall, 1990).

4. Morison, *The Oxford History of the American People*.

5. Ibid.

Chapter Two
What IQ Tells Us

1. F. Galton, *Inquiry into Human Faculty and Its Development* (London: Macmillan, 1883).

2. A. Binet and T. Simon, *The Development of Intelligence in Children* (1905; Baltimore: Williams & Wilkins, 1916).

3. Ibid.

4. R. L. Thorndike, E. P. Hagen, and J. M. Sattler, *Technical Manual for the Stanford-Binet Intelligence Scale*, 4th ed. (Chicago: Riverside, 1986).

5. Herrnstein and Murray, *The Bell Curve*.

6. J. R. Flynn, "Massive IQ Gains in 14 Nations: What IQ Tests Really Measure," *Psychological Bulletin* 101 (1987), 171–91.

7. D. K. Detterman and R. J. Sternberg, eds., *How and How Much Can Intelligence Be Increased?* (Norwood, N.J.: Ablex, 1982).

8. I. Lazar and R. Darlington, "Lasting Effects of Early Education: A Report from the Consortium for Longitudinal Studies," *Monographs of the Society for Research in Child Development* 47, nos. 2–3 (1982), Serial No. 195. E. Zigler and W. Berman, "Discerning the Future of Early Childhood Intervention," *American Psychologist* 38 (1983), 894–906.

9. M. J. Adams, coordinator, *Odyssey: A Curriculum for Thinking* (Watertown, Mass.: Mastery Education Corporation, 1986).

10. S. Messick, *The Effectiveness of Coaching for the SAT: Review and Reanalysis of Research from the Fifties to the FTC* (Princeton: Educational Testing Service, 1980).

11. R. J. Sternberg, "Most Vocabulary Is Learned from Context," in M. G. McKeown and M. E. Curtis, eds., *The Nature of Vocabulary Acquisition* (Hillsdale, N.J.: Lawrence Erlbaum, 1987), pp. 89–105.

12. J. B. Baron and R. J. Sternberg, eds., *Teaching Thinking Skills: Theory and Practice* (New York: Freeman, 1987).

Chapter Three
What IQ Doesn't Tell Us

1. C. A. Dweck, "Self Theories and Goals: Their Role in Motivation, Personality, and Development," in R. A. Dienstbier, ed., *Nebraska Symposium on Motivation, 1990: Perspectives on Motivation* (Lincoln: University of Nebraska Press, 1991), pp. 199–235.

2. R. J. Sternberg and D. K. Detterman, eds., *What Is Intelligence? Contemporary Viewpoints on Its Nature and Definition* (Norwood, N.J.: Ablex, 1986).

3. C. E. Spearman, " 'General Intelligence' Objectively Determined and Measured," *American Journal of Psychology* 15 (1904), 201–93. C. Spearman, *The Abilities of Man* (London: Macmillan, 1927).

4. P. C. Wason, "On the Failure to Eliminate Hypotheses in a Conceptual Task," *Quarterly Journal of Experimental Psychology* 12 (1960), 129–40.

5. B. Skyrms, *Choice and Chance: An Introduction to Inductive Logic,* 2d ed. (Encino, Calif.: Dickerson, 1975).

6. J. P. Guilford, "Cognitive Psychology's Ambiguities: Some Suggested Remedies," *Psychological Review* 89 (1982), 48–59.

7. R. B. Cattell, *Abilities: Their Structure, Growth and Action* (Boston: Houghton Mifflin, 1971).

8. A. Willner, "An Experimental Analysis of Analogical Reasoning," *Psychological Reports* 15 (1964), 479–94.

9. A. R. Jensen, "Psychometric *g* as a Focus of Concerted Research Effort," *Intelligence* 11 (1987), 193–98.

10. Ibid.

11. W. Mischel, *Personality and Assessment* (New York: Wiley, 1968).

12. E. B. Hunt, "Mechanics of Verbal Ability," *Psychological Review* 85 (1978), 109–30.

13. K. E. Stanovich, "Reconceptualizing Intelligence: Dysrationalia as an Intuition Pump," *Educational Researcher* 23, no. 4 (1994), 11–22.

14. P. T. Barrett and H. J. Eysenck, "Brain Evoked Potentials and Intelligence: The Hendrickson Paradigm," *Intelligence* 16 (1992), 361–81.

15. P. A. McGarry, R. M. Stelmack, and K. B. Campbell, "Intelligence, Reaction Time, and Event-Related Potentials," *Intelligence* 16 (1992), 289–313. T. E.

Reed and A. R. Jensen, "Conduction Velocity in a Brain Nerve Pathway of Normal Adults Correlates with Intelligence Level," *Intelligence* 16 (1992), 259–72. P. A. Vernon and M. Mori, "Intelligence, Reaction Times, and Peripheral Nerve Conduction Velocity," *Intelligence* 8 (1992), 273–88.

16. R. J. Haier, B. Siegel, C. Tang, L. Abel, and M. S. Buchsbaum, "Intelligence and Changes in Regional Cerebral Glucose Metabolic Rate Following Learning," *Intelligence* 16 (1992), 415–26.

17. J. C. Wickett and P. A. Vernon, "Peripheral Nerve Conduction Velocity, Reaction Time, and Intelligence: An Attempt to Replicate Vernon and Mori," *Intelligence* 18 (1994), 127–32.

18. A. E. Hendrickson and D. E. Hendrickson, "The Biological Basis for Individual Differences in Intelligence," *Personality & Individual Differences* 1 (1980), 3–33.

19. M. Mishkin and H. L. Petri, "Memories and Habits: Some Implications for the Analysis of Learning and Retention," in L. R. Squire and N. Butters, eds., *Neurophysiology of Memory* (New York: Guilford, 1984), pp. 287–96.

20. R. Serpell, "The Cultural Construction of Intelligence," in W. J. Lonner and R. S. Malpass, eds., *Psychology and Culture* (Boston: Allyn & Bacon, 1994).

21. R. Serpell, *The Significance of Schooling: Life Journeys in an African Society* (Cambridge, Eng.: University of Cambridge Press, 1993).

22. S. B. Sarason and J. Doris, *Educational Handicap, Public Policy, and Social History* (New York: Free Press, 1979).

23. H. J. Eysenck and L. Kamin, *The Intelligence Controversy: H. J. Eysenck versus Leon Kamin* (New York: Wiley, 1981).

24. S. J. Ceci, "How Much Does Schooling Influence General Intelligence and Its Cognitive Components? A Reassessment of the Evidence," *Developmental Psychology* 27, no. 5 (1991), 703–22.

25. R. B. Cattell and A. K. Cattell, *Test of g: Culture Fair, Scale 3* (Champaign, Ill.: Institute for Personality and Ability Testing, 1963).

26. A. R. Jensen, *Bias in Mental Testing* (New York: Free Press, 1980).

27. L. L. Thurstone, *The Nature of Intelligence* (New York: Harcourt Brace, 1924).

28. J. W. Berry, "Radical Cultural Relativism and the Concept of Intelligence," in J. W. Berry and P. R. Dasen, eds., *Culture and Cognition: Readings in Cross-Cultural Psychology* (London: Methuen, 1974), pp. 225–29.

29. P. Greenfield, "Testing in Collectivistic Cultures," *American Psychologist* (in press).

30. R. J. Sternberg and B. Rifkin, "The Development of Analogical Reasoning Processes," *Journal of Experimental Child Psychology* 27 (1979), 195–232.

31. Ceci, "How Much Does Schooling Influence General Intelligence."

32. D. A. Wagner, "Memories of Morocco: The Influence of Age, Schooling and Environment on Memory," *Cognitive Psychology* 10 (1978), 1–28.

33. S. J. Ceci and A. Roazzi, "The Effects of Context on Cognition: Postcards from Brazil," in R. J. Sternberg and R. K. Wagner, eds., *Mind in Context: Interac-*

tionist Perspectives on Human Intelligence (New York: Cambridge University Press, 1994), pp. 74–101.

34. S. J. Ceci and U. Bronfenbrenner, "Don't Forget to Take the Cupcakes Out of the Oven: Strategic Time-Monitoring, Prospective Memory and Context," *Child Development* 56 (1985), 175–90.

35. A. D. Schliemann and V. P. Magalhües, *Proportional Reasoning: From Shops, to Kitchens, Laboratories, and, Hopefully Schools* (Proceedings of the Fourteenth International Conference for the Psychology of Mathematical Education, Oaxtepec, Mexico, 1990).

36. H. Gardner, *Multiple Intelligences: The Theory in Practice* (New York: Basic Books, 1993).

37. D. Lubinsky and C. P. Benbow, "An Opportunity for 'Accuracy,' " *Contemporary Psychology* 40, no. 10 (1995), 939–40. R. J. Sternberg, "A Triarchic Model for Teaching and Assessing Students in General Psychology," *General Psychologist* 30, no. 2 (1994), 42–48.

Chapter Four
The Three Keys to Successful Intelligence

1. R. J. Sternberg, "Implicit Theories of Intelligence, Creativity, and Wisdom," *Journal of Personality and Social Psychology* 49 (1985), 607–27.

2. R. J. Sternberg, R. K. Wagner, and L. Okagaki, "Practical Intelligence: The Nature and Role of Tacit Knowledge in Work and at School," in H. Reese and J. Puckett, eds, *Advances in Lifespan Development* (Hillsdale, N.J.: Erlbaum, 1993), pp. 205–27. R. K. Wagner and R. J. Sternberg, "Practical Intelligence in Real-World Pursuits: The Role of Tacit Knowledge," *Journal of Personality and Social Psychology* 49 (1985), 436–58.

3. R. J. Sternberg, *In Search of the Human Mind* (Orlando, Fla.: Harcourt Brace College Publishers, 1995).

4. R. J. Sternberg, *Beyond IQ: A Triarchic Theory of Human Intelligence* (New York: Cambridge University Press, 1985).

5. M. Cole, J. Gay, J. Glick, and D. W. Sharp, *The Cultural Context of Learning and Thinking* (New York: Basic Books, 1971).

6. L. Spear-Swerling, Personal communication.

7. R. Edgerton, *The Cloak of Competence* (Berkeley: University of California Press, 1967).

8. L. Okagaki and R. J. Sternberg, "Parental Beliefs and Children's School Performance," *Child Development* 64, no. 1 (1993), 36–56.

9. S. B. Heath, *Ways with Words* (New York: Cambridge University Press, 1983).

10. C. E. Snow, W. S. Barnes, J. Chandler, J. F. Goodman, and L. Hemphill, *Unfulfilled Expectations: Home and School Influences on Literacy* (Cambridge, Mass: Harvard University Press, 1991).

11. R. J. Sternberg and P. Clinkenbeard, "A Triarchic View of Identifying, Teaching, and Assessing Gifted Children," *Roeper Review* 17, no. 4 (1995), 255–60. R. J. Sternberg, M. Ferrari, P. Clinkenbeard, and E. L. Grigorenko, "Identification, Instruction, and Assessment of Gifted Children: A Construct Validation of a Triarchic Model," *Gifted Child Quarterly* (in press).

12. Sternberg, *In Search of the Human Mind.*

13. M. Csikszentmihalyi, "Society, Culture, and Person: A Systems View of Creativity," in R. J. Sternberg, ed., *The Nature of Creativity* (New York: Cambridge University Press, 1988), pp. 325–39.

Chapter Five
Finding Good Solutions with Analytical Intelligence

1. R. J. Sternberg, "Intelligence and Nonentrenchment," *Journal of Educational Psychology* 73 (1981), 1–16.

2. M. T. H. Chi, R. Glaser, and E. Rees, "Expertise in Problem Solving," in R. J. Sternberg, ed., *Advances in Psychology of Human Intelligence,* vol. 1 (Hillsdale, N.J.: Erlbaum, 1982), pp. 7–75. J. Larkin, J. McDermott, D. P. Simon, and H. A. Simon, "Expert and Novice Performance in Solving Physics Problems," *Science* 208 (1980), 1335–42.

3. W. Mischel, Y. Shoda, and P. K. Peake, "The Nature of Adolescent Competencies Predicted by Pre-School Delay of Gratification," *Journal of Personality and Social Psychology* 54 (1988), 687–96.

4. M. Snyder, E. D. Tanke, and E. Berscheid, "Social Perception and Interpersonal Behavior: On the Self-Fulfilling Nature of Social Stereotypes," *Journal of Personality and Social Psychology* 35 (1977), 656–66.

5. R. R. Rosenthal and L. Jacobson, *Pygmalion in the Classroom* (New York: Holt, Rinehart & Winston, 1968).

6. E. Walster, V. Aronson, D. Abrahams, and L. Rottmann, "Importance of Physical Attractiveness in Dating Behavior," *Journal of Personality and Social Psychology* 4 (1966), 508–16.

7. E. Hatfield and S. Sprecher, *Mirror, Mirror . . . The Importance of Looks in Everyday Life* (Albany: State University of New York Press, 1986).

8. R. K. Wagner and R. J. Sternberg, "Executive Control in Reading Comprehension," in B. K. Britton and S. M. Glynn, eds., *Executive Control Processes in Reading* (Hillsdale, N.J.: Erlbaum, 1987), pp. 1–21.

9. G. Labouvie-Vief, "Beyond Formal Operations: Uses and Limits of Pure Logic in Life Span Development," *Human Development* 23 (1980), 141–61. G. Labouvie-Vief, "Wisdom as Integrated Thought: Historical and Developmental Perspectives," in R. J. Sternberg, ed., *Wisdom: Its Nature, Origins, and Development* (New York: Cambridge University Press, 1990), pp. 52–83. J. Pascual-Leone, "Attentional, Dialectic, and Mental Effort," in M. L. Commons, F. A. Richards, and C. Armon, eds., *Beyond Formal Operations* (New York:

Plenum, 1984). J. Pascual-Leone, "An Essay on Wisdom: Toward Organismic Processes That Make It Possible," in Sternberg, ed., *Wisdom*, pp. 244–78. K. F. Riegel, "Dialectical Operations: The Final Period of Cognitive Development," *Human Development* 16 (1973), 346–70.

10. A. Newell and H. A. Simon, *Human Problem Solving* (Englewood Cliffs, N.J.: Prentice-Hall, 1972).

11. T. Gladwin, *East Is a Big Bird: Navigation and Logic on Puluwat Atoll* (Cambridge, Mass.: Harvard University Press, 1970).

12. C. Lévi-Strauss, *The Savage Mind* (Chicago: University of Chicago Press, 1966).

13. I. Yanis and D. E. Meyers, "Activation and Metacognition of Inaccessible Stored Information: Potential Bases of Incubation Effects in Problem Solving," *Journal of Experimental Psychology: Learning, Memory, and Cognition* 13 (1987), 187–205.

14. B. F. Anderson, *Cognitive Psychology* (New York: Academic Press, 1975).

15. C. A. Kaplan and J. E. Davidson, *Incubation Effects in Problem Solving* (manuscript submitted for publication, 1989).

16. R. D. Luce and H. Raifa, *Games and Decisions* (New York: Wiley, 1957).

17. H. A. Simon, *Administrative Behavior*, 2d ed. (Totowa, N.J.: Littlefields, Adams, 1957).

18. D. Kahneman and A. Tversky, "Subjective Probability: A Judgment of Representativeness," *Cognitive Psychology* 3 (1972), 430–54.

19. L. Krantz, *What the Odds Are: A-to-Z Odds on Everything You Hoped or Feared Could Happen* (New York: Harper Perennial, 1992).

20. M. D. Shook and R. L. Shook, *The Book of Odds* (New York: Penguin, 1991).

21. Krantz, *What the Odds Are*.

22. Shook and Shook, *The Book of Odds*.

23. A. Tversky and D. Kahneman, "Availability: A Heuristic for Judging Frequency and Probability," *Cognitive Psychology* 5 (1973), 207–32.

24. B. Fischhoff, P. Slovic, and S. Lichtenstein, "Knowing with Certainty: The Appropriateness of Extreme Confidence," *Journal of Experimental Psychology: Human Perception and Performance* 3 (1977), 552–64.

25. B. Fischhoff, "Judgment and Decision Making," in R. J. Sternberg and E. E. Smith, eds, *The Psychology of Human Thought* (New York: Cambridge University Press, 1988), pp. 153–87.

Chapter Six
Finding Good Problems with Creative Intelligence

1. R. J. Sternberg and T. I. Lubart, *Defying the Crowd: Cultivating Creativity in a Culture of Conformity* (New York: Free Press, 1995).

2. Ibid.

3. J. Garcia and R. A. Koelling, "The Relation of Cue to Consequence in Avoidance Learning, *Psychonomic Science* 4 (1966), 123–24.

4. R. J. Sternberg, *Beyond IQ: A Triarchic Theory of Human Intelligence* (New York: Cambridge University Press, 1985). R. J. Sternberg, ed., *The Nature of Creativity: Contemporary Psychological Perspectives* (New York: Cambridge University Press, 1988). Sternberg and Lubart, *Defying the Crowd.*

5. R. C. Schank, *The Creative Attitude* (New York: Macmillan, 1988).

6. T. M. Amabile, *The Social Psychology of Creativity* (New York: Springer-Verlag, 1983).

7. Sternberg and Lubart, *Defying the Crowd.*

8. Amabile, *The Social Psychology of Creativity.*

9. B. A. Hennessey and T. M. Amabile, "The Conditions of Creativity," in Sternberg, ed. *The Nature of Creativity,* pp. 11–38.

10. T. I. Lubart and R. J. Sternberg, "An Investment Approach to Creativity: Theory and Data," in S. M. Smith, T. B. Ward, and R. A. Finke, eds., *The Creative Cognition Approach* (Cambridge, Mass: MIT Press, 1995), pp. 269–302.

11. R. J. Sternberg, *In Search of the Human Mind* (Orlando, Fla.: Harcourt Brace College Publishers, 1995). R. J. Sternberg and W. M. Williams, "Parenting Toward Cognitive Competence," in M. H. Bornstein, ed., *Handbook of Parenting,* vol. 4 (Mahwah, N.J.: Erlbaum, 1995), pp. 259–75.

12. Sternberg and Lubart, *Defying the Crowd.*

13. N. Kogan and M. A. Wallach, *Risk Taking: A Study in Cognition and Personality* (New York: Holt, Rinehart & Winston, 1964).

14. D. N. Jackson, L. Hourany, and N. J. Vidmar, "A Four-Dimensional Interpretation of Risk Taking," *Journal of Personality* 40 (1972), 483–501.

15. Amabile, *The Social Psychology of Creativity.*

16. Sternberg, *Beyond IQ.*

17. H. E. Gruber, "The Self-Construction of the Extraordinary," in R. J. Sternberg and J. E. Davidson, eds., *Conceptions of Giftedness* (New York: Cambridge University Press, 1986), pp. 247–63.

18. H. W. Stevenson and J. W. Stigler, *The Learning Gap* (New York: Summit, 1992).

19. G. Plimpton, ed., *Poets at Work* (New York: Viking Penguin, 1989), p. 8.

20. F. L. Holmes, *Lavoisier and the Chemistry of Life: An Exploration of Scientific Creativity* (Madison: University of Wisconsin Press, 1985).

21. P. A. Frensch and R. J. Sternberg, "Expertise and Intelligent Thinking: When Is It Worse to Know Better?" in R. J. Sternberg, ed., *Advances in the Psychology of Human Intelligence,* vol. 5 (Hillsdale, N.J.: Erlbaum, 1989), pp. 157–58.

22. M. Csikszentmihalyi, "Society, Culture, and Person: A Systems View of Creativity," in *The Nature of Creativity,* ed. R. J. Sternberg (New York: Cambridge University Press, 1988), pp. 325–39.

23. Amabile, *The Social Psychology of Creativity.*

Chapter Seven
Making Solutions Work with Practical Intelligence

1. R. J. Sternberg, "Implicit Theories of Intelligence, Creativity, and Wisdom," *Journal of Personality and Social Psychology* 49 (1985), 607–27.

2. D. C. McClelland, "Testing for Competence Rather than for 'Intelligence,'" *American Psychologist* 28 (1973), 1–14.

3. G. V. Barrett and R. L. Depinet, "A Reconsideration of Testing for Competence Rather than for Intelligence," *American Psychologist* 46 (1991), 1012–24.

4. L. S. Gottfredson, "Societal Consequences of the g Factor," *Journal of Vocational Behavior* 29 (1986), 379–410. J. Hawk, "Real World Implications of g," *Journal of Vocational Behavior* 29 (1986), 411–14. F. L. Schmidt and J. E. Hunter, "Employment Testing: Old Theories and New Research Findings," *American Psychologist* 36 (1981), 1128–37.

5. A. K. Wigdor and W. R. Garner, eds., *Ability Testing: Uses, Consequences, and Controversies* (Washington, D.C.: National Academy Press, 1982).

6. J. E. Hunter and R. F. Hunter, "Validity and Utility of Alternative Predictors of Job Performance," *Psychological Bulletin* 96 (1984), 72–98. Schmidt and Hunter, "Employment Testing."

7. Ibid.

8. R. Herrnstein and C. Murray, *The Bell Curve* (New York: Free Press, 1994).

9. Ibid.

10. C. Schooler, "Psychological Effects of Complex Environments During the Life Span: A Review and Theory," in C. Schooler and K. Warner Schaie, eds., *Cognitive Functioning and Social Structure over the Life Course* (Norwood, N.J.: Ablex, 1987), pp. 24–49.

11. U. Neisser, "General, Academic, and Artificial Intelligence," in L. Resnick, ed., *Human Intelligence: Perspectives on Its Theory and Measurement* (Hillsdale, N.J.: Erlbaum, 1976), pp. 179–89.

12. S. A. Williams, N. W. Denney, and M. Schadler, "Elderly Adults' Perception of Their Own Cognitive Development During the Adult Years," *International Journal of Aging and Human Development* 16 (1983), 147–58.

13. J. L. Horn and R. B. Cattell, "Refinement and Test of the Theory of Fluid and Crystallized Intelligence," *Journal of Educational Psychology* 57 (1966), 253–70.

14. J. B. Carroll, *Human Cognitive Abilities* (New York: Cambridge University Press, 1993).

15. R. A. Dixon and P. B. Baltes, "Toward Life-Span Research on the Functions and Pragmatics of Intelligence," in R. J. Sternberg and R. K. Wagner, eds., *Practical Intelligence: Nature and Origins of Competence in the Everyday World* (New York: Cambridge University Press, 1986), pp. 203–35.

16. N. W. Denney and A. M. Palmer, "Adult Age Differences on Traditional

and Practical Problem-Solving Measures," *Journal of Gerontology* 36 (1981), 323–28.

17. F. A. Mosher and J. R. Hornsby, "On Asking Questions," in J. S. Bruner, R. R. Oliver, and P. M. Greenfield, eds., *Studies in Cognitive Growth* (New York: Wiley, 1966).

18. S. W. Cornelius and A. Caspi, "Everyday Problem Solving in Adulthood and Old Age," *Psychology and Aging* 2 (1987), 144–53.

19. P. B. Baltes and M. M. Baltes, "Psychological Perspectives on Successful Aging: A Model of Selective Optimization with Compensation," in P. B. Baltes and M. M. Baltes, eds., *Successful Aging: Perspectives from the Behavioral Sciences* (Cambridge: Cambridge University Press, 1990), pp. 1–34.

20. T. A Salthouse, "Effects of Age on Skill in Typing," *Journal of Experimental Psychology: General* 113 (1984), 345–71.

21. S. Scribner, "Studying Working Intelligence," in B. Rogoff and J. Lave, eds., *Everyday Cognition: Its Development in Social Context* (Cambridge, Mass.: Harvard University Press, 1984), pp. 9–40. S. Scribner, "Thinking in Action: Some Characteristics of Practical Thought," in Sternberg and Wagner, eds., *Practical Intelligence*, pp. 13–30.

22. S. J. Ceci and J. Liker, "Academic and Nonacademic Intelligence: An Experimental Separation," in Sternberg and Wagner, eds., *Practical Intelligence*, pp. 119–42. S. J. Ceci and J. Liker, "Stalking the IQ-Expertise Relation: When the Critics Go Fishing," *Journal of Experimental Psychology: General* 117 (1988), 96–100.

23. J. Lave, M. Murtaugh, and O. de la Roche, "The Dialectic of Arithmetic in Grocery Shopping," in Rogoff and Lave, eds., *Everyday Cognition*, pp. 67–94.

24. Ibid.

25. T. N. Carraher, D. Carraher, and A. D. Schliemann, "Mathematics in the Streets and in Schools," *British Journal of Developmental Psychology* 3 (1985), 21–29.

26. D. Dörner and H. Kreuzig, "Problemlosefahigkeit und Intelligenz," *Psychologische Rundschaus* 34 (1983), 185–92. D. Dörner, H. Kreuzig, F. Reither, and T. Staudel, *Lohhausen: Vom Umgang mit Unbestimmtheir und Komplexitat* (Bern: Huber, 1983).

27. Sternberg, "Implicit Theories of Intelligence, Creativity, and Wisdom." R. J. Sternberg and D. Caruso, "Practical Modes of Knowing," in E. Eisner, ed., *Learning the Ways of Knowing* (Chicago: University of Chicago Press, 1985), pp. 133–58. R. K. Wagner, "Tacit Knowledge in Everyday Intelligent Behavior," *Journal of Personality and Social Psychology* 52 (1987), 1236–47. R. K. Wagner and R. J. Sternberg, "Tacit Knowledge and Intelligence in the Everyday World," in Sternberg and Wagner, eds., *Practical Intelligence*, pp. 51–83.

28. J. A. Horvath, G. B. Forsythe, P. Sweeney, J. McNally, J. Wattendorf, W. M. Williams, and R. J. Sternberg, "Tacit Knowledge and Military Leadership: Evidence from Officer Interviews," *ARI Technical Report* (Alexandria, Va.: U. S.

Army Research Institute for the Behavioral and Social Sciences, 1994). R. J. Sternberg, R. K. Wagner, W. M. Williams, and J. A. Horvath, "Testing Common Sense," *American Psychologist* 50, no. 11 (1995), 912–27.

29. Sternberg, Wagner, and Okagaki, "Practical Intelligence." Sternberg, Wagner, Williams, and Horvath, "Testing Common Sense."

30. Wagner, "Tacit Knowledge in Everyday Intelligent Behavior." R. K. Wagner and R. J. Sternberg, "Practical Intelligence in Real-World Pursuits: The Role of Tacit Knowledge," *Journal of Personality and Social Psychology* 49 (1985), 436–58.

31. W. M. Williams and R. J. Sternberg, *Success Acts for Managers* (Orlando, Fla.: Harcourt Brace, in press).

32. Wigdor and Garner, *Ability Testing*.

33. Wagner and Sternberg, "Practical Intelligence in Real-World Pursuits."

34. Williams and Sternberg, *Success Acts for Managers*.

35. A. R. Jensen, "Test Validity: *g* Versus 'Tacit Knowledge,'" *Current Directions in Psychological Science* 1 (1993), 9–10. M. J. Ree and J. A. Earles, "*g* Is to Psychology What Carbon Is to Chemistry: A Reply to Sternberg and Wagner, McClelland, and Calfee," *Current Directions in Psychological Science* 1 (1993), 11–12. F. L. Schmidt and J. E. Hunter, "Tacit Knowledge, Practical Intelligence, General Mental Ability, and Job Knowledge," *Current Directions in Psychological Science* 1 (1993), 8–9.

36. Wagner and Sternberg, "Practical Intelligence in Real-World Pursuits." R. K. Wagner and R. J. Sternberg, "Street Smarts," in K. E. Clark and M. B. Clark, eds., *Measures of Leadership* (West Orange, N.J.: Leadership Library of America, 1990), pp. 493–504.

37. A. S. Eddy, *The Relationship Between the Tacit Knowledge Inventory for Managers and the Armed Services Vocational Aptitude Battery* (master's thesis, St. Mary's University, San Antonio, Texas, 1988).

38. Wagner, "Tacit Knowledge in Everyday Intelligent Behavior." Wagner and Sternberg, "Practical Intelligence in Real-World Pursuits."

39. Sternberg, Wagner, and Okagaki, "Practical Intelligence."

40. *Ibid.*

41. R. J. Sternberg, L. Okagaki, and A. Jackson, "Practical Intelligence for Success in School," *Educational Leadership* 48 (1990), 35–39. H. Gardner, M. Krechevsky, R. J. Sternberg, and L. Okagaki, "Intelligence in Context: Enhancing Students' Practical Intelligence for School," in K. McGilly, ed., *Classroom Lessons: Integrating Cognitive Theory and Classroom Practice* (Cambridge, Mass.: Bradford Books, 1994), pp. 105–27.

42. W. Williams, T. Blythe, N. White, R. Sternberg, and H. Gardner, *Practical Intelligence for School* (New York: HarperCollins, 1996).

Chapter Eight
Self-activation Versus Self-sabotage

1. M. Lepper, D. Greene, and R. Nisbett, "Undermining Children's Intrinsic Interests with Extrinsic Rewards: A Test of the 'Overjustification' Hypothesis," *Journal of Personality and Social Psychology* 28 (1973), 129–37.

2. H. E. Gruber, "The Self-Construction of the Extraordinary," in R. J. Sternberg and J. E. Davidson, eds., *Conceptions of Giftedness* (New York: Cambridge University Press, 1986), pp. 247–63.

3. L. L. Thurstone, *The Nature of Intelligence* (New York: Harcourt Brace, 1924).

4. D. Stenhouse, *The Evolution of Intelligence: A General Theory and Some of Its Implications* (New York: Harper & Row, 1973).

5. E. R. Guthrie, *The Psychology of Learning* (New York: Harper & Brothers, 1935).

6. F. E. Fiedler and T. G. Link, "Leader Intelligence, Interpersonal Stress, and Task Performance," in R. J. Sternberg and R. K. Wagner, eds., *Mind in Context: Interactionist Perspectives on Human Intelligence* (New York: Cambridge University Press, 1994), pp. 152–67.

7. R. J. Sternberg, *The Triangle of Love* (New York: Basic Books, 1988).

8. D. C. McClelland, *Human Motivation* (New York: Scott, Foresman, 1985).

9. R. K. Wagner and R. J. Sternberg, "Practical Intelligence in Real-World Pursuits: The Role of Tacit Knowledge," *Journal of Personality and Social Psychology* 49 (1985), 436–58.

BIBLIOGRAPHY

Allen, B. A., and Boykin, A. W. "The Influence of Contextual Factors on Afro-American Children's Performance: Effects of Movement Opportunity and Music." *International Journal of Psychology* 26 (1991), 373–87.

Asch, S. "Forming Impressions of Personality." *Journal of Abnormal and Social Psychology* 41 (1946), 258–90.

Bandura, A. *Social Learning Theory.* Englewood Cliffs, N.J.: Prentice-Hall, 1977.

Berry, J. W. *Human Ecology and Cognitive Style: Comparative Studies in Cultural and Psychological Adaptation.* New York: Wiley, 1976.

Berscheid, E., and Walster, E. H. *Interpersonal Attraction.* 2d ed. Reading, Mass.: Addison-Wesley, 1978.

Boykin, A. W. "Reading Achievement and the Social Frame of Reference of Afro-American Children." *Journal of Negro Education* 53, no. 4 (1984), 464–73.

Bradley, R. H., and Caldwell, B. M. "The Relation of Infants' Home Environment to Achievement Test Performance in First Grade: A Follow-up Study." *Child Development* 52 (1984), 708–10.

Byrne, D. *The Attraction Paradigm.* San Diego, Cal.: Academic Press, 1971.

Cattell, J. M. "Mental Tests and Measurements." *Mind* 15 (1890), 373–80.

Cronbach, L. J. *Essentials of Psychological Testing.* 5th ed. New York: Harper & Row, 1990.

Dennis, W. *Children of the Crèche.* New York: Appleton-Century-Crofts, 1973.

Eysenck, H. J. "Intelligence Assessment: A Theoretical and Experimental Approach." *British Journal of Educational Psychology* 37 (1967), 81–98.

Gardner, H. *Creating Minds.* New York: Basic Books, 1994.

———. *Frames of Mind: The Theory of Multiple Intelligences.* New York: Basic Books, 1983.

Goddard, H. H. "Mental Tests and Immigrants." *Journal of Delinquency* 2 (1917), 243–77.

Goleman, D. *Emotional Intelligence.* New York: Bantam, 1995.

Gottfredson, L. S. "Societal Consequences of the g Factor." *Journal of Vocational Behavior* 29 (1986), 379–410.

Guilford, J. P. *The Nature of Human Intelligence.* New York: McGraw-Hill, 1967.

———. *Psychometric Methods.* New York: McGraw-Hill, 1954.

Herrnstein, R. J., Nickerson, R. S., de Sanchez, M., and Swets, J. A. "Teaching Thinking Skills." *American Psychologist* 41 (1986), 1279–89.

Horn, J. L. "Organization of Abilities and the Development of Intelligence." *Psychological Review* 75 (1968), 242–59.

———. "The Theory of Fluid and Crystallized Intelligence in Relation to Concepts of Cognitive Psychology and Aging in Adulthood." In F. I. M. Craik and Trehub, eds., *Aging and Cognitive Processes.* New York: Plenum, 1982, pp. 237–78.

Horn, J. L., and Knapp, J. R. "On the Subjective Character of the Empirical Base of Guilford's Structure of Intellect Model." *Psychological Bulletin* 80 (1973), 33–43.

Hunter, J. E. "Cognitive Ability, Cognitive Aptitudes, Job Knowledge, and Job Performance." *Journal of Vocational Behavior* 29 (1986), 340–62.

Jackson, D. N., Hourany, L., and Vidmar, N. J. "A Four-Dimensional Interpretation of Risk Taking." *Journal of Personality* 40 (1972), 483–501.

Kingston, W. *Innovative, Creativity, and Law.* Boston: Kluwer Academic, 1990.

Kogan, N., and Wallach, M. A. *Risk Taking: A Study in Cognition and Personality.* New York: Holt, Rinehart & Winston, 1964.

Labouvie-Vief, G. "Dynamic Development and the Nature of Autonomy: A Theoretical Prologue." *Human Development* 25 (1982), 161–91.

Larkin, J., McDermott, J., Simon, D. P., and Simon, H. A. "Expert and Novice Performance in Solving Physics Problems." *Science* 208 (1980), 1335–42.

Lazar, I., Darlington, R., Murray, H., Royce, J., and Snipper, A. "Lasting Effects of Early Education: A Report from the Consortium for Longitudinal Studies." *Monographs of the Society for Research in Child Development* 47, nos. 2–3 (1982), Serial No. 195.

Malkiel, B. G. *A Random Walk Down Wall Street.* 4th ed. 1973; New York: W. W. Norton, 1985.

Murtaugh, M. "The Practice of Arithmetic by American Grocery Shoppers." *Anthropology and Education Quarterly,* Fall 1985.

Nisbett, R. "Race, IQ, and Scientism." In S. Fraser, ed., *The Bell Curve Wars: Race, Intelligence and the Future of America.* New York: Basic Books, 1995, pp. 36–57.

Pascual-Leone, J. "An Essay on Wisdom: Toward Organismic Processes That Make It Possible. In R. J. Sternberg, ed., *Wisdom: Its Nature, Origins, and Development.* New York: Cambridge University Press, 1990, pp. 244–78.

Phillips, D. A. "The Illusion of Incompetence Among Academically Competent Children. *Child Development* 55 (1984), 2000–16.

———. "Socialization of Perceived Academic Competence Among Highly Competent Children." *Child Development* 58 (1987), 1308–20.

Phillips, D. A., and Zimmerman, M. "The Developmental Course of Perceived Competence and Incompetence Among Competent Children." In R. J. Sternberg and J. Kolligian, Jr., eds., *Competence Considered.* New Haven: Yale University Press, 1990, pp. 41–66.

Pinker, S. *The Language Instinct.* New York: Morrow, 1994.

Plimpton, G., ed. *Writers at Work: The Paris Review Interviews, Seventh Series.* New York: Viking, 1986.

Ramey, C. T., and Campbell, F. A. "Poverty, Early Childhood Education, and Academic Competence: The Abecedarian Experiment." In A. Huston, ed., *Children in Poverty*. New York: Cambridge University Press, 1992, pp. 190–221.

————. "Preventive Education for High Risk Children: Cognitive Consequences of the Carolina Abecedarian Project." *American Journal of Mental Deficiency* 88, no. 5 (1984), 515–23.

Sacks, O. *The Man Who Mistook His Wife for a Hat*. New York: Harper & Row, 1985.

Salovey, P., and Mayer, J. D. "Emotional Intelligence." *Imagination, Cognition and Personality* 9, no. 3 (1990), 185–211.

Scarr, S., and Weinberg, R. A. "IQ Test Performance of Black Children Adopted by White Families." *American Psychologist* 31 (1976), 726–39.

Schaie, K. W. "Toward a Stage Theory of Adult Cognitive Development." *International Journal of Aging and Human Development* 8 (1977/78), 129–38.

Scribner, S. "Studying Working Intelligence." In B. Rogoff and J. Lave, eds., *Everyday Cognition: Its Development in Social Context*. Cambridge, Mass.: Harvard University Press, 1984, pp. 9–40.

Simon, H. A. *Administrative Behavior*. 2d ed. Totowa, N.J.: Littlefields, Adams, 1957.

Singer, N. G., and Sattler, J. M. "Stanford-Binet Intelligence Scale, Fourth Edition." In R. J. Sternberg, ed., *Encyclopedia of Human Intelligence*, vol. 2. New York: Macmillan, 1994, pp. 1033–38.

Sternberg, R. J. *Intelligence Applied: Understanding and Increasing Your Intellectual Skills*. San Diego: Harcourt Brace Jovanovich, 1986.

————. "The Psychology of Verbal Comprehension." In R. Glaser, ed., *Advances in Instructional Psychology*, vol. 3. Hillsdale, N.J.: Erlbaum, 1987, pp. 97–151.

————. *The Triarchic Mind: A New Theory of Human Intelligence*. New York: Viking, 1988.

————. "Does the Graduate Record Examination Predict Meaningful Success in Psychology?" Manuscript submitted for publication.

Sternberg, R. J. and Williams, W. M. "Parenting Toward Cognitive Competence." In M. H. Bornstein, ed., *Handbook of Parenting*, vol. 4. Mahwah, N.J.: Erlbaum, 1995, pp. 259–75.

Thomas G. H. *The Factorial Analysis of Human Ability*. Boston: Houghton Mifflin, 1938.

Thurstone, L. L. *Primary Mental Abilities*. Chicago: University of Chicago Press, 1938.

Williams, W. M., Blythe, T., White, N., Sternberg, R. J., Li, J., and Gardner, H. I. *Practical Intelligence for School: A Handbook for Teachers of Grades 5–8*. New York: HarperCollins, 1996.

Wilson, M. N. "African Americans." In R. J. Sternberg, ed., *Encyclopedia of Human Intelligence*, vol. 1. New York: Macmillan, 1994, pp. 35–45.

INDEX